A
New
History of
Philosophy

MODERN

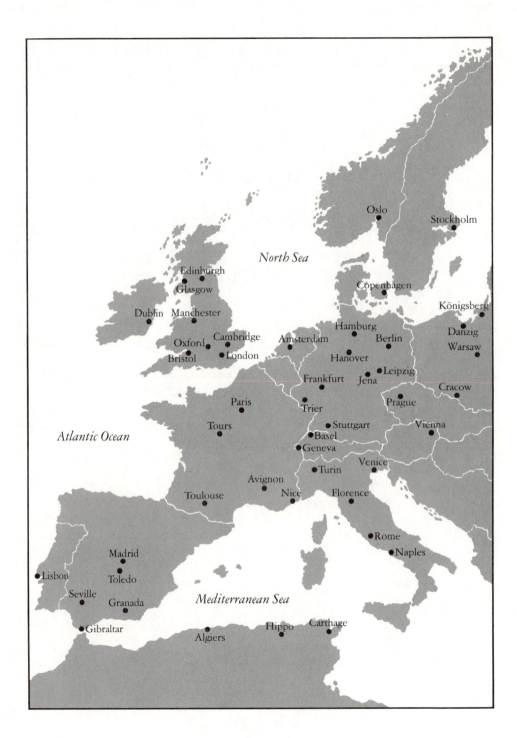

North Sea

Oslo

Stockholm

Edinburgh
Glasgow

Copenhagen

Königsberg

Dublin Manchester

Hamburg

Danzig
Warsaw

Berlin

Amsterdam

Oxford Cambridge

Hanover

Bristol London

Frankfurt

Leipzig
Jena

Cracow

Paris

Trier

Prague

Tours

Stuttgart

Vienna

Atlantic Ocean

Basel
Geneva

Venice

Avignon

Turin

Toulouse

Nice

Florence

Madrid

Rome

Naples

Lisbon

Toledo

Seville

Granada

Mediterranean Sea

Gibraltar

Algiers

Hippo

Carthage

Western and Central Europe

VOLUME II

A New History of Philosophy

MODERN

Wallace I. Matson
University of California, Berkeley

Under the general editorship of
Robert J. Fogelin
Dartmouth College

HARCOURT BRACE JOVANOVICH, PUBLISHERS

San Diego   New York   Chicago   Austin

London   Sydney   Tokyo   Toronto

Photo Credits: Page xviii (Vol. I): TAP Service, Athens; 146: © Leonard von Matt/Rapho, Photo Researchers; 180: Alinari/Art Resource, New York; 250: Giraudon/Art Resource, New York; 259: Smithsonian Institution/Courtesy AIP, Niels Bohr Library; 400: The Bettmann Archive/BBC Hulton; 427. 441: The Bettmann Archive; 446: UPI/Bettmann Newsphotos; 449: Brown Brothers; 473: © Archiv für Kunst und Geschichte, Berlin.

ISBN: 0–15–565729–1

Library of Congress Catalog Card Number: 85–82624

Printed in the United States of America

Copyrights and Acknowledgments

The author is grateful to the following publishers and copyright holders for permission to reprint material in this book:

BARNES & NOBLE BOOKS   For excerpts from *The Concept of Mind* by Gilbert Ryle. Copyright 1949 by Gilbert Ryle. Reprinted by permission of Harper & Row, Publishers, Inc.

BASIL BLACKWELL, LTD.   For excerpts from *Philosophical Investigations* by Ludwig Wittgenstein. Reprinted by permission of the publisher.

CLARENDON PRESS   For excerpts from *Philosophical Papers* and *Sense and Sensibilia*, both by J. L. Austin. Reprinted by permission of the publisher.

MACMILLAN PUBLISHING COMPANY   For excerpts from *Foundations of Metaphysics* by Immanuel Kant, translated by Lewis White Beck. Copyright © 1959 by Macmillan Publishing Company. Reprinted by permission of the publisher.

THE OPEN COURT PUBLISHING COMPANY   For excerpts from *Meditations* by Descartes. Reprinted by permission of the publisher.

Preface

Philosophy, the most important subject in the college curriculum, is unlike any other and must be taught differently.

What is to be studied is a series of discourses concerning the nature of human reason, how it can lead (if it can) to knowledge of how things are, and what it prescribes (if it prescribes anything) about satisfactory living. This is an interconnected literature—a discussion that has been going on for twenty-five centuries. A particular philosophy is a conscious response to its predecessors and cannot be understood apart from them: Aristotle is incomprehensible without Plato, Kant without Hume.

Students of the sciences begin by learning the elements and then proceed in logical progression to the state of knowledge so far attained. The budding astronomer can ignore the epicycles of Ptolemy, the chemist need know nothing of phlogiston. Not so in philosophy. There are no 'elements of philosophy'. And instead of one philosophy triumphing over its rivals and forcing them out, we find that a few conceptions of reason and the good life have stood the test of time, continually reappear modified to fit altered circumstances of life, and seem in no danger of being permanently discredited—however much their relative popularities may wax and wane.

Since for these reasons the possibility does not exist of studying philosophy apart from its history, the most orderly and efficient way is to begin at the beginning, with Thales' pronouncement that all is water, and to recapitulate the process of criticism and reformulation that led to the atomism of Democritus and beyond to the present day. For this study *there is no acceptable substitute for original documents*—the writings of Plato and his predecessors and successors. This book is offered only as an aid to reading in the primary sources. The earliest documents are fragmentary; and the later, though complete, are often puzzling if tackled with no explanation of the context in which they appeared. It is hoped that this book will serve as a preliminary survey map of the territory to be explored.

Why explore it?—Because somewhere in it you will find yourself.

I am grateful to James Clark, Robert Cornett, William Hayes, Richard Haynes, Max Hocutt, Meredith Moraine, George Sessions, Stephen Voss, and most especially to Robert Fogelin, for their friendly help and encouragement. I thank also Professors William E. Mann of the University of Vermont, Walter O'Briant of the University of Georgia, and William Bernard Peach of Duke University, who reviewed the manuscript.

Wallace I. Matson

CONTENTS

A
New
History of
Philosophy

MODERN

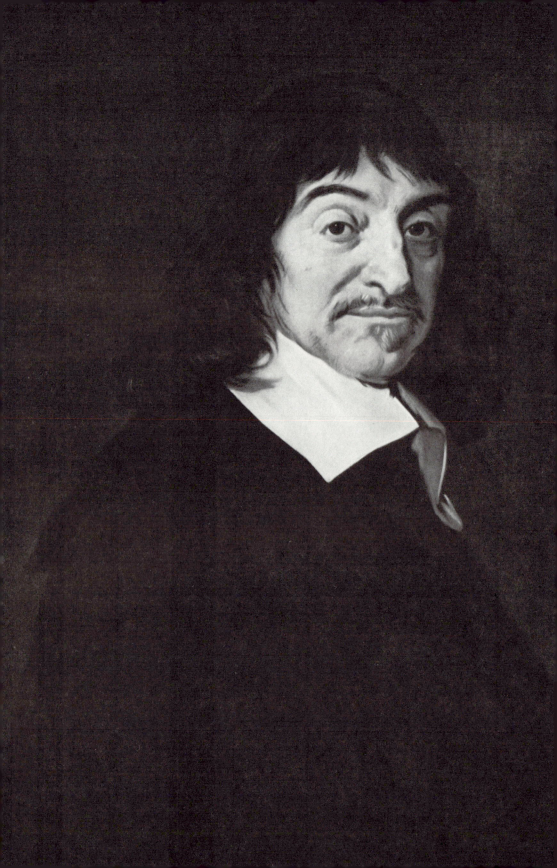

V

The Renaissance and the Scientific Revolution

Franz Hals, Portrait of Descartes, *seventeenth century. Oil. Louvre, Paris.*

32

The Renaissance

WILLIAM OF OCKHAM WAS the last of the great creative Scholastics. The three centuries following his death are a philosophical desert. Since the period is that of the hectic transition from medieval to modern Europe, this may seem surprising. But great philosophy is reflection after the fact—the effort of thoughtful people to make sense of the world once again after the old picture has become no longer believable.

Within the age known as the Renaissance—"Rebirth," a label better taken chronologically (*ca* 1350–1550) than as a significant metaphor—and the following century, it is possible to distinguish four overlapping epochs which reached their peaks in this order. First, in literature: the rediscovery of the Greek and Roman classics, and the arousal of obsessive interest in them. Second, in religion: the crisis of the Reformation and Counter-Reformation, extending on to the middle of the seventeenth century. Third, in natural science: a spectacular burst of progress, especially in astronomy and mechanics—the Copernican Revolution. Fourth, in philosophy: only after all these does a comparable revolution get under way. Concurrent with these movements and extending through the entire period (as well as before and after it) are the decline of the power of the Catholic Church, both politically and intellectually, and correlative increase in efficiency and dominance of secular governments—in particular the great kingdoms of Spain, France, and England.

Humanism

What was most definitely reborn in the Renaissance was knowledge and appreciation of Greek and Roman literature. The Roman poets, orators, and historians—hitherto neglected though not lost in the West—became central in the education of upper-class young men (and, occasionally, women). Learning no longer was the monopoly of clerics; theology no longer was able to claim the attentions and energies of the most vigorous intellects. The "vulgar" tongues—English, French, Provençal, Tuscan, Catalan—began to proliferate serious literatures. Latin, still the universal language, was recast in the florid rhetorical mould of Cicero; the clear, plain style of the scholastics was dismissed as barbarous. This back-to-the-classics literary movement was called Humanism, from its centering of attention on humanity rather than divinity.

For philosophy, the most significant incident in the revival of Roman literature was the discovery of Lucretius. Naturally the Epicurean moral indignation against religion, together with the picture of a purposeless universe, aroused furious antagonisms. The refutation of Lucretius, often in Latin verses, became a popular and profitable vocation for Humanists. Nevertheless, the alternative to a religious and supernatural worldview had again come explicitly to European consciousness.

The incomparably rich literature of Greece became available to the West toward the end of the fourteenth century, when regular instruction in the Greek language began in Florence. Greek refugees from the Turks, before and after the fall of Constantinople in 1453, spread their language and their manuscripts throughout Europe. At this time the complete dialogues of Plato became known and translated into Latin. Cosimo de' Medici, ruler of Florence, founded a school professing to be a revival of Plato's Academy. The interpretation of Plato favored in this school was Neoplatonic. It was fashionable to be anti-Aristotelian, therefore pro-Platonic, and to argue that Plato's philosophy was more compatible with Christianity. No doubt there was much truth in this contention.

The Religious Struggles

For nearly forty years at the end of the fourteenth century Christendom was accustomed to having two Popes. Each country of Europe adhered to one or the other of them, political considerations determining which. Thus secular rulers who according to the theory of St. Thomas Aquinas had their authority conferred on them by God only through His authorized representative the Pope, in practice turned the theory upside down and legitimized the Pope in their territories. This Great Schism was brought to an end by the Council of Constance, 1415–1417, and for a century afterward all Christians gave their obedience to a single Vicar of Christ.

Not, however, always ungrudgingly. The fifteenth century was one of great splendor in Rome. The Popes after all were the sovereigns of central Italy. Their enthusiasm for the new Humanism was often cultivated at the expense of what more earnest if less sophisticated Christians beyond the Alps regarded as the interests of true piety. The resentment was compounded by the fact that the cultural and artistic adornment of Rome was financed by revenues collected from all over Europe. Even the clergy, who had to bear many of the financial burdens, were disaffected. However, the Council of Constance treacherously burned at the stake John Hus, the Czech who was the leader of the protest movement, and ordered the body of John Wycliffe, the Englishman who had inspired him, to be dug up and burnt also. After this there was little effective opposition to papal policies for the rest of the fifteenth century.

The preoccupation of the Humanist popes with art, literature, and Italian politics accompanied a lack of zeal for doctrinal purity. Lorenzo Valla (1406–1457), a classical scholar who defended Epicurean hedonism and proved that the Donation of Constantine was a forgery, was rewarded by appointment as Apostolic Secretary to Pope Nicholas V. Pietro Pomponazzi (1462–1525) published in 1516 a book on the soul in which not only did he hold that Aristotle had denied immortality but that as a philosopher he had been right in doing so. He dwelt on the inconsistency of Aquinas in declaring that the soul is both the form of the body and also an entity that survives the body's dissolution. He pointed out that the observed facts of the close connection between soul and bodily conditions, particularly of the sense organs, make the hypothesis of immortality implausible. Finally, he rebutted the argument according to which morality would be impossible without heaven and hell. Virtue, Pomponazzi declared, is its own reward; actions performed from motives of hope of heaven or fear of hell are not really virtuous, being only expressions of prudential self-interest. To the objection that if the soul is mortal then all men are deceived, since all religions teach immortality, Pomponazzi replied that at best the majority of mankind *are* deceived—since of the three religions of Moses, Christ, and Mohammed, two at least must be false. (During the middle ages there were persistent rumors of a book *On the Three Impostors*, said to have been written by the skeptical—but heretic-burning— Emperor Frederick II. The book did not exist; nevertheless, it was very influential.) At the end of this devastating treatise the author stated that despite philosophy, we know by revelation that the soul *is* immortal. Having thus submitted himself to the Church, Pomponazzi continued in his post as lecturer in the University of Bologna.

On the other hand, the Papacy was quick and forceful in meeting challenges to its worldly position. Thus Alexander VI (Rodrigo Borgia, Pope 1492–1503) brought about the hanging and burning of Savonarola, the monk who in turning Florence from licentiousness to piety reflected unfavorably on the condition of the Papal Court.

The Reformation exploded not on account of any central point of Christian dogma but on the question of the Pope's income from the sale of indulgences. The issue was this. If you died in mortal sin—that is, if you had grievously offended God and had not repented and received His forgiveness through a priest— you would go to hell, there to burn eternally. The torment of hell was simply retribution for wickedness and not intended to produce repentance or reform. If you died "shriven," that is, not in mortal sin, you would go to heaven. But not at once: you would have to spend some time first in Purgatory, which was like hell except that its fires were intended to purify the soul of its unforgiven but venial sins by burning them away. The period to be spent in Purgatory would be proportional to the number and gravity of the sins committed when in this world. It might consume several centuries.

The Church could reduce the length of the sentence by granting indulgences. An indulgence was a remission—of so many days, months, or years—of the soul's sentence. Indulgences might be earned in this life by good works: by undertaking pilgrimages to holy places, for example. You might receive a plenary indulgence— exemption from purgatory for all the sins committed up to date—by visiting Rome in the year of jubilee; or even indulgence for all your sins including future ones if you went on Crusade and died fighting for the Cross in Palestine or Provence or Bohemia.

The theory was that the Church was custodian of the treasury of the practically infinite merits accumulated by the good works of the saints; it could draw on this repository to offset the sins of the penitents. Not only could you insure yourself against purgatory by this means, you could secure remissions for your loved ones who were already in that place. And the simplest kind of good work consisted of the payment of money into the Papal treasury.

Although the Church only reluctantly embarked on a policy of outright sale of indulgences, the practice became established and widespread in the fifteenth century and was soon a major source of revenue for Rome. Without it the building of the great Basilica of St. Peter could not have been undertaken. The industry was administered in an efficient and businesslike manner, with emotional advertising, standard fees, and sales commissions.

In Germany the sale of indulgences was opposed and even forbidden by many rulers who objected to the drain of money from their realms. When the Augustinian monk Martin Luther (1483–1546) announced in 1517 that he was prepared to defend in scholastic debate ninety-five theses against indulgences, he found to his surprise that he had become overnight a celebrity and a hero.

Luther's objections to indulgences were theological. He had read the Bible—a practice discouraged, if not actually forbidden, by the Church at that time—without finding therein a warrant for the business, nor indeed for the existence of Purgatory and the doctrine of justification by good works. He found to the contrary that St. Paul had taught that salvation is to be achieved through faith in Jesus Christ and by no other means.

The Papacy reacted furiously. Luther was driven to make public avowal of heretical opinions: he declared that neither the Pope nor a General Council possessed infallibility with respect to Christian doctrine. But the methods which a century earlier had been effective against John Hus did not prevail against Luther. At the crucial moment the Emperor Charles V, who abhorred Luther's heresy, was too busy with war against the Turks to deal with the monk's German protectors.

Luther went on discovering practices of the Church that lacked scriptural authority, for instance clerical celibacy. He proceeded then to marry a nun. His veneration for the Bible and desire to make it accessible to the people led him to translate it into German, by this act effectively creating German as a literary language.

His extreme position on salvation by faith implied that sacraments such as baptism, and indeed the whole apparatus of church and clergy, are unnecessary or even harmful—for faith is a relation directly between the believer and God. Luther, however, was not one to be deterred by consistency. Recognizing the necessity of institutionalizing his doctrines if they were to have any chance of surviving, he founded a church of his own with sacraments and rituals, a regular hierarchical organization of professional priests, and an explicit and rigid creed. A rash of prophets arose in Germany who, emboldened by Luther's example and his eloquence in exalting the individual conscience above Popish authority, proclaimed their own interpretations of Scripture and tried to attract followers. With Luther's enthusiastic approval, the Protestant (the term came into use after 1529) princes suppressed them by the same ruthless methods used against heretics in Catholic domains.

Much of northern Europe went over to Lutheranism in a short time, the region coinciding curiously with the lands that the Roman Emperors had not been able to conquer. England broke away from Rome in 1530 on account of Henry VIII's quarrel with the Pope over his divorce. John Calvin (1509–1564) worked out a theology more consistent, more heretical, and more frightening than Luther's—it laid primary emphasis on the Augustinian tenet that no man can do anything to save himself, salvation being predestined by God's arbitrary decree. Nevertheless, this doctrine captured the city of Geneva and much of Scotland and the Low Countries, and was supported by a large faction in France. It began to look as if the One Holy Catholic and Apostolic Church was about to collapse.

It did not collapse. The easygoing and gay Italian Renaissance collapsed. The cause of orthodoxy was defended primarily by the Spanish, under their King

Charles V, who was at the same time Holy Roman Emperor. Perceiving that there was substance in the complaints against Papal luxury, frivolity, and toleration, the fanatical Spanish demanded an end to them. An Imperial army invaded Italy and put the city of Rome itself to the sack in 1527.

The Council of Trent, which met at various times between 1545 and 1563, formulated Catholic doctrine explicitly and established important procedures for its defense, including the Index of Prohibited Books. But the most vigorous leadership of the Counter-Reformation, as it came to be called, was provided by the newly formed holy order the Society of Jesus.

A thirty-year-old Spanish soldier (in the army of Charles V), Iñigo Lopez de Recalde (1491–1556), while convalescing from almost fatal wounds, underwent a religious experience—including a vision of the Virgin and Child—that led him to vow to devote his life to the service of religion. The Spanish church authorities were impressed by his enthusiasm but required him to spend years in study before they would sanction his enterprise. He became a priest when he was 47 and a year later founded the Jesuit order.

It was organized on military lines with a General at its head. The vow of unquestioning obedience to superiors was especially stressed, and the order was put at the service of the Pope to use as he saw fit. The soldiers were not to aspire to ecclesiastical power: no Jesuit might become a bishop. From the beginning the members of the order concentrated on teaching and missionary endeavors—early reaching India, China, and Japan, as well as Central and South America. The excellence of Jesuit schools was acknowledged even by their enemies.

Jesuit education (and influence in high places), Spanish armies, and the revived Inquisition stemmed Protestant advances. After a century of hideous religious wars culminating in the Thirty Years' War (1618–1648) in Germany, the religious divisions of Europe stabilized about where they had been at the beginning.

The effect on philosophy of the fragmentation of Christendom was at first slight. Such as it was, it was adverse because of the intensification of fanaticism. Thus in 1619, Lucilio Vanini was strangled and burnt at Toulouse for having expressed opinions that Pomponazzi a century earlier had been able to publish with impunity. In the longer run the Reformation contributed greatly to the emancipation of thought, not because the reformers desired it but because in disunion there is weakness. Protestant churches were subordinate to secular rulers and not always able to use the machinery of the State as they wished. Moreover, a thinker persecuted in one country could usually find asylum in some other—usually Holland.

Science

The advances of the natural sciences, especially astronomy, in the sixteenth and seventeenth centuries made it necessary to discard the conception of the universe that had been current for two thousand years. The intellectual crisis occasioned was the most profound since the beginning of rational speculation in Miletus. It is still going on.

The literary Renaissance did not of itself advance the natural sciences. Scientific progress through the middle ages, though slow, was real at least from the twelfth century. Little or nothing of ancient science came to light at the Renaissance that was not already known, and in many instances already superseded. To the contrary, the passion for antiquity brought about a revival of superstitions that had been current in the ancient world but largely forgotten in the meantime. Astrology was the most curious of these, belief in witchcraft the most pernicious. It was the Humanist Pope Innocent VIII whose Bull for the suppression of witches, issued in 1484, initiated the most appalling persecution to occur in Europe before our century.

The notion dies hard that science made gigantic strides at the time of the Renaissance because people stopped reading Aristotle and started looking at nature. It is summed up in the image of Galileo (1564–1642) dropping cannonballs of unequal weights off the Tower of Pisa, noting that they struck the ground at the same instant and thereby refuting the Aristotelian dogma that velocity is proportional to weight. But this popular picture is not faithful to the facts. In the first place, the Aristotelian teaching was based on observation: everybody can see that bricks fall faster than leaves. The explanation that the difference is due to air resistance—and would disappear in vacuum—was an inference beyond observation and not confirmable until the invention of the air pump, several years after Galileo's theory had been worked out. Galileo himself applied the phrase "rape of the senses" to some of his own doctrines, for instance the subjectivity of colors. Second, although the cannonball experiment was performed in the sixteenth century, it does not appear that Galileo performed it or based any conclusions on it. On the contrary, he relied on a thought experiment. Suppose two bodies of equal weight were to be released together from a height: then, according to Aristotelian theory, they will fall with the same velocity. If they are close together, they will still fall this way. Now suppose them to be actually bolted together so that they form one object of twice the weight: how could this be a reason for any change in their (or its) velocity? Therefore, (air resistance aside) speed of free-fall must be independent of weight.

It is true, nevertheless, that there was heightened capacity for systematic and exact observation among the thinkers of the Renaissance. It was connected with developments in artistic techniques, as the work of Leonardo da Vinci (1452–1519) shows. To it is owed the great advance in knowledge of anatomy, as notably exhibited in Andreas Vesalius' book *On the Fabric of the Human Body*, published in 1543. (Vesalius got into difficulties with the Church because dissection was considered sacrilegious. He died while on a pilgrimage to the Holy Land prescribed as penance for his sins.) The biological sciences, which depend basically on accuracy of description, came to life again after slumbering since the days of Galen and Pliny.

In dynamics, the science of force and motion, Aristotle had held, following common sense and observation, that bodies have two kinds of motion: natural, which is down for heavy bodies, up for light ones, circular for the heavens; and violent, impressed by outside force. Violent motion, as of a stone thrown upward or horizontally, persists only as long as the mover continues in contact; left to itself, a body executes its natural motion as far as possible and then stops.

What then of the motion of a ball that goes on moving after it leaves the thrower's hand, or of an arrow when the bowstring is no longer touching it? Aristotle held, somewhat tentatively, that the motion of the hand or bowstring is communicated to the air, so that at every point the air in contact with the projectile continues to push it. William of Ockham refuted this explanation by pointing out that it would not account for the case of two projectiles sliding past each other: the same air would have to be moving them simultaneously in opposite directions.

Galileo Galilei, *seventeenth century. Wood engraving.*
Niels Bohr Library.

An alternative theory gained currency according to which the launcher imparted *impetus* to the projectile—an occult ("hidden," *i.e.* not perceptible by the senses) quality that faded rather quickly under resistance. This doctrine had a number of advantages, one of which was that it made possible the explanation of the motion of the heavens as due to the impetus given them by God; their motion was eternal because the bodies met no resistance.

Ockham used his Razor on this account also, as involving an unnecessarily postulated occult quality. But as his opinion on this point was not influential—Ockham's interest and work in physics was slight—it remained for Galileo to reassert it. In the impetus theory the mover communicates a certain quantity of impetus to the moving body. This impetus then causes the further motion of the projectile. Impetus was not motion; it was what explained motion. In Galileo's physics, on the other hand, the mover by applying force to the body accelerates it to a certain velocity. The mover does not endow the projectile with any quality, but simply moves it. When the force of the mover is withdrawn, the body in motion remains as it was: it keeps on moving, neither accelerating nor decelerating. The difference between the theories comes to this. Impetus was intended to explain motion (but it didn't, because the only way to determine the impetus of a body was to find out what its state of motion was); whereas for Galileo, nothing explained uniform (nonaccelerated) motion, because no explanation was needed. It is an ultimate fact about bodies that they are inertial, that is they persist in uniform motion (including rest: zero motion) precisely when *not* acted upon by anything. It is their accelerations and decelerations that demand explanation. Both are due to forces. Where the force is applied uniformly, as for example in the case of a body falling or rolling under the influence of gravitation, the acceleration is uniform.

These two principles, of inertia and of acceleration as proportional to force—which are better known as the first two of Newton's three Laws of Motion—corrected the error of Aristotle and thereby enabled physics to enter upon its triumphal and ever accelerating progress. They were fundamental to the explanation for the more spectacular discoveries in astronomy.

The Copernican Revolution

The model of the universe accepted by *nearly* everyone through the sixteenth century did not differ significantly from that depicted by Aristotle and Ptolemy. The cosmos consisted of a spherical motionless earth at the center of a nest of concentric crystalline spheres that revolved around the earth once every day and also performed various complicated motions relative to one another. The fixed stars were attached to the outermost sphere; the sun, moon, and five planets were embedded in the inner heavens. To account for the observed motions of these bodies on the assumption (which no one questioned) that all heavenly motions are circular, it was necessary to suppose that the planets were located not directly on the great spheres whose common center was the earth but on smaller spheres rolling on the surfaces of the great spheres: the famous epicycles. In Ptolemy's astronomy more than forty epicycles were required.

The techniques of positional astronomy were exact enough in the middle ages, and indeed even in antiquity, to detect difficulties in the model. The earth's supposed position at the center did not square with the observations; it would have had to be noticeably off to one side. But then how could the crystalline spheres glide smoothly over each other if they had no common center? Nevertheless, the model was not abandoned, as no one had a better one.

It was obvious even to the ancients that the system would be greatly simplified if, instead of having the heavens rush around the earth every day, the earth itself should be supposed to revolve. This suggestion was known and discussed in the middle ages. It was rejected mainly on two grounds: a daily revolution of the earth still would not explain the motions of the planets and—the psychologically compelling reason—it is just obvious that the earth *is* at rest, that we are *not* standing on a body rotating at incredible speed. And some theologians pointed to the Biblical texts (*Joshua* 10:1 and Psalm 93:1, for instance) that assert the fixity of the earth. However, these citations were not generally regarded as decisive, for it was recognized that scriptural language was accommodated to the conceptions of the people to whom it was addressed.

Aristarchus of Samos in the third century B.C. had suggested that the appearances could be accounted for most economically by assuming a double motion of the earth: once a day on its axis and once a year around the sun. This proposal did not win support. No more was heard in this vein until the sixteenth century. Then Nicolaus Copernicus (1473–1543), a Polish priest who was also an astronomer and mathematician, came independently upon the same hypothesis. In the bigoted atmosphere of the times, Copernicus naturally had misgivings about making his theory known. His book *On the Revolutions of the Heavenly Orbs*, to which he had devoted 33 years, was published only when its author knew himself to be on the point of death. It was dedicated to the Pope and included a preface, by another hand, asserting that the earth's double motion was set out only as a hypothesis and aid to calculation, not as a fact.

These precautions seem to have satisfied the Catholics, who in any case took little notice of the work for half a century. In the Protestant camp, Luther and his lieutenants bellowed in scornful laughter when they heard of the preposterous Polish theory. The most eminent astronomers also rejected it. At the time there were no compelling reasons for accepting it, and there were several objections that appeared cogent. For instance, if the earth rotated, should not a ball dropped from a tower fall to the side, since the earth would be slipping under it while it descended? This objection could be answered only after Galileo's formulation of the law of inertia. Moreover, even as an aid to calculation the theory was not spectacularly successful. Because Copernicus still retained the assumption of circular planetary orbits, he was obliged to assume epicycles, though only half as many as in the Ptolemaic system.

Yet Copernicus was not fated to fall into the obscurity of Aristarchus. His ideas were taken up by the two greatest astronomers of the succeeding generation, Kepler and Galileo.

Johannes Kepler (1571–1630) got his training as assistant to the Danish astronomer royal Tycho Brahe, who without a telescope attained astounding precision in his measurements. Kepler made his living as court astrologer to the King of Bohemia. At one time he had to devote all his energies to the defense (successful) of his mother against a charge of witchcraft. He was attracted to Pythagorean speculations and Sun worship, which predisposed him to be receptive to Copernicanism.

Kepler assumed the laborious task of modifying the Copernican theory to bring it into closer agreement with the observational data he had from Tycho Brahe. The fruits of his industry were the three laws of planetary motion. The first of these required the giving up of the assumption cherished since Plato's time that all heavenly motions are circular: it states that planetary orbits are ellipses with the sun at one focus. The psychological wrench of this was painful. Circles are perfect and orderly; why should a planet depart from this fitting kind of motion and take on that of a figure with only two axes of symmetry rather than an infinite number? Worse still, Kepler found that when a planet is on that stretch of its orbit that is closer to the sun, it moves faster than when it is on the opposite side. Again, there seemed to be no reason for such unseemly behavior. However, Kepler discovered and announced in his Second Law an elegant relation between position on the orbit and velocity: the line from the planet to the sun sweeps out equal areas in equal times. These laws were announced in 1609. Ten years later Kepler succeeded in establishing a third law showing a relation between the orbits of the different planets: the square of the time in which a planet completes its orbit (*i.e.* its "year") divided by the cube of the average distance of the planet from the sun is a number that is the same for every planet. Kepler sought for Pythagorean mathematical harmony in the heavens. He had found it—not so obvious as steady motion in circular paths, but perhaps even more aesthetically satisfying. The epicycles were at last abolished.

While Kepler was enunciating his first two Laws, Galileo Galilei was looking through the telescope he had made after having heard that there was such a thing in Holland. With it he discovered four satellites of Jupiter, the craters of the moon, sunspots, and the phases of Venus. All these observations tended to confirm Copernicus as against Aristotle. The "Medicean stars," as he tactfully named the Jovian moons in honor of his employer, if explainable at all on Aristotelian principles would have required an absurd number of extra crystalline spheres; the moon mountains and especially the sunspots dealt a blow to the notion of the supposed incorruptible matter of the heavenly bodies; whereas the phases of Venus could not be incorporated into the geocentric model at all. It is no wonder that one of Galileo's Aristotelian colleagues at the University of Padua refused to look through the telescope.

Soon afterwards the Catholic Church, locked in what seemed to be a struggle to the death with heresy and on that account not disposed to welcome new and unsettling ideas, began to scrutinize the new astronomy. In 1618, Copernicus' book was placed on the Index of Prohibited Books. Galileo was warned to cease advocating Copernicanism—so Catholic historians claim. In any case he published in 1632 a *Dialogue Concerning the Two Chief World Systems*, in which although neither side officially scored a victory, the author's preference for Copernicus was unmistakable. At this the Inquisition initiated proceedings against the author. The 68 year-old man, if not actually tortured, was at any rate shown the instruments that would be used if necessary. With express authorization by the Pope, the heliocentric theory was pronounced "absurd in philosophy and formally heretical, because expressly contrary to Holy Scripture." On June 22, 1633, Galileo was required to kneel in the church of Santa Maria sopra Minerva and "abjure the false doctrine that the sun is the central point of the universe and immovable, while the earth, on the contrary, is not the central point, and is in motion." (According to legend he was heard to mumble "*Eppur si muove*"—"Just the same, it *does* move." Whether true or not, the story is, as the Italians say, well-invented.) He had furthermore to swear that thereafter he would "neither by word of mouth nor in writing utter anything from which this doctrine might be inferred; but, on the contrary, would notify the Inquisition if he encountered a heretic, or anyone suspected of heresy." Until his death nine years later Galileo lived under house arrest. His last book, the *Discourses on Two New Sciences*, was smuggled out and published in Holland in 1638. It is the foundation work of modern physics. After Galileo, important scientific work was no longer done in Italy.

It is perhaps difficult for us to understand why the relative motions of sun and earth should have been thought to involve religious questions at all. And indeed much of the bitterness of the Galileo affair resulted from clashes of personalities. Nevertheless, the instincts of the princes of the Church who saw in Copernicanism a threat to religion were right. It is hard to believe simultaneously that (1) we live on a small spinning planet not at the center of the universe, not even at the center of the solar system, and that (2) the whole creation exists for our sake. The difficulty was increased once it was realized that if Copernicus was right, the so-called fixed stars must be at enormously greater distances from us than hitherto suspected—indeed, at "astronomical" distances. "The eternal silence of those infinite spaces strikes me with terror," Pascal wrote.[1]

Bruno

One man, however, far from being terrorized by the infinite, reacted with enthusiasm to the new idea, explored its implications, and thereby created the first original philosophy of the new era.

Giordano Bruno (1548–1600) was born in the south of Italy. At the age of 16 he entered a Dominican monastery. This irrevocable step he regretted almost immediately. Early suspected of heresy, he removed to Rome. When suspicion followed him there, he deserted the Dominican order, put on civilian clothes, and set out on his travels.

Bruno was restless, energetic, sensual, and quarrelsome. Geneva, under the dictatorship of Calvin, was hardly the place for such a character. Nevertheless, he went there and obtained a teaching post at the University. To do so he had to become formally a Protestant. Soon finding that he disliked Calvinism even more than Catholicism, he took steps to be reconciled with the Church, but without success since Rome refused to release him from his monkish vows and demanded that he penitently reenter the Dominican order.

So Bruno moved on to the University of Toulouse, then Paris, and in 1583 to Oxford. In England he wrote his most important works: the dialogues *On Cause, Principle, and Unity* and *On the Infinite Universe and the Worlds*.

Bruno had heard of Copernicus early in his life but did not take the new doctrine seriously until he learned mathematics and could follow Copernicus' reasoning, whereupon he became a convert to the heliocentric astronomy. He saw implications that Copernicus had not noticed. Copernicus had given up the notion that the earth was the center of the universe only to substitute the sun. He still supposed that the fixed stars were really fixed and on a sphere that was the outermost boundary of the universe. Bruno saw the need to abandon as meaningless the conception of a center of the universe. There is no foundation for it except prejudice, he pointed out. The notion is not even suggested by sense perception; wherever perception takes place is indifferently the "center," so that if we were on the moon that would be the center. Motion is not absolute but relative; nor is there any absolute distinction between motion and rest.

The so-called fixed stars Bruno declared to be suns like our own. The fact that they appear to be all at the same distance does not prove that they are; reason strongly suggests (he held) that they are scattered uniformly through infinite space. Each star must have planets revolving around it, with living creatures on them.

Bruno Neoplatonically conceived of God as the soul of the world—and as the soul of our souls too. An infinite cause ought to have an infinite effect, Bruno pointed out; thus the infinite world, far from posing a threat to religion, was more consistent with the Christian conception of divinity. Things are not moved from outside—there are no crystalline spheres with angels pushing them around. The universe is an interconnected whole, in which things move on account of their internal principles of motion. God *is* the principle of motion manifested in things: *Natura naturans*, the active aspect of nature, as opposed to *Natura naturata*, that which is moved but which is not really distinct from the moving principle. (These conceptions correspond to force and matter.) The motion of things is purposive; but it is at the same time fully intelligible in mechanical terms. Matter is not to be despised as lumpish and formless; it is active and "divine."

Bruno left England in 1586 and wandered in France and Germany. Homesick for Italy, in 1591 he let a young Venetian aristocrat persuade him to travel to Venice as his philosophy tutor. When the man found that Bruno was not going to teach him black magic, as he had expected, he worked off his vexation by denouncing the philosopher to the Venetian Inquisition. This was a relatively reasonable organization, as Inquisitions went. Bruno was frank with them, protested that he had always been a good Catholic, whose teachings were really consistent with those of the Church, and asked forgiveness. The Venetians might have let him go, but they yielded to a demand from the Roman Inquisition for his surrender.

Bruno spent six years in a Roman prison. The records of his trial have disappeared. It seems that he was required to recant eight "gross heresies." In the end he refused. On February 9, 1600, the customary sentence was pronounced: he was to be "delivered to the secular authorities, with the request that he be punished as mercifully as possible, and without the shedding of blood"—that is, that he be burnt at the stake. Bruno said to his judges: "You who pass judgment on me feel, maybe, greater fear than I who am judged." Eight days later the sentence was executed. Giordano Bruno is said to have borne his agony with nobility, not once uttering a groan. However, his mouth contained an iron tongue clamp to prevent him in his last moments from scandalizing the pious spectators with blasphemies.

Francis Bacon

In England the new age of science was eloquently proclaimed by Francis Bacon (1561–1626). Of a family important in politics, he studied law and entered Parliament at the age of 23. His public career, however, did not prosper during the reign of Elizabeth I. Advancement to great office came when James I ascended the throne. Knighted in the first year of the Stuart era, he occupied successively more important places in the King's legal service, becoming Baron and Lord Chancellor in 1618, Viscount St. Albans in 1624—the year of his downfall also. Accused and convicted by Parliament of taking bribes, he was deprived of office, sentenced to be imprisoned in the Tower of London, and assessed an enormous fine. Probably the charges against him, although not baseless, were motivated mainly by political enmity. In any case he remained in the Tower only a few days and never paid the fine. He retired to the country where two years later he died of pneumonia contracted while experimenting with snow.

In the manner of the Renaissance, Bacon's intellectual interests were boundless. His celebrated *Essayes* touch upon almost every topic of human interest. For philosophy and science, the central significance of his thought is in his conception of progress.

The notion that on the whole human affairs tend to get better—that the present age is an improvement on the past and the future will surpass the present—has not been dominant in human thought, not even in the Western world, which tends to be more optimistic than the East. Received opinion has usually held that we live in an iron age, a comedown from the silver and golden past—or at best that things go in cycles, the downs canceling the ups. Christian thought might seem to be otherwise framed; since the time after the life of Christ is the era of salvation, it is better to be living now than B.C. when damnation was inevitable for everyone. However, there is here no idea of progress as a process—we have the advantage of accessible salvation, but we do not have more of it than the early Christians had. And Christianity incorporates the myth of a Fall more disastrous than any that Hesiod or Empedocles lamented.

Nor did the literary Renaissance, an antiquarian movement, look toward the possibility of improvement beyond the recovery of ancient perfection.

One department of human affairs—and one only—is obviously progressive: technology. Woven textiles must have come later than metallurgy, Lucretius observed, because certain parts of looms have to be made of metal. At the end of the fifth book of *On the Nature of Things* the Roman poet reconstructed, *a priori* but with uncanny accuracy, the outlines of technological and sociological development. He concluded

> Thus time by degrees brings each several thing forth before men's eyes and reason raises it up into the borders of light; for things must be brought to light one after the other and in due order in the different arts, until these have reached their highest point of development.[2]

But the Epicureans were reserved in their admiration for progress. Lucretius noted that although civilization had liberated people from the fear of being eaten by wild beasts, it had created compensating dangers of massacre and poisoning.

Moreover, in antiquity and in the middle ages there was little sense of connection between knowledge of the sort philosophers and other learned men gathered, and technological advance. Archimedes, we are told, invented some engines of war using principles he had developed in his theoretical studies, but he was ashamed of having done so. Engineering, in which there was no dearth of remarkable examples, was not thought of as "applied science." The alchemists tried to deduce practical recipes from general theories, but as their theories were fantastic and their goals impossible of attainment they came to nothing. Although there are interesting anticipations, such as the prognostications of Roger Bacon, science and technology can hardly be said to have become linked even tenuously before Leonardo da Vinci at the end of the fifteenth century. But when Galileo worked out the mathematical theory of projectiles, it began to be apparent that theoretical physics might help to win battles. Governments consequently began to subsidize scientists.

Ideas taken for granted in our age, that technology enriches life—or at any rate can do so if properly employed—and that pure science nourishes technology, came to consciousness in Francis Bacon's writings. The Renaissance worship of the wisdom of the ancients he denounced as resting on fallacy: if reverence is due to age, then we should revere ourselves, for the so-called ancients lived when the world was young; *we* are the old ones with the experience of ages behind us. Bacon denounced Aristotle in particular. This was not unusual, but his reason was. Bacon did not reject Aristotle in favor of Plato or Augustine but because Aristotle's science bore no fruits of practical utility. Printing, gunpowder, the magnet had transformed the world; the philosophers had had nothing to do with any of them. This needed changing.

Bacon set out to change it, to develop a philosophical program for the advancement of learning and its application to useful ends. Like all revolutionary thinkers he deemed the first necessary step to be the clearing of the field—getting rid of traditional errors and prejudices, thus to leave the mind of the investigator a pure white tablet fit for the impression of truth. In his *New Organon* (that is, as we should say, *New Methodology of Science*—the old *Organon* was Aristotle's works on logic and scientific inference) Bacon classified prejudices under the metaphor of four kinds of Idols, choosing this word, no doubt, because of its double significance of mere image without substance and of unworthy object of worship.

The Idols of the Tribe are prejudicial modes of thinking common to humanity as such. The tendency to wishful thinking is the principal one. We overvalue what agrees with our preconceptions and overlook negative instances. It is a universal human trait also, Bacon thought, to explain things animistically and anthropomorphically.

> The Idols of the Cave are the idols of the individual man. For every one . . . has a cave or a den of his own, which refracts and discolours the light of nature, owing either to his own proper and peculiar nature, or to his education and conversation with others, or to the reading of books, and the authority of those whom he esteems and admires, or to the differences of impressions, accordingly as they take place in a mind preoccupied and predisposed or in a mind indifferent and settled, or the like. So that the spirit of man . . . is in fact a thing variable and full of perturbation, and governed as it were by chance.[3]

Some people are liberals, others are conservatives. Some like to understand by analysis, some look at things organically. We ride our hobbies: "Aristotle . . . made his natural philosophy a mere bondservant to his logic, thereby rendering it contentious and well nigh useless . . . Gilbert also, after he had employed himself most laboriously in the study and observation of the loadstone, proceeded at once to construct an entire system in accordance with his favorite subject."[4]

The Idols of the Market Place are the infirmities of language: "the ill and unfit choice of words wonderfully obstructs the understanding."[5] Bacon is not deploring the deficiencies of an individual's vocabulary but the defects of language itself, which he thinks has words it should not have, such as Fortune and Prime Mover, which signify nothing that exists; and vague and ambiguous words, such as humid, earth, generate, corrupt, alter, heavy, light, rare, and dense. They come from "faulty and unskilful abstraction."

"But the Idols of the Theatre are not innate, nor do they steal into the understanding secretly, but are plainly impressed and received into the mind from the playbooks of philosophical systems and the perverted rules of demonstration."[6] These are the systems of philosophy—Aristotelianism, Scholasticism, and the like, which are "but so many stage plays, representing worlds of their own creation after an unreal and scenic fashion."[7] In their grip we fail to notice what the world is like because we are persuaded we already know what it must be like.

Despite its celebrity this classification of impediments to objective thought as Idols is more misleading than useful. That we should strive to avoid wishful thinking, and that we should try to be conscious of our own prejudices and allow for them, are doubtless pieces of good advice, and that is why they are so often given. But the attack on language under the label Idols of the Market Place was largely gratuitous. Granted that Prime Mover signifies nothing real, the fault is not that of language but of a philosophical system, Aristotelianism, outside which the phrase has no meaning. So we have in this case an Idol not of the Market Place but of the Theatre, and Bacon has misclassified his own example. His objection to words like 'dense' seems to have been that there is no precise context-free rule for deciding of any thing—a crowd, a cloud, an intellect—whether it is dense or not. What Bacon apparently wanted was a language containing nothing but words whose application could be specified precisely in advance. Bacon was one of the first but by no means the last of philosophers who yearn for an artificial and exact language. Lastly, the Idols of the Theatre—besides being properly a subclass of Idols of the Cave and not a separate division—constitute in reality merely an occasion for a lively but outrageously prejudiced attack on Aristotelianism, damned as "sophistical"; William Gilbert, dismissed as merely "empirical"; and Pythagoras and Plato, condemned as "superstitious" because they mixed up philosophy and theology.

Bacon, whether consciously or not, continued the Ockhamite tradition in his insistence on separating science and religion. Religion in his view is based on revelation. It therefore need not be rational; indeed, the more incredible a revelation is, the more we honor God in believing it. A point of impingement of religion on science he found in the doctrine of Final Causes, which he compared to nuns: of religious importance, but barren. Natural science should seek mechanical explanations exclusively; its sphere is the material world.

What we should do as natural scientists, once we have expelled the Idols from our minds and insulated ourselves from supernaturalist thinking, is this: we are to perform systematic observations and experiments aiming at the discovery of the Forms. "The Form of a thing," we are told, "is the very thing itself."[8] This sounds like Aristotelian Essence—and so it is, though at the same time it is Law. "When I speak of Forms, I mean nothing more than those laws and determinations of absolute actuality which govern and constitute any simple nature . . . Thus the Form of Heat or the Form of Light is the same thing as the Law of Heat or the Law of Light."[9]

Bacon illustrates his somewhat obscure directions for discovering Forms with the extended example of Heat. The first step is to make a list of instances where heat is present: sunlight, meteors, friction, fresh horse dung, and so on. Then a second list is compiled, as like the first as possible except that heat is absent: moonlight, rubbing of smooth or oily bodies—Bacon lists 27. Third, a list of instances where heat is present but varies in degree with the degree of something else. With these tables before us, we are to perform an Induction: "upon a review of the instances, all and each, to find such a nature as is always present or absent with the given nature, and always increases and decreases with it, and which is . . . a particular case of a more general nature."[10] We reject natures that are present in both the first and second tables, or (from the third) do not vary when the nature under investigation varies. This process will shorten the tables drastically. At this point we "make an essay of the Interpretation of Nature in the affirmative way; on the strength both of the instances given in the tables, and of any others it may meet with elsewhere. Which . . . I call . . . the *First Vintage*."[11] By this Bacon means what we should call a hypothesis. In the example it is this: "Heat is a motion, expansive, restrained, and acting in its strife upon the smaller particles of bodies. . ."

Bacon had high hopes for his method.

> The course I propose for the discovery of science is such as leaves but little to the acuteness and strength of wits, but places all wits and understandings nearly on a level. For as in the drawing of a straight line or a perfect circle much depends on the steadiness and practice of the hand, if it be done by aim of hand only, but if with the aid of rule or compass, little or nothing; so is it exactly with my plan.[12]

It has been the dream of many philosophers from Plato onward—not including Aristotle—to discover the royal road. Bacon advanced about as far as any one yet has done. His method is one that can be and is systematically, routinely, and successfully applied by technicians to make discoveries. Discoveries, however, of such things as what is wrong with a malfunctioning television receiver, not what is the cause of cancer or what quasars are—though the Baconian induction may play a part in the preliminaries. Genius has not been rendered superfluous.

Why not, is a long and still imperfectly understood story. But part of the answer lies in the necessity for conceptual reformulation that Bacon overlooked. The rules for Baconian induction take for granted that the phenomena under investigation can be satisfactorily described in the current vocabulary and that the Form we are looking for will be somewhere on our lists—that is to say, we already possess all the concepts we need. But, to take a simple example, the phenomena of magnetism cannot be adequately characterized without the notion of the magnetic "pole." This was understood by Bacon's older contemporary, William Gilbert (1544–1603), "the most distinguished man of science in England during the reign of Queen Elizabeth, and the father of electric and magnetic science."[13] Gilbert was one of the first English advocates of Copernican astronomy (which Bacon rejected), and like Bruno suggested that there was no reason to suppose that the fixed stars are all at the same distance. Gilbert's book *Of the Magnet and Magnetic Bodies, and of the Earth a Great Magnet* (1600), which Bacon ridiculed, was and is a paradigm of how important scientific discoveries are in fact made.

33

Descartes

RENÉ DESCARTES, THE MAN generally considered the initiator of modern philosophy, was born near Tours on the 31st of March 1596 of a noble and moderately wealthy family. He was educated by the Jesuits and formed early an attachment to intellectual pursuits, mathematics especially. He did not, however, enter the Church or attend a university; he was a gentleman amateur, as almost all the great philosophers of the succeeding two centuries were to be.

On leaving school Descartes went to Paris where for a few years he lived a life appropriate to his rank and income. But as he became more and more engrossed in studies, he found the social whirl so distracting that he took what may seem a curious step toward ensuring leisure and quiet for meditation: he joined the army of Bavaria. This was at the beginning of what was to become the Thirty Years' War. Campaigns took place only in summer; the months when the army was encamped in winter quarters afforded the desired freedom from distractions. On the 10th of November 1619, he "discovered the foundations of a wonderful science." The reflections which thus culminated when he was 23 were embodied in his *Discourse on Method*. The wonderful science was not a body of knowledge but a certain way of investigating, the rules of which were these.

> The first was to accept nothing as true which I did not clearly recognize to be so: that is to say, carefully to avoid precipitation and prejudice in judgments, and to accept in them nothing more than what was presented to my mind so clearly and distinctly that I could have no occasion to doubt it.
>
> The second was to divide up each of the difficulties which I examined into as many parts as possible, and as seemed requisite in order that it might be resolved in the best manner possible.
>
> The third was to carry on my reflections in due order, commencing with objects that were the most simple and easy to understand, in order to rise little by little, or by degrees, to knowledge of the most complex, assuming an order, even if a fictitious one, among those which do not follow a natural sequence relatively to one another.
>
> The last was in all cases to make enumerations so complete and reviews so general that I should be certain of having omitted nothing.[1]

What Descartes here describes is in effect the order of presentation of a deductive system, for instance Euclidean geometry, beginning with "clear and distinct" indubitable axioms and proceeding "in due order" to "knowledge of the most complex." We must read these precepts not as giving a recipe for making discoveries but as affording a framework onto which the investigator could attach the results already attained and which would guide further search.

Descartes assures us that by adhering strictly to these somewhat platitudinous precepts he was able to make a number of important discoveries and clear up some ancient puzzles in a short time. These advances were in mathematics and optics. To Descartes the world chiefly owes analytic geometry, which is the reduction of geometry to algebra by means of representing points in space by three numbers—the "Cartesian coordinates"—that specify their distances from three mutually perpendicular lines. While the idea of the graph is found in the work of Nicholas Oresme (*d.* 1382), Descartes originated the use of coordinate numbers and variables in algebraic equations to describe lines and curves. This system facilitates the handling of geometrical problems to much the same extent as the introduction of Arabic numerals simplified arithmetical calculations. Without it modern physical science and engineering would be scarcely conceivable.

Descartes abandoned the military life after three years, but until 1629 he seldom stayed long in one place. Then he settled in Holland where he remained for most of the rest of his life. Holland was quieter than Paris and, more importantly, safer.

Descartes was a good Catholic, one indeed whose efforts were consciously directed toward strengthening the intellectual position of the Church. It is hard to understand how his writings could have received anything but grateful praise from the clergy. But the age was one of extreme bigotry. In 1624 a scholar was expelled from Paris for announcing that he would defend atomism in a public debate. Later the same year the Parliament of Paris forbade *all* intellectual innovation under pain of death. In 1633 Galileo had to perjure himself by recanting his Copernican views. One consequence of the Galileo affair was that Descartes decided not to publish his book, *The World*, in which he affirmed the earth's motion. In 1634 occurred the affair of the Devils of Loudun: Urbain Grandier, a handsome young priest, being accused of having infected certain hysterical nuns with devils, was hideously tortured and then burnt at the stake—this at the personal direction of Cardinal Richelieu, the effective ruler of France. Even in Holland freedom from persecution was not absolute. One Protestant preacher agitated to have Descartes burnt at the summit of the highest (or only) hill in Holland, whence the fire would be visible in three provinces. Descartes' books were banned and even burnt. A professor of philosophy at Utrecht who was so rash as to defend Cartesianism was dismissed. The Dutch government, however, sometimes opposed these excesses.

But Descartes had influential friends. He was "the celebrated Monsieur Descartes" long before he had published anything. He corresponded with all the leading intellects of Europe. In 1637 he was prevailed upon to publish a volume of *Philosophical Essays* containing the *Discourse on Method* besides works on optics, phenomena of the heavens, and the foundation of analytic geometry. His principal philosophical work, the *Meditations on First Philosophy*, appeared in 1640. *The Principles of Philosophy* (1644) and *The Passions of the Soul* (1649) were his only other writings to appear during his lifetime.

Descartes was admired by royal ladies: the brilliant Elizabeth, Princess Palatine—daughter of the deposed King of Bohemia and niece of Charles I of England—and Christina, the young Queen of Sweden. Correspondence with the latter led to Descartes' untimely death. Christina invited him to Stockholm and would not be refused. She sent a warship to convey him to the "land of bears, ice, and rocks," as he privately called her kingdom. Descartes loved to be warm; ever since his school days he had made a practice of meditating in bed until late in the morning. The Queen required him to give her lessons in philosophy at five a.m. in her drafty castle. Descartes caught pneumonia and died, aged 54.

In 1663 Descartes' writings were placed on the Catholic Index of Prohibited Books. The proscription was issued at the behest of the Jesuits, who had educated Descartes and whom he had tried in vain throughout his life to placate. In 1667 Descartes' body was brought from Sweden for reburial near Paris. The Chancellor of the University of Paris intended to deliver a eulogy on the occasion but was forbidden to do so by order of King Louis XIV.

Cartesian Doubt

It was unkind of the Church to take this stance, for Descartes only wanted to help. He aimed in fact to be the St. Thomas Aquinas of his day, reconciling the teachings of the Church with the new science. St. Thomas met with clerical opposition but his followers triumphed in the end. Descartes' ecclesiastical supporters lost.

To be sure, the crisis of the seventeenth century was more profound than that which beset Christendom in the thirteenth. Aristotle's worldview, being one according to which understanding of things is in terms of purposes, was fundamentally of the same kind as the Christian, so that reconciliation required mainly accommodations in details and shifts of emphases, and in particular a heightened concern and respect for this world of nature. But in the seventeenth century not only was the religious world picture suddenly rendered implausible by Copernicanism, more seriously perhaps if less spectacularly the whole traditional way of looking at the world was threatened by the success of mechanistic explanations and the consequent tendency to reject objective purposes. The intellectual shock was comparable to that of only one previous era: Plato's time, when the Greeks were confronted with the science of Anaxagoras and Democritus.

Plato and Descartes had much in common besides. Both were mathematicians, both aimed to put knowledge on a firm foundation by generalizing mathematical methods, and both believed that the indispensable first step for reconstructing knowledge was to get rid of confusions by means of a critique of hitherto received opinions. Both, in consequence, conceded much to the skeptics around them while remaining fundamentally hostile to skepticism.

The first sentence of Descartes's first *Meditation* is this.

> There is no novelty to me in the reflection that, from my earliest years, I have accepted many false opinions as true, and that what I have concluded from such badly assured premises could not but be highly doubtful and uncertain.

He proposes to make a heroic attempt to purge thinking of all elements that are in the least doubtful in order to find out what if anything remains. But since one cannot list, much less examine, all one's beliefs one by one, they must be divided into categories according to their foundations—that is, the reasons for holding them.

Now what we believe, we accept either because someone has told us so or because we have found out for ourselves. Descartes spends no time on establishing the doubtfulness of everything believed merely on grounds of the testimony of others. For clearly this cannot be an original ground of belief.

So Descartes can begin by noting that "everything which I have thus far accepted as entirely true has been acquired from the senses or by means of the senses." But seeing is not always believing. The fact that a distant tower looks round is not sufficient warrant for concluding that it certainly is round. But what of things seen close up in a good light? Descartes does not say that in fact he can doubt whether such things exist and are as they seem. You do not doubt, and as a matter of psychology probably you cannot make yourself doubt, that you are at this moment reading a book. Yet doubt can be cast on such experiences indirectly, by means of the celebrated argument from dreams.

It goes back to Plato's *Theaetetus*. Dreams, at least the vivid kind, do not present themselves to us *as* dreams; while they are going on they seem just like ordinary (waking) experiences. "I have been misled, while asleep," Descartes says, "and there are no conclusive indications by which waking life can be distinguished from sleep." Perhaps you have sometime dreamed that you were reading a book on Descartes' philosophy; we will use this example, but any other would do. To dream that you are reading a book is not to be (really) reading a book. In order to be reading a book you must be awake, you must have a book in your line of sight, your eyes must be open. None of these conditions is met when you are asleep. But when you dream you are reading a book, you *think* you are reading a book. So you are deceived. From your inward point of view everything is just as it would be if you really were reading a book. But you are mistaken. In order not to be mistaken, you would have to know—be aware while dreaming—that you were dreaming. This awareness does not occur, or at any rate it does not always occur—as we know, because sometimes we wake up and are surprised to find that what we dreamed was only a dream.

At least sometimes dreams are accompanied by a feeling of certainty that you are really experiencing whatever you are dreaming about. This is as much as to say that sometimes when you are asleep you feel certain that you are awake. Therefore, if the question is *now* raised whether you are awake or dreaming *now*, it does no good to invoke the feeling of certainty that you *now* have as justifying your assertion that you are indeed awake. But there does not seem to be any other evidence that you might produce, for whatever you suggest might be duplicated in a dream.

However, Descartes was not interested primarily in the fact (if it is a fact) that you cannot prove that you are awake. The dream hypothesis is invoked as a stratagem to show that there is no impossibility in all experience's being, so to speak, one long dream. The alleged fact that dream experiences are not intrinsically distinguishable from waking experiences is enough, he thinks, to show that we cannot know with absolute certainty that any particular experience is of a reality existing independently of our thoughts. Nor can we know that even one of our experiences is of this kind. Therefore, all sense experience is infected with doubt: none of it necessarily reveals what things are really like.

If all knowledge comes from the senses and all sense experience falls short of certainty, Descartes ought to be able to conclude at once that everything is doubtful. But he is more cautious. He next observes that some kinds of knowledge retain their validity no matter whether one is awake or dreaming. These are the truths of mathematics. "For whether I am awake or whether I am asleep, two and three together will always make the number five, and the square will never have more than four sides." By following the reasoning already outlined I can perhaps make myself somewhat doubtful of whether anything I think I see is really out there. But this does not suffice to make me feel the slightest doubt that the two things that look like books on my left and the three other things that seem to be books on my right together comprise five whatever-they-are's.

In order to cast doubt on even these kinds of beliefs, Descartes introduces the hypothesis of "a malignant demon, who is at once exceedingly potent and deceitful, who has employed all his artifice to deceive me." (If he lived in our century, Descartes would write of a great hypnotist or brainwasher.) Is it not possible, conceivable, that I am in the power of such a horrid being, who for his evil amusement makes me think always that two and three are five, whereas they really are (say) six and a half? The possibility cannot be rejected, Descartes thinks, and it is only the bare possibility that is in question. Descartes set out to determine whether there was any belief of his that could not possibly be mistaken, no matter what the circumstances. Thus if it is possible to describe a situation however queer in which a belief would in fact be mistaken, then that belief cannot be considered absolutely proof against doubt. The hypothesis of the deceitful demon suffices to prove that even mathematical truths of the simplest kind are not indubitable in the absolute sense.

Thus at the end of the first *Meditation*, Descartes is left in the condition of doubting whether there is an external world, even doubting whether his beliefs about simple arithmetic and geometry have any truth in them.

Descartes here carried doubt systematically further than it had been brought by the ancient skeptics or even by the revived Pyrrhonism in vogue in the France of his day. The demon hypothesis was original with him. It has been suggested[2] that the idea came out of the Loudun affair and its horrible absurdities. Devils were there required to testify in court (under oath!), speaking through the tongues of the possessed nuns; and the Faculty of Theology of the University of Paris (to whom Descartes dedicated the *Meditations*) pondered the question of what credence was to be given to these depositions.

"I Think, Therefore I Am"

"What then could still be thought true? Perhaps nothing else, unless it is that there is nothing certain in the world." Descartes has managed to doubt both his senses and his ability to manipulate simple notions validly, as in adding and counting. But—says Descartes—not everything has slipped away. One thing remains, conspicuous against the background of general ruin. There is, after all, one matter that no deceiver, however powerful and malignant, could possibly deceive him about: his own existence! He may be a bodiless spirit floating in a void, imagining all his surroundings and counting them up wrong—but the kind of mistake that would consist in supposing that he was something, when in fact he was nothing at all, could not possibly occur.

"This proposition: *I am, I exist*, is necessarily true every time I pronounce it or conceive it in my mind." The more famous phrase employed in the *Discourse on Method*, "Cogito, ergo sum" is traditionally put into English as "I think, therefore I am," although a more accurate rendering would be "I am thinking, therefore I exist."

Skepticism therefore cannot be total, for there is one statement that cannot possibly be false. One must be careful, however, in describing just what it is that is absolutely certain. This certainty is restricted to the first-person form. "I am thinking, therefore I exist" expresses *my* certain knowledge when I say it or think it; but "*You* are thinking, therefore *you* exist" does not have this certainty for *me*. And what am *I*? It is not certain at this point that I exist as a body, as a "mechanism." For if I believe that I have a body, this belief likewise is based on sense experience, which is still under suspicion. It is possible that there are no bodies at all. Only this is certain: I exist as a thinking being. "Thought is an attribute that belongs to me; it alone is inseparable from my nature."

And the certainty exists only as long as the thinking does. (In this context Descartes uses 'thinking' in the very broad sense of including everything we ordinarily mean by being conscious: reflecting, imagining, and perceiving.) I do not know, yet, that I continue to exist when (as we would say) I fall into dreamless sleep.

Can the certainty thus attained be expressed more fully than in the disappointingly short sentence that I think and exist? Yes. It is certain that I am thinking. Hence it is certain that my thoughts, considered just as thoughts, are what they are. Now it seems to me that I am sitting at a desk, at night, with the light on, with socks on but shoes off, writing about Descartes. And although it is not certain that I really am writing about Descartes, and so forth, I can derive a multitude of absolute certainties from this situation. (1) It is certain that it seems to me that I am sitting at a desk. (2) It is certain that it seems to me that there is a light overhead. (3) It is certain that it seems to me that I am writing about a man whom I seem to remember having read about, who lived in what I was told was seventeenth-century Holland. And so on, indefinitely. In general—though I may be mistaken, partly or wholly, about what really *is* out there—I can never possibly be mistaken about what *seems to me* to be there. This point, which may appear trivial, is of fundamental importance for philosophy from Descartes to the present day.

Knowledge and certainty are, then, to be found in the mind, though it will be said—and Descartes would agree—that if nothing is certain except statements prefaced by "It seems to me that . . .", then we are still a long way from the kind of certainty we desire. But at this point Descartes is engaged in establishing that knowledge is an attribute of the mind and never of the senses only.

For this purpose he embarks on a digression. Abandoning for the moment our doubts about the world external to our minds, let us suppose that there is a piece of wax in front of us. We say "There is a piece of wax." If, as we are supposing, the statement expresses knowledge, what is its source? Perhaps we think it is a simple matter of sense experience—we see it, touch it, taste it, and so forth—and on this basis conclude that it is wax. Not so, says Descartes. What is given in sense perception may be entirely altered by melting the wax: "what remained of the taste is exhaled, the smell evaporates, the color alters, the figure is destroyed, the size increases, it becomes liquid, it heats, scarcely can one handle it, and when one strikes it, no sound is emitted." Despite this total alteration we know that it is wax, the very same wax. It is the understanding, then—a faculty different from mere sense perception—whereby the wax is known. The senses provide us with data without which the understanding would have nothing to work on. Nevertheless, it is "an inspection by the mind" of the sense data that produces knowledge.

Descartes reinforces the point with another example. From the window he looks at passersby in the street below, attired in the flowing cloaks and broad-brimmed hats of the *Three Musketeers* era. What does he really, directly, see? Only hats and cloaks. But he *judges* that there are people under them. We must not be misled into supposing that at any rate he has direct and infallible knowledge of the existence of hats and cloaks outside his window. Someone might be carrying a scene painting, or it might be some elaborate and pointless optical illusion, or he might be dreaming or having a hallucination. But any statement whatsoever that goes beyond the "It seems that . . ." stage involves something more than pure sense experience. One must think about the data—'think' here in the more usual and restricted sense of 'judge'. In making judgments, there is always the possibility of error. The problem of knowledge for Descartes, then, is just the problem of finding out how to guarantee these judgments against error.

Solipsism and Skepticism

The predicament that Descartes finds himself in at the end of the first *Meditation* is solipsism—self-alone-ism—the view that nothing exists except the consciousness of the thinker, or at any rate that no valid reasons can be offered for thinking otherwise. This is not to say that Descartes is committed to the truth of solipsism—far from it; but he is faced with the problem, at this juncture seemingly insoluble, of producing reasons for not being a solipsist.

How did Descartes get into this distressing situation? Seemingly by a straightforward argument that can be paraphrased thus: Sometimes solipsism *is* true, so to speak, namely when I am dreaming. For the dream, no matter what it seems to be, is nothing but the content of my consciousness. But there is no way to distinguish, with certainty, waking from dreaming. Therefore, there is no way to be sure that solipsism is not true absolutely.

This argument depends crucially on an assumption made by Descartes and by most of the philosophers who have followed him: that the immediate objects of awareness are mental images, bits of consciousness, ideas, impressions, sense data—the labels are multifarious but they refer in common to something supposed to be private and inner and not identical with objects in the external world. When I am aware, so the argument runs, I must be aware of something. In dreams and hallucinations, the something I am aware of is nothing but my own consciousness. But on reflection it turns out that even when I am awake my awareness is *directly* of the content of consciousness—how could it be otherwise? I cannot really, literally, have a tomato in my mind; that is nonsense. What is in my mind must be something mental, at best an image of something nonmental. Here is where a perplexing problem shows itself: how can I know that this mental picture is a faithful picture, or indeed a picture at all, of something out there? We are back with Democritus and his lament "In truth we know nothing, but each thing is the flow toward us"—if it is not too optimistic to believe that there has to be a flow.

There are two approaches in philosophy, which we may call the outside-in and the inside-out. The outside-in philosophy begins with an account of the world, and at or near the end it explains the human mind and its knowledge in the terms developed in that account. Thus in Aristotle's philosophy we survey the world and learn that it is an articulated whole, the activities and interactions of whose parts typically are movements from potentiality to actuality. Having reached these conclusions, we then examine sense perception and proceed to fit it into the theory: it is to be understood as the reception of the form of the object without the matter. Since to know is to know forms, there is not any problem of how or whether we know the external world. Indeed it is not necessary, or strictly even possible, to draw a distinction between the external world and the inner or mental realm.

Plato illustrates the inside-out philosophy. He takes the existence of knowledge as his starting point, and asks what reality has to be like in order for us to have the knowledge we do have. The answer is that it must consist of Ideas, which are either numbers or like them.

From Plato to Descartes, however, the inside-out approach was not taken by the philosophers who aimed to reach positive views about the world. And indeed Plato does not afford a clear case of it. Only the Skeptics insisted that any honest investigator must begin with nothing but what is given to the individual consciousness. Once we realize that this object of direct acquaintance is only appearance and that it is hopeless to seek for a means of extracting from appearance the reality supposed to lie—unperceived and unperceivable—behind it, we will be led to the skeptical suspense of judgment, the modest wisdom of knowing that we do not know, together with such peace of mind as comes with the elimination of worry about being mistaken.

In the seventeenth century skepticism was put to another use in religious controversy. Skepticism in the ancient world had implied a conservative social philosophy. If nothing was certain, then among the uncertain things was the necessity or desirability of reform. The rule of skeptical life therefore was to behave conventionally. In the context of the Reformation, this attitude was adopted by people like Erasmus of Rotterdam (1466–1536). If neither reformers nor counterreformers could legitimately claim certainty for their dogmas, the prudent course was to persist in the traditional worship. Skeptical arguments were also used, as they had been by some of the earliest Christian apologists, to undermine the arguments of those who would oppose reason to revelation and authority.

The Cartesian philosophy was distinctive in its attempt to build positive results on a skeptical foundation. Descartes, however, would probably not approve of this way of putting it. He would say, like Plato, that his use of skeptical arguments was for the purpose of clearing away rubble from the site on which knowledge was to be erected. The foundation of his philosophy, according to him, was the *Cogito*.

God to the Rescue

Having fallen, in the first two *Meditations*, into the abyss of skepticism, Descartes hoists himself out in the third and fourth. What he needs, as any mountain climber knows, is a skyhook; this he fashions for himself in the third *Meditation*, where he proves that there must be at least one Being in the world besides Descartes—God. But since God, the perfect Being and cause of everything—including Descartes' thoughts—could not be a deceiver, it follows that Descartes' thoughts correspond with an external reality. At any rate most of them do.

"I think, therefore I am." This is certain. But how do I know that it is certain? "There is nothing else which assures me of its truth but the clear and distinct perception of what I affirm." If we ask what Descartes means by clarity and distinctness, the answer is not entirely clear.

> I term that clear which is present and apparent to an attentive mind, in the same way as we assert that we see objects clearly when, being present to the regarding eye, they operate upon it with sufficient strength. But the distinct is that which is so precise and different from all other objects that it contains within itself nothing but what is clear.[3]

This feeling of certainty upon inspection by the "attentive mind" is taken as the criterion of truth, and must be, in any nonskeptical but inside-out philosophy. "Everything which we conceive very clearly and very distinctly is wholly true."

The problem of knowledge for Descartes at this point, then, has been reduced to that of inspecting his fund of ideas, of how things seem, to discover whether any of them exhibits with sufficient clarity and distinctness a truth about how things are outside Descartes' mind. Although ideas seem to fall into three classes—(1) those that are innate, such as simple mathematical propositions not requiring validation by experience, (2) others that come from outside, such as notions of bodies and other persons, and lastly (3) mere fictions—there cannot at this point be certainty that any of them represents reality. They might all belong to the third class.

Now, however, Descartes reexamines his stock of ideas according to their content of what he calls "objective reality." Descartes uses the word 'idea' in its modern sense, as signifying a bit of consciousness, a usage that has nothing in common with Plato's. And all ideas, considered just as bits of consciousness, are equal; none is more an idea than any other.

> But considering them as images, of which some represent one thing and some another, it is evident that they differ greatly among themselves. For those that represent substances are undoubtedly something more, and contain in themselves, so to speak, more objective reality, or rather, participate by representation in a higher degree of being or perfection, than those which represent only modes or accidents.

Descartes here brings in a Scholastic distinction between two kinds of reality, *formal* and *objective*. To get this distinction straight it is of utmost importance to banish from our attention the modern distinction between subjective and objective; for while there is a rough correspondence between the two sets of distinctions, Scholastic 'objective' goes with modern '*subjective*'! It may help to recall to mind Anselm's proof of the existence of God. Anselm says that everyone will agree that God exists in the mind; the question is whether He also exists in reality outside the mind. Put in terms of the Scholastic distinction, we have: Even the Fool admits that God has *objective* reality; that is, He exists as object of the Fool's idea—which is to say no more than that there really is an idea in the Fool's mind that is *about* God. All sorts of purely imaginary things have objective reality, just in case somebody really imagines them: mermaids, centaurs, unicorns. (Of course fish, cows, and horses also have objective reality—they too are objects of ideas.) Formal reality on the other hand is existence independent of thought—what *we* would call (plain) reality (or even 'objective' reality as opposed to being 'merely subjective'!). However, there is a further complication. The Scholastics held that there are degrees of reality: substances (such as people, horses, and tomatoes) have more (formal) reality than modes (the round shape of the tomato) or accidents (the color of the horse's hide); and, analogously, the idea of a substance (woman or mermaid) has more objective reality than the idea of a substance's mode (the woman's solidity) or of an accident (the mermaid's eye color).

To give Descartes his due, we should admit that these distinctions, while unfamiliar to modern thought, cannot be dismissed as merely arbitrary. There is an intuitively convincing sense in which an apple can be regarded as "more real" than its color or its taste—for the apple can exist on its own while its color and taste cannot—and in which correspondingly our idea of Los Angeles can be said to have more "objective reality" than our idea merely of L.A. smog.

Now that all this is perfectly clear and distinct we can continue with Descartes' argument.

Ideas can thus be ranked in order of their degree of objective reality. At the top must be the idea "by which I conceive a supreme God, eternal, infinite, immutable, omniscient, omnipotent, and the universal creator of all things that exist outside of Himself—that idea, I say, certainly contains in itself more objective reality than do those by which finite substances are represented." That is, whether or not God exists (has formal reality), it cannot be denied that the idea of God exists; and since God, if He exists, has the highest degree of formal reality conceivable, the idea of God must (whether God exists or not) have the highest degree of objective reality that any idea could possibly have.

Now we come to the crux of the argument. Descartes enunciates a principle declared to be "manifest by the light of nature": "There must be at least as much reality in the efficient and total cause as in its effect." Moreover, he tells us, "this is not only evidently true of those effects, whose reality is actual or formal, but likewise of ideas, whose reality is only considered as objective." The cause of a stone must contain all that enters into the stone. When a thing is heated, the cause of heat must be "of an order at least as perfect [*i.e.* complete, real] as heat."

> But further, even the idea of the heat, or of the stone, cannot exist in me unless it be put there by a cause that contains at least as much reality as I conceive existent in the heat or in the stone: for, although that cause may not transmit into my idea anything of its actual or formal reality, we ought not on this account to imagine that it is less real; but we ought to consider that, as every idea is a work of the mind, its nature is such as of itself to demand no other formal reality than that which it borrows from our consciousness, of which it is but a mode.

Here Descartes conceives of ideas as particular entities which are put into me and have reality put into them. There must be something, some cause, that puts them into me. The idea of heat is not itself hot; that is what Descartes means when he says "the cause may not transmit into my idea anything of its actual or formal reality." Nevertheless, the idea must have a cause that is not itself an idea and that cause must have a formal reality that is commensurate with the objective reality of the idea. To assert this amounts to denying that the mind can produce ideas all by itself. It can put ideas together and come up with the idea of a mermaid, but it cannot produce the simple components of such a fantasy.

This thought is continued.

> But in order that an idea may contain this objective reality rather than that, it must doubtless derive it from some cause in which is found at least as much formal reality as the idea contains of objective; for, if we suppose that there is found in an idea anything which was not in its cause it must of course derive this from nothing. But,

however imperfect may be the mode of existence by which a thing is objectively or by representation in the understanding by its idea, we certainly cannot, for all that, allege that this mode of existence is nothing, nor consequently, that the idea owes its origin to nothing.

In this passage Descartes relies on an assumption that the degrees and varieties—formal and objective—of reality are related so closely that one of them can be the cause of the other. In accordance with this assumption, Descartes concludes that the objective reality of ideas cannot in the last analysis be derived simply from other objective reality, but at some point there must be a cause of them that has commensurate formal reality. Some ideas may have no causes but other ideas, yet at some point the chain must hang on a peg.

I am thus clearly taught by the light of nature that ideas exist in me as pictures or images, which may in truth readily fall short of the perfection of the objects from which they are taken, but can never contain anything greater or more perfect.

In the next step Descartes examines his stock of ideas to see whether according to these principles there is enough formal reality in himself to cause them. If so, then he may be left in the skeptical abyss; if not, "it is a necessary consequence that I am not alone in the world, but that there is besides myself some other being who exists as the cause of that idea."

He finds ideas that purport to represent corporeal things, inanimate things, angels, animals, and other people. But, Descartes avers, he should not be so modest as to deny that he might be capable of being the source of the few clear and distinct elements in these; while the rest, such as heat, are so obscure that they may be false, that is, represent nothing real, hence "proceed from nothing."

There only remains, therefore, the idea of God, in which I must consider whether there is anything that cannot be supposed to originate with myself. By the name God, I understand a substance infinite, eternal, immutable, independent, all-knowing, all-powerful, and by which I myself, and every other thing that exists, if any such there be, were created. But these properties are so great and excellent, that the more attentively I consider them the less I feel persuaded that the idea I have of them owes its origin to myself alone. And thus it is absolutely necessary to conclude, from all that I have before said, that God exists: for though the idea of substance be in my mind owing to this, that I myself am a substance, I should not, however, have the idea of an infinite substance, seeing I am a finite being, unless it were given me by some substance in reality infinite.

That is how René Descartes proved the existence of God.

The argument is puzzling both in itself and in its context. It is unsettling to encounter an author who tells us that for all he *knows* he may be alone in the world, without a body, mistakenly believing that two and three are five; who with triumph commensurate to the difficulty of the task succeeds in proving his own existence (though not the existence of his body); and who then, a few pages on, announces in the most insouciant manner "it is manifest by the light of nature that there must be at least as much reality in the efficient and total cause as in its effect." Surely, we tend to think, anyone who could doubt whether two and three are five should have not the slightest difficulty in doubting *that*. And the most gullible person in the world ought to be able to doubt whether "this is not only evidently true of those effects, whose reality is actual or formal, but likewise of ideas, whose reality is only considered as objective." What happened? Did Descartes suddenly abandon altogether his supreme effort to doubt, and drop even the pretense of being a skeptic?

Yet we are not at liberty to suppose that a great philosopher would proceed so erratically. There must have been some reason, sufficient to Descartes' mind, why the causal principle should escape the *débâcle* of the first two *Meditations*. And the reason is not hard to find. Two categories of beliefs were not there scrutinized by Descartes: beliefs about language and about logic.

Among the things it is possible to doubt, if you are a virtuoso doubter, is constancy of meaning. Words notoriously do change their meanings over the years: for example 'objective', as we have just seen. We can imagine the process to be speeded up. The deceiving demon might have deceived Descartes into supposing that he had always meant the same state of affairs by the string of words 'All men are mortal', whereas in fact five minutes earlier they had conveyed to him the notion now suggested by 'The cat is on the mat'. Furthermore, while it is hard to conceive how the conclusion 'Socrates is mortal' should be wrongly drawn from the premises 'All men are mortal, and Socrates is a man', the possibility of error here must be at least as significant as that of being wrong in getting five as the sum of two and three.

In fact Descartes forgot to doubt meaning constancy and logic. Why, we cannot tell. It is easy to see, however, that if he had subjected these to doubt, the *Meditations* would have had to end forthwith. If we deem it doubtful whether our words convey the meanings we intend, it becomes pointless to go on writing, even merely in a private notebook. And if we doubt the validity of simple logical inferences, we cannot continue to argue. The upshot is that the method of doubt if pursued *thoroughly* leads into a black hole from which there is absolutely no hope of escape, not even with the aid of Omnipotence.

Now perhaps we see why the causal principle escaped Cartesian doubt. It was regarded by Descartes as a principle of logic. The bond between cause and effect was generally held, in Descartes' time, to be the same as that between premises and conclusion in a syllogism: given the one the other *must* follow—the sense of necessity being the same for events as for inferences. This assumption, that there are necessary connections in nature, was made by all the principal modern philosophers before Hume.

Skepticism Overthrown

Having established the existence of God, Descartes could easily reestablish and repeople the world. God is the most real, therefore the most perfect being. Therefore, he cannot be evil, for evil is imperfection. Therefore He is not the deceiving demon. But he *would* be the deceiving demon if He had built into His creature, Descartes, such a strong propensity to believe in the existence of a physical world when in fact there was none. Therefore the physical world is real.

Indeed, in the fourth *Meditation* there is a curious reversal of the approach and problems considered in the first two. There the method was systematic doubt, and the problem—made to seem for a while almost hopeless—was how we could assure ourselves that any of our beliefs were true. In the fourth, on the contrary, the principal puzzle becomes that of how it can be possible for any of God's creatures ever to be mistaken about anything. Everybody is from time to time mistaken in his or her beliefs; that unassailable truth was what started the *Meditations* off. But if it is a fault or defect in us to make mistakes, and we are God's handiwork, does it not follow that God has not done so well in making us as a perfect being ought? The problem for Descartes, then, is to show the compatibility with God's perfection of His creatures' being liable to fall into error.

Descartes' procedure is ingenious. God has made us with limited intellects—finite faculties of understanding and imagination. There is no cause for reproach in this, since as far as they go they are not defective. But one of our faculties, that of volition, is infinite—there is nothing that we cannot *will*. We have no cause for complaint at God's bounty in this respect. Now mistakes are the results of the disparity between the finite judgment and the infinite will: we willfully leap at conclusions that go beyond the limitations of our intellectual faculties. Hence our mistakes are our own fault, not God's.

This problem of error, discussed in the fourth *Meditation*, is a subproblem under that of Evil: How can there be anything bad in a world created by the infinitely wise, powerful, and good God? Descartes' blaming error on human free will is a special application of one of the typical solutions: all evil is due to human free will, for which God is not to blame.

The Cartesian Compromise

The principal positive result that Descartes claimed for his method of doubt was that it established the real distinction of thinking and extended substances. This it did because it turned out to be possible to doubt the existence of one's body (the extended part of oneself) but not to doubt the existence of oneself as a thinking thing. Descartes held that if the existence of *A* can be doubted while that of *B* cannot, then *A* and *B* must be distinct things. So a human being is, as Plato held, really two things at once: a space-occupying body and a nonspatial soul.

The body is like "a machine, so built and composed of bones, nerves, muscles, veins, blood, and skin that even if there were no mind in it, it would not cease to move in all the ways that it does at present when it is not moved under the direction of the will, nor consequently with the aid of the mind." Descartes held that all animals except man are mere stimulus-response mechanisms without consciousness. (Cartesian biologists cited this doctrine in defense of vivisection: the howls of the cut-up dog were compared to the squeaks of an unlubricated machine.)

Descartes intended thus to reconcile the new mechanical philosophy with the traditional religious interpretation of the world by separating two spheres of reality in such a way that science would be supreme and unchallenged in the one, theology in the other. Body, including the human body, is unthinking extended substance, the proper subject for scientific physical investigation. Mind or soul, unextended thinking substance, lies entirely outside the sphere of physical investigation. There can be no conflict between science and religion because the combatants are to be kept separate—though theology would have the last word, since God is the source of everything, body and mind alike, and the only substance in the strict sense of that which can exist no matter what else does or does not.

This diplomatic solution was not found satisfactory, even in Descartes' lifetime, because it immediately generated the problem of interaction between mind and body. Obviously body and mind, however distinct as substances, act upon each other: a blow to the head causes seeing-stars or lapse of consciousness; the (mental) urge to kill causes the (physical) movement of muscles holding a dagger. But how is it possible to conceive of nonphysical substance moving gross matter, or the converse? Moreover, physical science would be thrown into confusion if it were not possible in principle to explain all physical events completely in physical terms. Likewise, in the mental sphere the ascription of praise or blame, salvation or damnation, would be compromised if these should turn out to be dependent on the operations of deterministic mechanistic bodily motions.

Descartes' notorious hypothesis about the mechanism of interaction was that it takes place in the so-called pineal gland, a small region in the center of the brain. He thought that the afferent nerves—which he pictured as tubes containing a thin fluid, the "animal spirits"—brought the stimulus to this point, presenting sensations to the mind, whereupon the mind freely activated the efferent nerves, in response, by directing the animal spirits through appropriate valves. Unfortunately this hypothesis, besides its inherent implausibility and lack of histological confirmation, was found to be incompatible with the fundamental physical law of the conservation of momentum.

Geulincx and Malebranche

Some Cartesians deemed it necessary to deny the reality of mind-body interaction. Arnold Geulincx (1625–1669) propounded the theory known as Occasionalism. There are two independent series of events, mental and physical. Neither acts on the other; but God, Who created them both, has so arranged them that they correspond just as if there were interaction. When in the physical series my head is hit by a baseball bat, there is simultaneously in the mental series the phenomenon of seeing-stars. The series are like two clocks, one of which strikes when the other points the hour, not because either influences the other but because the Clockmaker has made them that way.

Nicholas Malebranche (1638–1715) went even further, denying all causal efficacy except that of God. Events whether mental or physical merely succeed each other; the only real cause in the universe is God, Who directly produces every thing and event in such harmonious array that they seem to us to produce each other.

Ultimately the enormous influence of Descartes tended in the direction of materialistic mechanism. Once Descartes had suggested that a dog was a machine and could be understood completely as such, there was no escaping the extension of the theory to man himself. The Church was perhaps right after all in its instinctive hostility to Cartesianism, as it had been to Galileo and every other advance of the mechanistic viewpoint, no matter how many provisos ostensibly safeguarded the spiritual interest.

Cartesian dualism is by no means a dead theory today. Probably the theory that soul and body are distinct entities, which in the individual human being somehow interact, is the view held at least implicitly by more "unphilosophical" people than any rival conception. Nor is it without its distinguished partisans in this century. For instance, Sir Charles Sherrington, the most eminent brain physiologist of his generation, Nobel Prize winner and president of the Royal Society, wrote in 1940

The sun's energy is part of the closed energy-cycle. What leverage can it have on mind? Yet through my retina and brain it is able to act on my mind. The theoretically impossible happens. In fine, I assert that it does act on my mind. Conversely my thinking "self" thinks that it can bend my arm. Physics tells me that my arm cannot be bent without disturbing the sun. Physics tells me that unless my mind is energy it cannot disturb the sun. My mind then does not bend my arm. If it does, the theoretically impossible happens. Let me prefer to think the theoretically impossible does happen. Despite the theoretical I take it my mind *does* bend my arm, and that it disturbs the sun.[4]

34

Hobbes

THOMAS HOBBES, THE FIRST of the really modern philosophers, was born on April 5, 1588—prematurely, due to his mother's fright at the approach of the Spanish Armada. His father was vicar of Westport, near Malmesbury; a quarrelsome man who destroyed his career by getting into a fistfight with another clergyman in front of his own church door. He fled to London, deserting his family. Fortunately, a wealthy relative rescued them. Thomas received a good education, including Greek, then a novelty. When he was 14 he translated the *Medea* of Euripides into Latin verses. In the same year he entered Magdalen Hall, Oxford, where he remained for six years, though without enthusiasm for the Aristotelian logic-chopping that formed the principal part of the curriculum.

Hobbes' second stroke of good fortune came when upon receipt of his Oxford B.A. degree he was employed as tutor to William Cavendish, the young Earl of Devonshire. His Lordship was only two years younger than Hobbes. For the next eighteen years, which he said were the pleasantest of his life, Hobbes was a member of the Cavendish household. His position with this great family gave him opportunity to meet influential men and to travel. With the Earl he made the grand tour of France and Italy. From time to time between 1621 and 1626 he acted as secretary to Francis Bacon, following him around "in his delicious walks in Gorhambury" and writing down the great man's words. Although Hobbes was not a Baconian in his philosophy, he shared the Lord Chancellor's enthusiasm for the application of scientific principles to the improvement of human life.

Hobbes' fortieth year, 1628, was eventful for him. He published his first book, a translation of Thucydides' *History of the Peloponnesian War*. The 1620s were years of growing popular opposition to the policy of Charles I. Hobbes wanted to make Thucydides accessible to his countrymen because the Greek historian had shown the appalling consequences of letting governmental policy be decided by the people. ("It must be admitted," Sir Leslie Stephen wrote in his book on Hobbes, "that this method of meeting democratic tendencies was decidedly roundabout.") In the same year his friend and patron died. Hobbes then accompanied the son of Sir Gervase Clinton in his travels on the Continent for a year and a half. Most importantly for his philosophical development, which really began in this year, he discovered geometrical reasoning.

> Being in a Gentleman's Library, Euclid's Elements lay open, and 'twas the [47th Proposition of Book I—the Pythagorean Theorem]. He read the Proposition. *By G--*, sayd he (he would now and then sweare an emphaticall Oath by way of

emphasis) *this is impossible!* So he reads the Demonstration of it, which referred him back to such a Proposition; which proposition he read. That referred him back to another, which he also read. And so on that at last he was demonstratively convinced of that trueth. This made him in love with Geometry.[1]

About the same time there occurred a conversation about the senses, in which someone asked "But what is sensation?" and no one present could reply. The answer Hobbes gave at length—that sensation is motion in the brain—is the basis of his conception of human nature.

In 1631 Hobbes was received back into the Cavendish family as tutor to the third Earl, the son of his old friend. In 1634 he made his third visit to the Continent. By this time Hobbes was "the celebrated English philosopher," received in the intellectual salons of Paris and invited to propose Objections to Descartes' *Meditations*, then being circulated in manuscript. In Florence he visited and made the friendship of old Galileo, whose new science of motion was to become the underpinning of Hobbes' philosophy.

In the late 1630s resistance to the King had grown to the point where Parliament could and did make things dangerous for supporters of royal power. Hobbes, returned to England, had written and circulated (though not printed) a pamphlet defending the King's claim to certain rights including that of levying taxes directly. When in 1640 the Parliament imprisoned the Bishop of St. David's for having preached this doctrine, Hobbes deemed it time to look to his own safety. He removed to Paris, "the first of all who fled," as he later half-boasted.

There he wrote his principal books: *De Cive (The Citizen)*, part of *De Corpore (On Body)*, and finally *Leviathan*. Soon Paris began to fill up with aristocratic refugees, including the young heir to the throne. Hobbes' reputation and connections secured him appointment as mathematics tutor to the Prince, 1646–1648. Charles grew fond of Hobbes, but opposition, especially among the bishops at the court in exile, became so intense that he was at length dismissed and told not to enter the royal presence again. The clerics had reason to be shocked. When Hobbes was ill and thought to be dying, "the Divines came to him, and tormented him (both Roman Catholic, Church of England, and Geneva). Sayd he to them, Let me alone, or els I will detect all your Cheates from Aaron to yourselves."[2] He defended monarchy, but not on the officially approved ground of divine right. And his attack in *Leviathan* on the "Kingdome of Darknesse," that is, the Catholic Church, made him odious to the French as well.

In these circumstances he found it prudent to flee from the refugees. In the winter of 1651 he returned to England, "not well assured of safety there," he wrote, "but there was no other place where I could be safer. It was cold, the snow was deep, I was an old man, the wind was sharp. A skittish horse and rough road were troublesome too."[3] He submitted himself to Cromwell's Council of State, which allowed him to live in peace, writing and publishing as he pleased. He finished *De Corpore*, which was published in Latin in 1655 and the next year in English.

In that book Hobbes—who was a good geometer for one who had started so late, but thought himself even better—set out a method, as he claimed, of squaring the circle. This led to a protracted, furious, and unseemly quarrel with John Wallis, the Professor of Geometry at Oxford. To his death Hobbes never confessed his error, though it was he who wrote "for who is so stupid, as both to mistake in Geometry, and also to persist in it, when another detects his error to him?"[4] This enmity was the principal reason why Hobbes was never elected to membership in the Royal Society. (In Hobbes' defense it should be pointed out that his process for circle squaring, while deficient in geometrical rigor, contained the germ of the idea of the infinitesimal calculus, for which Newton and Leibniz were to gain so much glory in the next generation.)

King Charles II, soon after his restoration to the throne in 1660, went out of his way to be gracious to his former tutor. He gave orders that Hobbes was to be allowed to come to court whenever he pleased and awarded him a pension of a hundred pounds annually, which however was not regularly paid. On one occasion royal influence seems to have rescued Hobbes from real danger. After the great plague followed by the great fire of 1666, which the religious interpreted as signs of divine displeasure at wicked Londoners, "in Parliament . . . some of the Bishops made a Motion to have the good old Gentleman burn't for a Heretique."[5] All that eventually happened was that Hobbes was forbidden to publish any more books on politics and religion. His subsequent works were printed in Holland. *Leviathan* became a rare item in England and sold for large sums.

Hobbes was sickly when young, but after severe illnesses in his late fifties his constitution changed dramatically for the better. He was always busy, and played tennis up to the age of 75. But palsy and partial paralysis vexed him in old age. In his eighties he translated Homer into English verse to keep occupied. Finally in 1675 he retired to Chatsworth—one of the Earl of Devonshire's country estates—where he lived for four more years, dying on December 4, 1679, in his ninety-second year.

> That he was a Christian 'tis cleare, for he received the Sacrament of Dr. Pierson, and in his confession to Dr. John Cosins, on his (as he thought) death-bed, declared that he liked the Religion of the Church of England best of all other . . .
>
> He was put into a Woollen Shroud and Coffin, which was covered with a white Sheet, and upon that a black Herse cloth, and so carryed upon men's shoulders, a little mile to Church. The company consisting of the family and neighbours that came to his Funerall, and attended him to his grave, were very handsomely entertained with Wine, burned and raw, cake, biscuit, etc.[6]

First Philosophy

Hobbes defined philosophy as

> *such knowledge of effects or appearances, as we acquire by true ratiocination from the knowledge we have first of their causes or generation: And again, of such causes or generations as may be from knowing first their effects.*[7]

That is to say, he makes philosophy to be reasoned knowledge of nature. It thus includes, or indeed is the same as, science as we think of it. It excludes theology, because God has no cause and also because in Hobbes' opinion we know God only by revelation, which is not "ratiocination."

First philosophy, which is reasoning about reasoning, or philosophy of philosophy, tells us what ratiocination is: computation. Here Hobbes' fascination with geometry asserted itself. The nature of reasoning in geometry, "the only science that it hath pleased God hitherto to bestow on mankind," is this. The axioms are definitions, explicit presentations of the simple notions that enter into the subject.

After J. Wright, Thomas Hobbes, *c. 1669–1670. Oil.*
National Portrait Gallery, London.

The theorems consist in adding these notions together and noting the equalities that result. Thus it turns out that the meanings of 'equal', 'three', 'angle', 'side', and 'triangle' are such that the names 'equiangular triangle' and 'equilateral triangle' name the same objects. Hobbes is using 'addition' in a sense such that whenever an axiom or previous theorem is cited in the proof of a theorem, its content is said to be added. Any kind of reasoning in which we start from definitions and proceed to deduce their consequences is reasoning by what Hobbes calls the compositive or synthetical method—that is, putting-together.

There is a complementary form of reasoning, the analytic or resolutive, by which we attain understanding of a complex thing by resolving its notion into its simple components. In this way we proceed to definitions, which are first principles. Hobbes illustrates: We can resolve 'unjust' into 'fact against law', 'law' in turn into 'command of him or them that have coercive power'. 'Unjust' thus means 'fact against the command of him or them that have coercive power'. (The analysis can be carried further.)

A consequence of Hobbes' doctrine of computation is that "Every proposition, universally true, is either a definition, or part of a definition, or the evidence of it depends upon definitions."[8] In modern terminology, every true proposition of science is analytic, hence necessarily true. A false general statement is at bottom incoherent, self-contradictory.

Hobbes says that scientific exposition begins with definitions, which are "arbitrary." These so-called definitions, however, should include causes of the things defined; they really amount to what we should call scientific hypotheses. His description of the typical method of science as "partly synthetical and partly analytical" amounts to this: By the analytical method we propose a definition. Then using the synthetical method we investigate the consequences of this definition in combination with other definitions. At some point in the proceedings we can compare these consequences with our observations, to see whether these "arbitrary" definitions in fact describe anything actually existing in the world. If so, good; if not, we must try another "definition." This is in its essentials what is now called the hypothetico-deductive method that is said to be the proper method of scientific investigation: elaboration of a hypothesis, deduction of observational consequences, and experimental verification or falsification. Hobbes, furthermore, was the first to make a clear statement of its nature.

Body

To the question "What is there to philosophize about?" Hobbes' answer is starkly simple: Bodies. There are no universal things; everything that exists is a particular individual, "that which, having no dependence upon our thought, is coincident or coextended with some part of space."[9] Bodies move. In doing so they move other bodies; that is all that happens. Hence the science of motion is ultimately the only science. Geometry Hobbes thought of as the first and most abstract part of this science, for he conceived of geometrical figures not as static entities but as paths of motions: the circle as the motion of a point at a fixed distance from another point, the sphere as the motion of a semicircle around its diameter. The second part of philosophy is the contemplation of the effects of moving bodies on one another in altering their mutual motions. Third, we must investigate the causes of seeing, hearing, tasting, smelling, and touching. Fourth, the sensible qualities—such as light, sound, and heat. These Hobbes calls in Aristotelian fashion Physics. Then we may consider more particularly the motions of the mind (*i.e.* brain): the passions of love, anger, envy, and the like, and their causes, which comprise moral philosophy. Lastly, civil philosophy is the study of the motions of men (including their larynxes and tongues) in commonwealths. While moral and civil philosophy are thus linked in principle to the study of simple motions, Hobbes was aware that it is and will remain impractical to treat of them by the synthetical method appropriate to the abstract sciences. They are therefore to be pursued by the analytical method, which turns out to be in these cases observation of the way of the world helped out by introspection of our own passions.

Bodies are distinguished from one another by their *accidents*—properties, qualities, relations. "Bodies are things, and not generated; accidents are generated, and not things." The notion of an accident is too simple to be defined, Hobbes thought—but examples are extension, motion, color, sound, rationality. Hobbes did say that accident is "the manner by which any body is conceived; . . . that faculty of any body, by which it works in us a conception of itself."[10] Now the way in which bodies get themselves conceived by us is by pressing, directly or through a medium, our sense organs. Therefore, every accident is reducible to some configuration of moving bodies or parts of bodies.

Phantasms

Hobbes held with Galileo, however, that only the extension, mass, and motion—what later came to be called the primary qualities—of bodies are in the objects perceived. Color, sound, taste, and smell are really "in us." This brings us to the vexing subject of the *phantasm* in Hobbes' philosophy.

'Phantasm' is the Greek word meaning something that appears, apparition. In medieval theory of perception the word was used as a technical term for that which is, directly and immediately, in the soul when perception takes place. When I look at a tomato there is no tomato in my soul; there must be a "conversion to phantasm" in order for there to be a perception.

Hobbes used the word similarly to signify that which is in us when we perceive. But what is in us is motion of matter, for there is nothing else in the world. In meditating on the question, What is sensation?, it occurred to Hobbes that if all motion were to cease, perception would cease with it. Therefore, perception must be motion.

> Sense . . . can be nothing else but motion in some of the internal parts of the sentient. . . . And so we find what is the subject of our sense, namely, that in which are the phantasms; and partly also we have discovered the nature of sense, namely, that it is some internal motion in the sentient. . . . The subject of sense is the sentient itself, namely, some living creature; and we speak more correctly, when we say a living creature seeth, than when we say the eye seeth. The object is the thing received; and it is more accurately said, that we see the sun, than that we see the light. For light and color, and heat and sound, and other qualities which are commonly called sensible, are not objects, but phantasms in the sentients. For a phantasm is the act of sense, and differs no otherwise from sense than *fieri*, that is, being a doing, differs from *factum esse*, that is, being done; which difference, in things that are done in an instant, is none at all; and a phantasm is made in an instant.[11]

Here Hobbes is telling us that colors and the like, our sensations, really are motions in the head. Unfortunately, in several passages Hobbes neglected this doctrine in favor of a distinction between things and their appearances.

> There is nothing without us (really) which we call an image or colour. . . . The said image or colour is but an apparition unto us of the motion, agitation, or alteration, which the object worketh in the brain, or spirits, or some internal substance of the head.[12]

> All which qualities, called sensible, are in the object, that causeth them, but so many several motions of the matter, by which it presseth our organs diversely. Neither in us that are pressed, are they any thing else, but diverse motions; for motion produceth nothing but motion. But their appearance to us is fancy, the same waking, that dreaming.[13]

There seem to be two "us"es in these passages: one that is matter in motion, another that is the dupe of appearances. Any attempt to show how consciousness is just a kind of motion is apt to lead into these reverberative problems of the relation of motion to the appearance of motion: is the appearance of motion another motion? If so, motion of what? If not, has not something besides motion been sneaked into the philosophy?

Man

> For seeing life is but a motion of Limbs, the beginning whereof is in some principall part within; why may we not say, that all *Automata* (Engines that move themselves by springs and wheeles as doth a watch) have an artificiall life? For what is the *Heart*, but a *Spring*; and the *Nerves*, but so many *Strings*; and the *Joynts*, but so many *Wheeles*, giving motion to the whole Body, such as was intended by the Artificer?[14]

In this simile we have one of the first appearances of the man-a-machine motif in philosophy, though some of Leonardo da Vinci's drawings had compared skeleto-muscular anatomy to mechanical devices. Descartes indeed had pronounced the human body to be a machine, but inasmuch as he made the unextended thinking substance to be the real person, it remained for Hobbes to work out the first thoroughly mechanistic theory of human nature.

Against such a view the objection would be urged that men have free will while machines can do only what their design necessitates. Hobbes during his stay in Paris in the 1640s engaged in controversy concerning freedom of the will with Dr. Bramhall, refugee Bishop of Derry. Hobbes believed the whole problem arose from muddled thinking and would be dissolved once we attained clarity about the ideas involved. What is the will? For Hobbes it is not enlightening to say that it is a faculty—as if our cognitive faculty surveyed the situation and made its report to another headquarters, the Will, which then decided what orders to issue. We deliberate about what to do—deliberation being an imagination of consequences of proposed action, giving rise in us to succession alternately of appetite and fear. The will is just "the last appetite in deliberation." When our action proceeds from this last appetite, that is when we do what we want to do and are not constrained by external obstacles, our actions are voluntary. But "The will is not voluntary: for, a man can no more say he will will, than he will will will, and so make an infinite repetition of the word; which is absurd, and insignificant."[15]

If freedom of the will means absence of determining causes for our appetites and fears, there is no freedom of the will; these, like everything else, are necessitated by their causes. But *we* are free, at least sometimes: liberty, "the absence of external impediments to motion," is compatible with necessity, as water is both free and necessitated to run downhill. To the objection that determination of the will would make advice, reward, and punishment ineffective, Hobbes replied that on the contrary these can be of use only if they are among the factors that determine the will. If the will is not determined at all, then it is not determined by advice, reward, and punishment, and efforts expended in these activities are indeed wasted.

The Bishop pointed out in horror that if the will is strictly determined, then in the end it is God Who determines it. Therefore, He both causes us to sin and punishes us with hellfire for doing so. Hobbes did not shrink from affirming this conclusion. Citing St. Paul he answered that "the *power* of God alone without other helps is sufficient *justification* of any action he doth . . . *Power irresistible justifies all actions, really and properly.*" Hobbes suggested, however, that this doctrine, though true, should perhaps not be stated openly. His writing against Bramhall was published against his wishes.

We are to understand people, then, by studying what impels them to action, the "interior beginnings of voluntary motions; commonly called the Passions." To find out about them we must observe what people do and, most importantly, we must look into ourselves. For we are so much alike that if we know what we do and upon what grounds—when we think, reason, hope, or fear—we learn at the same time why others behave as they do. "When I shall have set down my own reading orderly, and perspicuously, the pains left another, will be onely to consider, if he also find not the same in himself. For this kind of Doctrine admitteth no other Demonstration."[16]

The small beginning of motion, which Hobbes called Endeavour, is defined to be "motion made in less space and time than can be given; that is, motion made through the length of a point, and in an instant or point of time."[17] It sounds absurd to talk of motion through the length of a point; but in fact Hobbes, here as in his circle squaring, was trying to express the fundamental idea of the infinitesimal calculus. He was also, as a materialist must, striving to avoid thinking of dispositions as real potentialities not reducible to actualities.

The many different passions (emotions, we would say) are based upon two: Appetite, Desire, or Love, defined as endeavor toward something which causes it, and Aversion or Hatred, which is "Endeavour fromward." Each of us calls the object of desire good, the object of aversion evil. But although the specific objects of desire are various, it is possible to generalize about "the Felicity of this life." It

> consisteth not in the repose of a mind satisfied. For there is no such *Finis ultimus*, (utmost ayme,) nor *Summum Bonum*, (greatest Good,) as is spoken of in the Books of the old Morall Philosophers. Nor can a man any more live, whose desires are at an end, than he, whose Senses and Imaginations are at a stand. Felicity is a continuall progresse of the desire, from one object to another; the attaining of the former, being still but the way to the later. . . .
>
> So that in the first place, I put for a generall inclination of all mankind, a perpetuall and restlesse desire of Power after power, that ceaseth onely in Death.[18]

Hobbes held that what we desire is always some good for ourselves. Thus he defined Pity as "*Griefe*, for the Calamity of another, . . . [which] ariseth from the imagination that the like calamity may befall himselfe."[19] He did not deny, however, that personal satisfaction can be obtained from the happiness of another. When charged with inconsistency for giving money to a poor and infirm old man, he replied that he did it "Because I was in paine to consider the miserable condition of the old man; and now my almes, giving him some reliefe, doth also ease me."[20]

Life is a continual competition, which Hobbes compared to a race in a grand metaphor of all the passions.

> To endeavour, is *appetite*.
> To be remiss, is *sensuality*.
> To consider them behind, is *glory*.
> To consider them before, is *humility*.
> To lose ground with looking back, *vain glory*.
> To be holden, *hatred*.
> To turn back, *repentance*.
> To be in breath, *hope*.

To be weary, *despair.*
To endeavour to overtake the next, *emulation.*
To supplant or overthrow, *envy.*
To resolve to break through a stop foreseen, *courage.*
To break through a sudden stop, *anger.*
To lose ground by little hindrances, *pusillanimity.*
To fall on the sudden, is disposition to *weep.*
To see another fall, is disposition to *laugh.*
To see one out-gone whom we would not, is *pity.*
To see one out-go whom we would not, is *indignation.*
To hold fast by another, is to *love.*
To carry him on that so holdeth, is *charity.*
To hurt one's-self for haste, is *shame.*
Continually to be out-gone, is *misery.*
Continually to out-go the next before, is *felicity.*
And to forsake the course, is to *die.*[21]

Political Philosophy

One might expect that a philosopher entranced thus with a picture of human beings as restless selfish seekers of power after power would think of government and morality as Thrasymachus and Callicles in Plato's dialogues did: as two more obstacles for the strong to overcome. But Hobbes to the contrary based the necessity of government on reason and human nature, and argued, as few have done before or since, that no restrictions should be put on its authority—or hardly any.

Hobbes was the first major political theorist since Aristotle to keep politics separate from theology. In the middle ages, whenever the question was raised "Why do I have an obligation to obey the laws?" the answer was some variant of "Because it is God's commandment." "The powers that be are ordained of God," St. Paul had pronounced. The principal question remaining was whether the power of the State was transmitted from God to the King via the Pope (St. Thomas Aquinas) or via the people (Marsiglio of Padua, William of Ockham) or directly (Dante, King James I of England). Sir Robert Filmer, a contemporary of Hobbes, argued that the King should be obeyed because he was, "or ought to be reputed to be," the direct heir of Adam in the male line!

Hobbes paid his respects to God as the ultimate source of everything, including human reason, but after that his theory was independent of religion. Indeed one of his principal aims was to defend the secular State against priestly interference. Unlike almost all his predecessors, moreover, he began with an assertion of the fact of human equality.

> Nature hath made men so equall, in the faculties of body, and mind; as that though there bee found one man sometimes manifestly stronger in body, or of quicker mind then another; yet when all is reckoned together, the difference between man, and man, is not so considerable, as that one man can thereupon claim to himselfe any benefit, to which another may not pretend, as well as he.[22]

Given luck or aid, the weakest can kill the strongest; and as for wisdom, "there is not ordinarily a greater signe of the equall distribution of any thing, than that every man is contented with his share."

Because of this natural equality, people have equal hope of succeeding in competition for scarce goods; therefore they are at enmity with their rivals, therefore at war. For we are naturally quarrelsome on account of the prevalence of competition, diffidence (fear of what others will do to us if we do not do it to them first), and glory (the universal tendency to demand honor from others).

Consequently, human beings living in a state of nature—with no common power over them all strong enough to keep them in awe—would be at war each with all the rest.

> In such condition, there is no place for Industry; because the fruit thereof is uncertain: and consequently no Culture of the Earth; no Navigation, nor use of the commodities that may be imported by Sea; no commodious Building; no Instruments of moving, and removing such things as require much force; no Knowledge of the face of the Earth; no account of Time; no Arts; no Letters; no Society; and which is worst of all, continuall feare, and danger of violent death; and the life of man, solitary, poore, nasty, brutish, and short.[23]

This famous description is part of a thought experiment. In spite of some remarks about "the savage people in many places of *America*," Hobbes was not speculatively reconstructing history. He was thinking rather of the anarchy that occurs in the midst of civil war, such as he had witnessed from the safety of France, as well as the relations between sovereign States.

In the state of nature

> nothing can be Unjust. The notions of Right and Wrong, Justice and Injustice have there no place. Where there is no common Power, there is no Law: where no Law, no Injustice. Force, and Fraud, are in warre the two Cardinall vertues.[24]

Right and Law of Nature

But competitive, diffident, and glory-seeking men are also fearful of death and desirous of a less nasty and brutish existence. And they are, to some extent, rational. Therefore, finding themselves in the state of nature, they would do (so Hobbes believed) what reason dictated as necessary to get out of that condition.

What reason tells us is twofold. In the absence of a power over us, each one of us has a right, the Right of Nature, to do anything judged necessary or convenient for preserving life. Hobbes in calling this a right apparently meant only that no one can blame me for defending myself by any means I choose to employ; this is not a right that imposes an obligation on anyone else. I have the right to shoot you if I deem you dangerous to me, but you likewise have the right to shoot back. Since, however, reason tells both of us that as long as everybody has and exercises this right no one can be secure, we come to another precept: *"That every man, ought to endeavour Peace, as farre as he has hope of obtaining it."* This is the first and fundamental Law of Nature.

The Social Contract

How can we get peace? It would be unreasonable for me to resolve to be peaceable if the others did not. I can be required only to be willing, when others are so too, to abandon my right to all things and to be content with as much liberty against others as I would allow others against myself. If all of us make this agreement among ourselves, well and good, provided the agreement is enforceable. For "covenants, without the sword, are but words, and of no strength to secure a man at all." We must therefore not only make this covenant with one another, but at the same time authorize some one or some group to enforce it, and provide the enforcer(s) with sufficient means to do so. We are to say to one another

> *I Authorise and give up my Right of Governing my selfe, to this Man, or to this Assembly of men, on this condition, that thou give up thy Right to him, and Authorise all his Actions in like manner.* This done, the Multitude so united in one Person, is called a COMMON-WEALTH ... This is the Generation of that great LEVIATHAN, or rather (to speake more reverently) of that *Mortall God*, to which wee owe under the *Immortal God*, our peace and defence.[25]

Hobbes' language suggests that if a group of us found ourselves on a desert island, we could escape anarchy by reciting this formula en masse and delivering our weapons to some person or some committee—or even by retaining them in our possession, since Hobbes allowed the possibility of the sovereignty inhering in the whole people. That was not his meaning. The Leviathan must be a "reall Unitie of them all, in one and the same Person." Such unity can be attained only if all—or at least the preponderant majority—of parties to the agreement really do resolve to put themselves at the service of the sovereign, to abide by decisions officially announced, and actively to assist in terrorizing the recalcitrant (if any) still remaining in the state of nature. Because Hobbes was so insistent on this point, his theory was repugnant to many people. He would allow no reservations in submission to the sovereign, for any such could not but weaken the supreme authority and tend to dissolve the always precarious structure of the "Mortall God." The sovereign is not a party to the Hobbesian covenant, thus can never justly be accused of violating an agreement.

The social contract, to repeat, is a thought experiment. If we found ourselves in anarchy, and if we were rational, we would get out of that state by the only means we could, which would be to subscribe explicitly and sincerely to this sort of contract, recognizing that only thus could the interests of each of us be secured. Therefore, even when we have not formally subscribed in this manner, it is as if we had. If someone is inclined to ask "But why should I obey the laws of the land?" the answer is "Because you have, in effect, covenanted to do so." If this answer does not satisfy you, the only further thing to say is, "All right, then *don't* respect the sovereign. In that case you put yourself back into the state of nature, and you have no right to complain if the rest of us employ all the terrors of war against you." Thus the sovereign's rights are just the same whether derived from the formula explicitly, or acquired by conquest or even usurpation. The sovereign is legitimate just as long as in fact the peace is kept at home and the country is defended abroad. There can be no justification for rebellion. Tyranny, Hobbes remarked, is simply a word that people apply to monarchy when they dislike the monarch.

The rights of sovereignty Hobbes summarizes as follows.

> His Power cannot, without his consent, be Transferred to another: He cannot Forfeit it, He cannot be Accused by any of his Subjects, of Injury: He cannot be Punished by them: He is Judge of what is necessary for Peace; and Judge of Doctrines: He is Sole Legislator; and the Supreme Judge of Controversies; and of the Times, and Occasions of Warre, and Peace: to him it belongeth to choose Magistrates, Counsellours, Commanders, and all other Officers, and Ministers; and to determine of Rewards, and Punishments, Honour, and Order.[26]

Except for "Judge of Doctrines," that is, of religion, there is nothing on this list that is not claimed as the prerogative of government in the United States of the present day, and every other nation in the world.

Because the subject submits to the sovereign for the sake of security, all those rights are retained the abrogation of which would be inconsistent therewith. These comprise the right to refuse to commit suicide even if ordered to do so; to refuse to incriminate oneself; and, in some cases, to refuse to be drafted into military service!

Monarchy is preferable to aristocracy and democracy because it is more efficient—and because there is bound to be harmony between monarch and people, for the monarch's and the people's power and security go together. Constitutional monarchy, or cabinet rule, Hobbes compared to a game of tennis played from a wheelbarrow with several men holding each handle.

Political Pathology

"Though nothing can be immortall, which morals make; yet, if men had the use of reason they pretend to, their Commonwealths might be secured, at least, from perishing by internall diseases."[27] Except for "want of Mony," the infirmities of commonwealths that Hobbes enumerates consist in limitations on the power of the sovereign—all of which open up ways for successful resistance by subjects. As the first of "seditious doctrines" Hobbes mentions "That every private man is Judge of Good and Evill actions."[28] This is perhaps surprising to find—coming 144 pages after the definitions of Good and Evil in terms of objects of desire and aversion, and insistence on their relativity to the individual. Hobbes defends himself against the reproach of inconsistency by arguing that all men as a matter of fact desire peace. Therefore—as far as they are rational—they desire the necessary condition for peace, which is Commonwealth; in consequence, not only do they consent implicitly to the decisions of the sovereign, they desire whatever the sovereign desires! Conscientious scruples against the sovereign's command must not be tolerated, else the Commonwealth will be on the way to collapse.

Besides denouncing the doctrine of private judgment, Hobbes deplored as seditious the views that it is sin to act against conscience and that sanctity is inspired (breathed) into the soul by the Holy Spirit—which would make a prophet of every one who claimed inspiration. These were tenets of the Presbyterians, who had subverted the monarchy of Charles I. They had been helped along, he thought, by the teachings of Sir Edward Coke (1552–1634)—the great advocate of Common Law and antagonist of Stuart absolutism—who had held that the King is subject to the common Law; that the right of private property, including tenure of judicial office, is absolute and not to be abrogated by the sovereign; and that since King and judiciary are supreme in their own spheres, the sovereignty is divisible.

Religion

Perhaps Hobbes was a good Anglican Christian, as his biographer Aubrey believed him to be. Or perhaps, as a nineteenth-century writer asserted, "he knew, better probably than even the bishops, how thoroughly he deserved to be burnt."[29] In the seventeenth century, less prudent men than Hobbes deemed it vital to conceal their opinions on certain points of religion. But there is little ground for supposing that Hobbes' voluminous writings on religion do not express what he believed, and all that he believed.

He thought that the existence of God could be proved from the necessity of a first cause, but that we can know nothing of His attributes. We call Him infinitely wise, good, loving, and the like to do Him honor, not to describe Him. (But since "incorporeal substance" was Hobbes' stock example of "insignificant speech," Bishop Bramhall was able to force him into the position of having to say of God that He is an invisible *body*!) Early in *Leviathan*[30] he entertains us with an essay on the absurd religious practices of mankind, which he ascribes to fear and ignorance. In his notorious definition of religion, he distinguishes it from superstition only by its having the approval of the sovereign.

> *Feare* of power invisible, feigned by the mind, or imagined from tales publiquely allowed, RELIGION; not allowed, SUPERSTITION.[31]

To which he blandly adds

> And when the power imagined, is truly such as we imagine, TRUE RELIGION.

Elsewhere we are told that religion rests entirely on revelation, which it is unprofitable to discuss.

> For it is with the mysteries of our Religion, as with wholesome pills for the sick, which swallowed whole, have the vertue to cure; but chewed, are for the most part cast up again without effect.[32]

True religion is presumably that which is evidenced by genuine revelations. The question, which revelations are genuine and which spurious, is to be decided by the sovereign.

Of the four parts into which *Leviathan* is divided, two are devoted almost exclusively to religious questions. In Part III Hobbes sought to establish, by minute scrutiny of the Holy Scriptures, two theses: that Christianity consists in adhering to one proposition only, namely that Jesus is the Christ, and that the Scriptures consistently teach subordination of religious to secular power. The last Part, entitled "Of the Kingdome of Darknesse," exposes the pretensions of the Papacy as based on wrong scriptural interpretation motivated by greed for power and money.

Hobbism

Though Hobbes may have been right in his claim that nothing in *Leviathan* was against the doctrine of the Church of England, in one way and another the book did carry out his threat to the clergy to expose all their cheats from Aaron to themselves. This fact, together with widespread rumors of his downright atheism, accounts for much of the ferocious clerical opposition to him, and for the public burning of *Leviathan* in Oxford. It was Hobbes' First Philosophy, however—the view of the universe including humanity as nothing but bodies in motion—that was absolutely incompatible with religion.

Dozens of writings exposing the errors of the Monster of Malmesbury appeared, to loud applause, in the latter part of the seventeenth century. Only one pamphlet was published in defense of Hobbism—anonymously.

35

Spinoza

THE MONARCHS OF SPAIN in 1492 and Portugal in 1497 required all Jews living in their dominions to adopt the Christian religion. Many who were baptized continued at enormous risk to practice Judaism secretly. Near the beginning of the seventeenth century some of these *marranos*, as they were known, made their way to Holland—almost the only place in western Europe where Jews were allowed to immigrate.

Baruch Spinoza (or Espinosa) was born in Amsterdam in 1632 to Portuguese *marrano* parents, members of the large and prosperous Jewish colony by then established in that city. Early showing signs of an extraordinary intellect, he was trained to be a rabbi, and received education not only in the traditional Hebrew and Arabic literature but also—a novelty—in Latin, "the priests' tongue." He was instructed by one Frans van den Ende, a man of independent and indeed heretical disposition who familiarized him with the Cartesian philosophy.

In his early twenties Baruch expressed certain doubts about the immortality of the soul and the existence of angels. The authorities of the Jewish community, anxious to avoid offending their Christian hosts (to whom such views would be extremely offensive), tried to bribe the young man into silence. When this was refused, things came to such a pass that a formal sentence of excommunication was pronounced with this curse in the handsome Amsterdam synagogue.

> With the judgment of the angels and the sentence of the saints, we anathematize, execrate, curse and cast out Baruch Spinoza, the whole of the sacred community assenting, in presence of the sacred books with the six hundred and thirteen precepts written therein, pronouncing against him the malediction wherewith Elisha cursed the children, and all the maledictions written in the Book of the Law. Let him be accursed by day, and accursed by night; let him be accursed in his lying down, and accursed in his rising up; accursed in going out and accursed in coming in. May the Lord never more pardon or acknowledge him; may the wrath and displeasure of the Lord burn henceforth against this man, load him with all the curses written in the Book of the Law, and blot out his name from under the sky; may the Lord sever him for ever from all the tribes of Israel, weight him with all the maledictions of the firmament contained in the Book of the Law; and may all ye who are obedient to the Lord your God be saved this day.
>
> Hereby then are all admonished that none hold converse with him by word of mouth, none hold communication with him by writing; that no one do him any service, no one abide under the same roof with him, no one approach within four cubits length of him, and no one read any document dictated by him, or written by his hand.[1]

Shortly afterwards an attempt was made on his life. Baruch changed his given name into its Latin equivalent, Benedictus ("Blessed"), and went to live in a suburb of Amsterdam as a lodger in the house of a Mennonite family. When five years later these good people moved to Rijnsburg near Leiden, Spinoza went with them. Afterwards he lived in the house of a widow in the Hague, later with an artist's family.

The 21 years between his excommunication and his death were outwardly uneventful. In keeping with the tradition of rabbinical students, he had learned a manual trade: lens grinding. In his room he ground enough lenses to pay for rent, clothing, bread, cheese, beer, tobacco, paper, ink, and books; he required hardly anything more. The rest of his time he spent in writing and conversing. He was not solitary, despite being shunned by the pious of his former community. His trade, and soon his reputation as a philosopher, brought him into contact with important men of science such as Huyghens, the greatest Dutch scientist of the era; Leibniz; and Oldenburg, the secretary of the Royal Society in London, with whom he carried on an extensive philosophical correspondence. There was always a group of young men, many of them physicians, who met to discuss his philosophy in more or less formal seminars. His fame spread to the extent that when he was 41 he was offered the position of professor of philosophy in Heidelberg University. "You will have the most ample freedom in philosophical teaching," the invitation read, "which the Prince is confident you will not misuse, to disturb the religion publicly established." Spinoza replied: "I do not know the limits, within which the freedom of my philosophical teaching would be confined, if I am to avoid all appearance of disturbing the publicly established religion."[2] He tactfully declined the offer on the ground that public teaching would not leave him time for his researches. Four years later he died of the tuberculosis that had afflicted him for many years.

He had friends, too, among merchants—one of whom insisted on settling a regular income on him—and statesmen, including the De Witt brothers, for years the liberal leaders of the Dutch government. When in 1672 they fell from power and were lynched at the Hague by an Orangist mob, Spinoza lost his philosophic calm—the only time in his life, as far as is known. He wanted to rush into the street and denounce the murderers. Friends locked him in his room, probably saving his life.

Spinoza published only two books in his lifetime: *Principles of Cartesian Philosophy* (1663), an expository work, and in 1670, anonymously, the *Theologico-Political Treatise*, which went through five editions before it was banned by the government under pressure from Calvinist preachers. Although the great *Ethics Demonstrated in Geometrical Order* was substantially completed by 1665, Spinoza made no attempt to publish it until ten years later. In a letter to Oldenburg he related what happened.

DISTINGUISHED AND ILLUSTRIOUS SIR—When I received your letter of the 22nd July, I had set out to Amsterdam for the purpose of publishing the book I had mentioned to you. While I was negotiating, a rumor gained currency that I had in the press a book concerning God, wherein I endeavored to show that there is no God. This report was believed by many. Hence certain theologians, perhaps the authors of the rumor, took occasion to complain of me before the prince and the magistrates; moreover, the stupid Cartesians, being suspected of favoring me, endeavored to remove the aspersion by abusing everywhere my opinions and writings, a course which they still pursue. When I became aware of this through trustworthy men, who also assured me that the theologians were everywhere lying in wait for me, I determined to put off publishing till I saw how things were going, and I proposed to inform you of my intentions. But matters seem to get worse and worse, and I am still uncertain what to do.[3]

He did nothing. Only after his death did his friend the physician Ludwig Meyer take upon himself the risk of publishing it, along with an unfinished *Political Treatise*, a *Hebrew Grammar*, and the author's surviving Correspondence.

Political Philosophy

Like Hobbes' *Leviathan*, the *Theologico-Political Treatise* combines two oddly assorted topics, political theory and Biblical criticism, whose union is to be explained only by the odd conditions existing in the seventeenth century. Spinoza was defending the liberalism of the Dutch Republic against the Calvinist bigotry influential with the House of Orange. Like Hobbes, Spinoza made the authority of the State rest on a virtual social contract by which people give up their right of doing as they see fit to a social agency, the sovereign, created to enforce peace and protect them. Spinoza also drew the Hobbesian consequence that the power of the State cannot be limited, and in particular the State must be supreme over the Church.

In two respects, however, Spinoza opposed Hobbes' doctrine. The subtitle of the *Treatise* is "Containing Certain Discussions Where is Set Forth that Freedom of Thought and Speech not only May, without Prejudice to Piety and the Public Peace, be Granted; but Also May Not, without Danger to Piety and the Public Peace, be Withheld." This book is, after Milton's *Areopagitica* (1644), the first great plea for general freedom of speech—a novel position in its time; the law everywhere made words as well as deeds punishable when deemed subversive. Spinoza conceded the right of government to regulate speech; he argued only that it was foolish and unprofitable for it to make the attempt. In the nature of things it is impossible for us to abdicate our natural right to judge, each of us, of truth and falsity, right and wrong. The State can only punish us for expressing our views. But if it does so, it will be subverting its own end.

> No, the object of government is not to change men from rational beings into beasts or puppets, but to enable them to develop their minds and bodies in security, and to employ their reason unshackled; neither showing hatred, anger, or deceit, nor watched with the eyes of jealousy and injustice. In fact, the true aim of government is liberty.[4]

The second point of difference from Hobbes is that Spinoza considered democracy—the constitution in which all respectable men who are of age have the vote—to be the "most natural" and best form of government. He would have developed this idea in the *Political Treatise* had he lived to finish it.

Most of the *Theologico-Political Treatise* is concerned with Biblical criticism. It was a pioneer work in this discipline. Spinoza soberly and calmly scrutinized the Holy Scriptures as he might any other ancient literary remain. He reached such conclusions as that the first five books of the Old Testament could not have been written entirely by Moses, as tradition had it, since (among other reasons) *Deuteronomy* concludes with an account of Moses' death and burial. The prophets, he pointed out, were notable for superior piety and imagination, not for intelligence or learning. Moreover, to be understood by their fellows they had to speak according to the manner and general beliefs of the day. We therefore ought to be edified by their moral teaching, but it is no duty of religion to believe the prophetical narratives to be literally true descriptions of facts.

The part that gave most offense was the chapter on Miracles. Nearly everyone supposed that the credibility of the Holy Scriptures stood or fell with the veracity of the accounts of miracles that they related. Furthermore, the occurrence of miracles was deemed the surest proof of the existence of God. Spinoza argued that the notion of a miracle presupposes a view of reality as consisting of two opposing powers: Nature, on the one hand, going her own way in accordance with her accustomed laws except on those special occasions when God, on the other hand, sees fit to abrogate them. But the laws and power of Nature *are* the laws and power of God. Everything occurs necessarily as it follows from the divine nature. If there were miracles they would render the existence of God doubtful, for it is only on the basis of the fixity of nature that we can ground any inference to a fact not self-evident, including that of God's existence. Biblical stories of miracles are to be taken either as relations of natural (though striking and puzzling) events or to be interpreted in a "spiritual sense," for instance, the resurrection of Jesus.

The Aim of Philosophy

The identification of God with the animating force of the world reminds us of the Stoics. There are other respects in which Spinoza's philosophy is parallel to Stoicism. Spinoza, like Epictetus, philosophized for the sake of attaining a peace of mind that could not be disturbed by external circumstance.

> After experience had taught me that all the usual surroundings of social life are vain and futile; seeing that none of the objects of my fears contained in themselves anything either good or bad, except in so far as the mind is affected by them, I finally resolved to inquire whether there might be some real good having power to communicate itself, which would affect the mind singly, to the exclusion of all else: whether, in fact, there might be anything of which the discovery and attainment would enable me to enjoy continuous, supreme, and unending happiness.[5]

Again as with the Stoics, Spinoza found this chief good to consist in cultivating a character with "knowledge of the union existing between the mind and the whole of nature," and in helping others to attain the same condition. This aim is not so forbiddingly intellectualistic as it may sound, for in Spinoza's philosophy intellect, will, and emotion are not ultimately distinct. Clear perception by the mind turns out to be the very same thing as freedom and the feeling of joy.

What Understanding Is

Descartes, before embarking on a program for understanding human nature and the world, deemed it necessary first to establish the reality of knowledge. Scepticism had to be overcome by the process, perhaps itself rather dubious, of proving that God exists and is not a deceiver. God could deceive us but He does not. The validity of reason, then, depends on the will of God. Since the will of God is not necessitated, the rationality of the world and consequent possibility of knowledge must be admitted to be a brute fact incapable of any explanation.

Spinoza, like Hobbes, denied the need for these preliminaries. The world exists and is intelligible; the human mind is adequate for knowing it. These propositions may be assumptions, but they are bedrock. There is no more ultimate standpoint from which we might prove them. But it is a mistake to suppose that before we can know anything we must first make sure that we know that we know something. If we did, before that we would have to know that we know that we know, and so on in a vicious regress.

Spinoza rejected also the Cartesian metaphor of "foundations of knowledge," according to which knowledge if worthy of the name must rest on indubitable truths, ultimately on the *Cogito*. We must not argue, Spinoza tells us, that since tools cannot be made without the aid of preexisting tools, therefore there are no tools. Complicated tools in fact have been made by the use of simpler and less efficient ones. In the same way more extensive and certain knowledge may develop from a previous condition of partial ignorance, error, and confusion.

To understand anything is to know what its causes are—which is the same as to know what the reasons are that necessitate it to be as it is. Cause and reason are, as in Hobbes, not ultimately distinct notions. It follows of necessity, from certain statements about extension, that the circle is the figure of greatest area for a given perimeter. Once we understand these reasons, the fact becomes for us the reasoned fact. But it also follows of necessity from certain statements known to astronomers that an eclipse of the sun will take place at such and such a time. And of necessity the mob lynched the De Witt brothers, although all the causes of that event were not and perhaps never could be known to any finite intellect. Nevertheless, there are no facts that are in their own nature brute and unintelligible. All true statements are necessarily true. Physics and psychology do not differ in principle from geometry. Ethics can be demonstrated in the geometrical manner.

"But," Spinoza cautions us, "by the series of causes and real entities I do not mean the series of particular and mutable things, but only the series of fixed and eternal things."[6] An avalanche is a series of particular and mutable things, falling one on the other, the effect of one fall being the cause of the next. But understanding an avalanche, knowing its cause, consists in apprehending the law of falling bodies, $s = \frac{1}{2} gt^2$. Further understanding consists in knowing how this law follows of necessity from the more general law of gravitation: that every body attracts every other body with a force proportional to the product of their masses and inversely proportional to the distance between them. This is a "series of fixed and eternal things."

The central conviction of Spinoza is that the series of fixed and eternal things forms a structured whole, a unity. This whole is nature, and it is God.

God

All the truths about a unity of the sort Spinoza had in mind must be related by logical entailments. These truths, then, can be arranged in a deductive order, the model for which had been established for all time by Euclid's *Elements of Geometry* in the third century B.C. Beginning with explicit definitions of the concepts to be treated, and a few unproved but presumably self-evident axioms, the remaining propositions are stated and demonstrated by explicitly deductive arguments citing only the axioms and propositions previously proved. Spinoza's *Ethics Demonstrated in Geometrical Order* expounded his system of philosophy in this way. However, the book abounds in Explanations, Scholia, Prefaces, and Appendices, in which the author slips out of his logical straitjacket.

Part I, "Of God," begins with eight Definitions and seven Axioms into which Spinoza's whole metaphysics is packed. Let us begin with the first Axiom, "Everything which is, is either in itself or in another." By "in" Spinoza means "causally dependent on." Keeping in mind his conception of causation as fixed, eternal, and rational, we see that to say of something that it is "in another" means that it cannot exist or be understood without reference to that other. If it is "in itself," it is self-explanatory. Now Definition 3 tells us that Substance is to be the name for whatever is "in itself" and Definition 5, that Mode is whatever is "in another." These are traditional definitions; however, Spinoza applies them in a surprising way. Descartes referred to particular thoughts and colors as modes, for they have no independent existence: a thought must be in some mind, a color must be of some body. But the mind and the body are individuals, independently existing, and therefore substances. (To be sure, Descartes affirmed thinking and extended substances to depend on God for their creation and continued existence. However, a mind for him was something that could conceivably exist all by itself.) Spinoza rejected this view. No individual man, horse, pyramid, or planet is a thing that could exist on its own and be understood without going beyond. Every individual is in constant interaction with its environment and understandable only through reference to its external causes. A wave or a hurricane may look like an individual and might even be named Frances, but a moment's reflection shows that these are but modifications—modes—of the sea and atmosphere. Further reflection should convince us that we too are modes, not substances.

Modes of what? That which exists in itself, and can be conceived through itself alone, is substance. The definition can fit nothing less than the totality (or, more accurately, the cause of the totality) of everything there is, and has been, and will be: the universe, Nature. There cannot be more than one substance; it is infinite, and it is God. We, then, and waves and hurricanes, are modifications of God, Who is not distinct from us: God is not our creator, like a clockmaker, but our cause and sustaining energy.

A Cartesian would object that even so we should distinguish two substances, thought and extension, each infinite and each "in itself." Spinoza grants these the status of "attributes" of substance, "that which the intellect perceives of substance as constituting its essence." Substance, being infinite, has an infinity of attributes, that is it exists in an infinite number of ways, but we are capable of perceiving only two of them. Substance exists as thinking, and substance—the same substance—exists as extended body. What this means, and how it is possible, we shall discuss later.

God, "Being absolutely infinite, that is to say, substance consisting of infinite attributes, each one of which expresses eternal and infinite essence," necessarily exists. Spinoza's main proof of this proposition looks like the argument of Anselm: God must exist because His essence (the very conception of God) involves existence. God is "cause of Himself," that whose nature cannot be conceived unless existing. However, Spinoza's proof is perhaps resistant to some objections urged against Anselm's (and Descartes'). If God were defined simply as the totality of things, it would indeed follow necessarily, though trivially, that He (or It) exists. Since in Spinoza's system God is in addition the self-explanatory Being, that in terms of which everything else is to be explained, the proof is not quite so trivial; for to assert that this kind of God exists is to declare that there is an ultimate explanation of things, indeed that it is inconceivable that there should not be.

The way in which Spinoza's God explains the world is, however, so unusual as to be a revolution in theological thought—if indeed it can be called theological. Hitherto, God had rendered the universe intelligible by either being or determining its final cause—in Aristotle, by moving the heavens "as the beloved moves the lover"; in Augustine and in most Christian thought, by being author/producer of the drama of salvation. Leibniz, in the next generation after Spinoza, would announce that things could not be otherwise than they are because they are God's choice of the best. Not only did the divine purpose provide the ultimate explanation, it also accounted for the particular constitutions of things: the admirably efficient constructions of the human eyes and limbs, the nesting instincts of birds, were ascribed to God's intelligent and benevolent design.

In the Appendix to Part I of the *Ethics*, Spinoza sweeps all this away. "Nature has set no end before herself, and all final causes are nothing but human fictions." The notion is begotten of our natural ignorance of causes united to our consciousness of desire for what profits us. Hence we think that we are free, for we know our desires but not their causes. Reasoning by analogy, when we find in nature something that is useful to us we infer that some invisible super-person must have made it for our benefit.

"The attempt, however, to show that nature does nothing in vain (that is to say, nothing which is not profitable to man), seems to end in showing that nature, the gods, and man are alike mad." In the final-cause theory, everything is centered on us and our welfare. Whatever is injurious in nature is conceived as divine punishment—despite our uniform experience that earthquakes and plagues strike down the virtuous and the wicked indifferently. The final-cause doctrine, moreover, overturns nature: "that which in truth is the cause it considers as the effect, and vice versa." And it is incompatible with the theologically essential tenet of God's perfection: for despite evasive maneuvers, it cannot but lead to the conclusion that God is in need of something.

As for design in nature

> So, also, when they behold the structure of the human body, they are amazed; and because they are ignorant of the causes of such art, they conclude that the body was made not by mechanical but by a supernatural or divine art, and has been formed in such a way so that the one part may not injure the other. Hence it happens that the man who endeavours to find out the true causes of miracles, and who desires as a wise man to understand nature, and not to gape at it like a fool, is generally considered and proclaimed to be a heretic and impious by those whom the vulgar worship as the interpreters both of nature and the gods. For these know that if ignorance be removed, amazed stupidity, the sole ground on which they rely in arguing or in defending their authority, is taken away also.

God has these properties: He is eternal, simple, infinite, indivisible, and perfect—that is, He lacks nothing that perfectly expresses Being.[7] But "neither intellect nor will pertain to the nature of God,"[8] though God is the cause of the intellect and will in us. At any rate, "if intellect and will pertain to His eternal essence, these attributes cannot be understood in the sense in which men generally use them, for the intellect and will which could constitute His essence would have to differ entirely from our intellect and will, and could resemble ours in nothing except in name. There could be no further likeness than that between the celestial constellation of the Dog and the animal which barks."[9] Our intellects learn things of which they were previously ignorant; our knowledge is an effect of what it is the knowledge of. Our wills aim at the production of things we need; and these are essential properties of intellect and will as we know them. But nothing of the sort is attributable to God. It is doubtful, then, whether in any sense meaningful to us we may ascribe personality to God.

It is hazardous to try to say what Spinoza's God is. But if we were allowed only one word for it, the word would have to be Energy. If we asked the physicist of today to tell us in a word what the world consists of, we would be told that matter—extended substance—is a modification of energy, or convertible with it; and that the world is at bottom a pattern of energy redistributing itself in a regular manner, that is, according to patterns of action which we sum up in the laws of physics. These laws, we understand, are not external standards that energy obeys; they are simply descriptive of the essence of energy. This picture, it seems, is Spinoza's—at any rate very much like the way he thought of the universe.

Although physics tells us that energy and matter are fundamentally the same, we tend to think of energy as active and matter as what energy acts on. This attempt at a distinction is parallel to Spinoza's division of things into *natura naturans*, nature as active, and *natura naturata*, nature as the divine product. The one is "God considered as a free cause," as determined by nothing but Himself; the other is "all the modes of God's attributes in so far as they are considered as things which are in God, and which without God can neither be nor can be conceived."[10]

God is free, for there can be nothing to compel His action; but that does not mean that He selects one course of action out of a plurality of possible alternatives. "From the necessity of the divine nature infinite numbers of things in infinite ways (that is to say, all things which can be conceived by the infinite intellect) must follow."[11] "Things could have been produced by God in no other manner and in no other order than that in which they have been produced."[12] "In nature there is nothing contingent, but all things are determined from the necessity of the divine nature to exist and act in a certain manner."[13] Everything that is possible is actual; whatever does not exist is impossible, ultimately self-contradictory, or at least excluded by the nature of the causal order. Contingency is only a name we give to things of whose necessity or impossibility we are ignorant.

In a world so rigidly determined, time is hardly real. Tomorrow's effects are logically entailed by today's causes, so that in a sense they are already there. There are games of solitaire in which the player has no choices to make: the cards must be played as they turn up, in accordance with rules that allow no alternatives. In this kind of game, the outcome is already there in the order of the cards when the player begins the deal. A sufficiently powerful intellect knowing the original order of the cards would know the outcome, so that the dealing out and playing of the game would be unreal in that it added nothing to what was already there. This intellect would view the cards "under the form of eternity (*sub specie aeternitatis*)," in Spinoza's famous phrase.

Atheism?

More than a century after Spinoza's death, the German poet Novalis called him "the God-intoxicated man." But in his own time, and long afterwards, he was execrated as the arch-atheist. Who was right?

It all depends, no doubt, on what you mean by God. But the question, though verbal, is not trivial. Religious thinkers in Western culture, if they are to be taken seriously, must emancipate themselves from a grossly anthropomorphic conception of God. The question is how far they can go in doing so while still retaining some basis for an institution recognizably religious.

Spinoza went as far as possible in purging the conception of God from anthropomorphism. But there is scarcely a single respect in which predecessors of his conception cannot be found among the most orthodox of medieval theologians. All agreed that God's intellect is not discursive, that is it does not turn its attention to one thing after another as ours must, but perceives and knows everything all at once. Yet what it would be like to do this, no one could imagine. When Spinoza made thought one of the attributes of God and wrote of "the infinite idea of God," he asserted just this. It might seem that Spinoza departed from the tradition when he declared God to be the immanent cause of the world, that is, the ordering principle in it rather than its external creator. This is Pantheism, which is incompatible with both Christianity and Judaism. But perhaps even here the difference is more apparent than real. Catholic theologians insisted that God sustains the universe; the created world is not something that He left to its own devices.

It comes to this. Spinoza and the theologians, if not in agreement, were fairly close in their positive and literal conceptions of the nature of God. But the theologians strove, by emphasizing the mysteriousness of God, to reconcile their conception of Him with much that Spinoza utterly rejected: miracles, a creation in time, the divinity of Jesus, His literal resurrection from the dead, a last judgment, heaven and hell for resurrected souls. The crucial difference was the professional necessity for the theologians of preserving God as a being to whom one might pray—though these men had to admit when pressed that the will of God could not possibly be altered. Spinoza, under no necessity to preserve traditional notions or to put a good face on popular religion, said aloud what the theologians could only whisper to one another.

Mind and Body

There is and can be only one God, one infinite substance. We perceive the essence of this substance as thought, mind, also as extension, body. But these attributes—essential characteristics—cannot be distinct; if they were, it would be at least possible (as Descartes believed it was actual) for there to be both thinking nonextended substance and an extended nonthinking substance—that is, two Gods.

Spinoza was driven by this reasoning to affirm the identity of mind and body. The interaction problem was avoided, but only at the expense of raising the difficult question of how the identity can be conceived.

When we think of Spinoza's philosophy, or feel a stabbing pain, or look at a lawn, certain things are happening in our bodies, specifically in the nerves and the brain. These are events of the sort studied by biochemists: chemical reactions take place and electrical discharges occur that can be measured by suitably placed instruments. We have (the Cartesian dualist will say) two things: the neural discharge and the sensation of green color. One is the cause of the other; they are distinct, and can be at least conceived as happening one without the other. They are correlates in two series, the physical and the mental.

Spinozism declares that on the contrary there is but a single happening, which however is conceived in two ways, under the attributes of thought and extension.

If you had a window in your skull so that the occurrences in your brain literally could be observed through a microscope, it would be possible to see your sensation of green color. That is not to say that it would look green; it would presumably look bloody-gray. Now there is a temptation at this point to expound Spinoza's doctrine by saying that the vivisectionist would see your sensation from the outside while you, looking at the grass, would perceive the sensation from the inside. But that would not be right. The investigator sees your sensation; but *you* do not *see* it, you *have* it. The sensation is (part of) your consciousness at the moment—not something that the consciousness is aware *of*, but the consciousness itself. Thus objections to the identity theory, based on the allegation that thoughts and brain events are perceived to be altogether different, can be parried. If they are perceived to be different, they must both be perceived; but although the brain event can be perceived, the conscious experience cannot be—it can only be lived through.

This at any rate seems the most plausible interpretation to put on Spinoza's doctrine of mind and body as "one and the same thing expressed in two ways."[14] It avoids the disastrous distinction between reality (the brain event) and appearance (the "phantasm") that Hobbes deemed it necessary to introduce. As Spinoza did not concern himself unduly with considerations of plausibility, he was in the main content to assert identity as a consequence of the unitary conception of God, and leave it at that.

Will and Intellect

Spinoza denied also the division of psychic functions into emotion, will, and intellect. Emphasis on unity, organism, and explanation of part by whole did not blind him to the fact that everything that exists is particular; in his terminology, God is manifested only in His modes. In the attribute of thought there are only particular thoughts, not Thought over and above them. But no more is there Will over and above particular acts of deciding and exerting effort. There is no such thing, for example, as love (emotion) without an idea (cognition) of a beloved object; nor is there will (volition) without a belief about the end pursued; nor are pure volitions and the like even imaginable. These distinctions do not mark off separate faculties, though they may have some use when employed in the analysis of particular acts.

This fact is the key to blessedness, which is the aim of philosophy. For happiness consists in a certain disposition of the mind. It is possible, then, to ensure the desired disposition by a change in ideas: by the replacement of inadequate ideas by adequate ones.

The Emotions

Our minds sometimes act, sometimes they are acted upon. To act, to be the adequate cause of anything, requires that we have an adequate idea of what we are doing. Insofar as our ideas are not adequate, we are buffeted about by powers that we do not comprehend. Our passions consist in the inadequacy of our ideas.

Spinoza defines 48 emotions in terms of three basic ones: Desire (or Appetite), the endeavor to persevere in being, which is "the essence itself of man"; Joy, "man's passage from a less to a greater perfection"; and Sorrow, the opposite passage. Love, for example, is joy together with the idea of an external cause. The good, as for Hobbes, is whatever is the object of desire: "we neither strive for, wish, seek, nor desire anything because we think it to be good, but, on the contrary, we adjudge a thing to be good because we strive for, wish, seek, or desire it."[15] Much of Spinoza's penetrating discussion of the emotions is concerned with love, hate, and their multifarious derivatives.

There is only one active emotion: fortitude, which Spinoza divides into courage, "the desire by which each person endeavors from the dictates of reason alone to preserve his own being" and generosity, "the desire by which from the dictates of reason alone each person endeavors to help other people and to join them to him in friendship."[16] Spinoza does not counsel us, however, to suppress all our passions and be moved by courage and generosity alone. That would be impossible, for we are parts of nature, so that our doings and sufferings are necessarily the effects of external causes. We necessarily are always subject to passions.

But some passions are better than others. Hatred, for example, is never good. Cheerfulness is never bad. The emotions act and react on each other; the only way to restrain or remove an emotion is by an opposed and stronger one. Human bondage consists in subjection to those emotions based on sorrow—which include humility, repentance, and pity.

Human Freedom

There is no free will, nor is there any free cause except God. Nevertheless, there is a sense in which one person can be called a slave, another called free. The slave is led by emotion or opinion alone, behaving—whether willingly or not—in ignorance of causes. The free man is led by reason, hence does the will of no one but himself.

"To act absolutely in conformity with virtue is, in us, nothing but acting, living, and preserving our being (these three things have the same meaning) as reason directs, from the ground of seeking our own profit."[17] But reason recognizes nothing to be profitable that does not conduce to understanding.

> It is therefore most profitable to us in life to make perfect the intellect or reason as far as possible, and in this one thing consists the highest happiness or blessedness of man; for blessedness is nothing but the peace of mind which springs from the intuitive knowledge of God, and to perfect the intellect is nothing but to understand God, together with the attributes and actions of God, which flow from the necessity of His nature. The final aim, therefore, of a man who is guided by reason, that is to say, the chief desire by which he strives to govern all his other desires, is that by which he is led adequately to conceive himself and all things which can be conceived by his intelligence.[18]

Knowledge is a remedy against passion, for "an emotion which is a passion ceases to be a passion as soon as we form a clear and distinct idea of it"[19]—step back, so to speak, and take a look at it and its causes. We should remember too that "our sorrows and misfortunes mainly proceed from too much love towards an object which is subject to many changes, and which we can never possess. For no one is troubled or anxious about any object he does not love, neither do wrongs, suspicions, hatreds, etc., arise except from love towards objects of which no one can be truly the possessor."[20] Love toward God, an immutable object, is safer.

There are grades of knowledge. After mere hearsay, the lowest form is knowledge of the unconnected fact, such as that water puts out fire. Scientific knowledge of causes and of their necessity accustoms us to view things "under the form of eternity." But there is a yet higher knowledge, the "third kind," intuitive knowledge combining the necessity of scientific theorizing with the immediacy of sense perception. It has been compared to knowing the world as the sympathetic physician knows the patient. Spinoza admitted that he had succeeded in knowing few things this way; nevertheless, "the more we understand things in this manner, the more we understand God."[21] This is the intellectual love of God, identical to the love with which God loves Himself. This is what Spinoza sought when he "resolved to inquire whether there might be some real good . . . the discovery and attainment of which would enable me to enjoy continuous, supreme, and unending happiness."[22]

The final Proposition of the *Ethics* reads

> Blessedness is not the reward of virtue, but is virtue itself; nor do we delight in blessedness because we restrain our lusts; but, on the contrary, because we delight in it, therefore are we able to restrain them.

And its Scholium:

> I have finished everything I wished to explain concerning the power of the mind over the emotions and concerning its liberty. From what has been said we see what is the strength of the wise man, and how much he surpasses the ignorant who is driven forward by lust alone. For the ignorant man is not only agitated by external causes in many ways, and never enjoys true peace of soul, but lives also ignorant, as it were, both of God and of things, and as soon as he ceases to suffer ceases also to be. On the other hand, the wise man, in so far as he is considered as such, is scarcely ever moved in his mind, but, being conscious by a certain eternal necessity of himself, of God, and of things, never ceases to be, and always enjoys true peace of soul. If the way which, as I have shown, leads hither seems very difficult, it can nevertheless be found. It must indeed be difficult since it is so seldom discovered; for if salvation lay ready to hand and could be discovered without great labor, how could it be possible that it should be neglected almost by everybody? But all noble things are as difficult as they are rare.

Some Remarks in Criticism

Spinozism is the most philosophical of philosophies. Benedictus de Spinoza considered all the questions philosophers are supposed to ponder, and he gave them definite unevasive answers. If he is obscure, he is never obscurantist. Never before or since was a system of the world presented more systematically and elegantly. Spinoza explicitly claimed to have discovered the true philosophy. Perhaps he alone could make this announcement without irritating his reader.

Spinoza sought to compel rational assent by his geometrical order. Granting that he committed no vitiating errors in logic, the compulsion is nevertheless not absolute. For terms like essence, substance, infinity, free, and necessary—which occur in the definitions—possess hardly the simplicity and clarity of point, line, plane, and equality. Nor does the axiom "Everything which is, is either in itself or in another" have the luminosity of "Two lines cannot enclose a space."

Nonetheless, the picture Spinoza presents of an integrated, deterministic, non-purposive, and impersonal universe is consistent with the spirit of the new science arising in his day—perhaps even defines that spirit. If for the ordinary church- (or synagogue-) going European it was too great an intellectual wrench to be told that God is the energy manifested in the cosmic process, at least this announcement would have been intelligible to many if not most religious philosophers clear back to the Pre-Socratics, who also were accustomed to call the ground of things "divine."

As for the psychological and ethical parts of the *Ethics*, it is no doubt true that many of us have more trouble in life than we might otherwise have because of excessive emotional involvements and cultivation of unprofitable urges, such as for revenge. We stand in need then of counsels to be active not passive, to practice philosophical calm, and of directions for attaining it. Doing science—astronomy especially—and taking long views are helpful in these respects. Whether, however, noninvolvement and the conquest of the passions, especially the sexual ones, deserve to be lauded as "blessedness" is something one must decide for oneself.

VI

The Enlightenment

36

Locke

JOHN LOCKE WAS BORN near Bristol in 1632, the same year as Spinoza, but his first publication did not appear until several years after Spinoza's death. Like Hobbes, Locke was exceptional in the late development of his philosophical interests.

He attended Oxford nearly half a century after Hobbes had been there, receiving much the same sort of education and reacting with similar dissatisfaction. Locke intended at first to enter the Church, but his undogmatic mind did not find congenial the views then required for advancement. He switched to medicine, but delayed taking the degree for several years and never set up a public practice. Instead he became personal physician and confidant to the Earl of Shaftesbury, in whose household he lived for much of his life—thereby gaining entry to the great world as Hobbes had through the Cavendishes.

Lord Shaftesbury was one of the most prominent English politicians under both Cromwell and King Charles II. His downfall came when in the early 1680s he staked everything in an attempt to keep the English throne from passing to a Catholic. King Charles, whose Catholicism was an ill-kept secret, had no legitimate offspring. Hence at his death the monarchy would pass to his brother James, Duke of York, who was openly and enthusiastically Catholic; he resigned all his official posts when Catholics were excluded from public employment. The only position in government still open to him was King! Shaftesbury tried to correct this oversight by an Exclusion Bill that would have made Catholics ineligible to be monarchs as well as clerks. The House of Commons passed it, but Charles' strenuous opposition defeated it in the Lords. Shaftesbury, accused of treason by the King's henchmen, withdrew to Holland where soon afterwards he died.

In the same year, 1683, Locke also found it prudent to take up residence in Holland. James came to the throne two years later. Early in his reign the Duke of Monmouth, Protestant bastard of Charles II, was induced to lead an invasion and insurrection, which was put down in the bloodiest manner. Locke was accused of complicity and demand was made to the Dutch government for his surrender. Locke went into hiding. The Dutch King, William, did not search for him very diligently. This was hardly surprising, for early in 1689, after the bloodless overthrow of James II, William and his wife Mary, James' daughter, accepted the invitation to become joint sovereigns of England. Locke was in favor with the royal couple, and returned to England on the same ship with Mary.

After G. Kneller, John Locke, *1704. Oil. National Portrait Gallery, London.*

Locke's principal works were mostly written during his stay in Holland, and were all published in a period of six years: the *Letter Concerning Toleration*, 1689; the *Essay Concerning Human Understanding*, 1690; *Two Treatises of Civil Government*, also 1690; *Some Thoughts Concerning Education*, 1693; and *The Reasonableness of Christianity*, 1695. From 1691 until his death in 1704, Locke lived as paying guest in the country estate of his friend Sir Francis Masham, whose learned wife was something of a philosopher in her own right.

Like Aristotle, Locke had the happy faculty of being able to articulate in philosophical terms, and with sincerity, the views held by the influential men who typified enlightened common sense in his day. This was true in the highest degree of his political philosophy, in which he was the acknowledged spokesman for the more liberal politicians and tycoons who brought in William and Mary; he was, so to speak, the Whig party theoretician. In religion, Locke was somewhat more in advance of his times; but his (in Anglican terms) extremely Broad Church position was the one toward which opinion was moving. His advocacy of toleration was entirely successful in the century after his death, perhaps because the practical advantages came to be recognized. Thus Locke enjoyed in his own country an honor such as comes to few prophets.

The Essay

In the Preface to his *Essay Concerning Human Understanding*, Locke relates how "five or six friends meeting at my chamber, and discoursing on a subject very remote from this, found themselves quickly at a stand, by the difficulties that rose on every side. After we had a while puzzled ourselves, not coming any nearer solution of those doubts which perplexed us, it came into my thoughts, that we took a wrong course; and that before we set ourselves upon inquiries of that nature, it was necessary to examine our own abilities, and see what objects our understanding were, or were not, fitted to deal with."

The "subject very remote from this" was God and morality. Twenty years later Locke completed and published his examination of the human intellect. The passages in it concerning God and morality are brief and incidental. The book, however, is very long, and served as the groundwork of British philosophy for two and a half centuries. Its influence on the Continent, especially in France, was so great that the Age of the Enlightenment is customarily dated from its publication.

Locke's purpose, announced at the outset, was "to inquire into the original, certainty, and extent of human knowledge, together with the grounds and degrees of belief, opinion, and assent." He thus allied himself with Descartes (to whom he acknowledged great indebtedness) in supposing that the human mind can usefully undertake a general survey of its own powers, to establish in advance both what subjects it can profitably investigate and which ones its nature precludes it from knowing. (The assumption may be plausible, but it is not a self-evident truth. If there are some questions that cannot be answered, "What questions cannot be answered?" may be one of them.)

Ideas

Deeming the certainty and extent of human knowledge to depend upon its origin, Locke proceeded by the "historical, plain method" of inquiring into "the original of those ideas . . . which a man observes." The mind is something that has ideas in it. Knowledge consists in the perception of the agreement or disagreement of ideas. Whether a piece of alleged knowledge is genuine depends, then, on whether the ideas in question have a right to be in the mind. The "historical" method consists in finding out their histories—that is, how they got into the mind, and from where. (The sense of the word 'history' here is that in which we speak of the medical history of a patient.) The credentials of the ideas are to be scrutinized; if they cannot provide the proper birth certificates, so to speak, then they must be rejected, they can have no role in proper knowledge.

'Idea' is defined as "whatsoever is the object of the understanding when a man thinks." Ideas are "in men's minds." Thus if you think about Moscow, you must not suppose that the object of your understanding is Moscow the city—the cathedrals, the Kremlin, and so on. No, the object of your understanding is your idea of Moscow—that is what you are "observing," it is something "in the mind"—and what relation it has to the city of Moscow is a question later to be pondered. But even if you go to Moscow and stand in Red Square gazing at Lenin's tomb, your immediate object is not a marble building but another idea.

Locke did not deem it necessary to argue for the proposition that there are ideas in this sense—entities "in the mind" (a phrase not defined), distinct from cities and tomatoes but representing them. "I presume it will be easily granted me," he presumed, "that there are such ideas in men's minds. Every one is conscious of them in himself." He argued at great length, however, that there are no innate ideas or principles in the mind. Despite the celebrity of this polemic, it is hard to determine whom and what it was directed against. Descartes indeed had professed to discover in his mind an idea of God that could have been neither self-generated nor derived from sensation. However, the idea of God or of His existence does not seem to be the target of Locke's attack. Examples of supposedly innate principles that Locke mentions are "Whatever is, is" and "Nothing can both be, and not be." Locke observes, truly enough, that children and idiots do not have these propositions imprinted in their minds. What this is supposed to prove, and whom refute, is obscure, as is also the reason for Locke's vehemence on the point.

At any rate, Locke proceeded to lay it down that originally the mind is like white paper or a blank tablet, and that all the ideas with which it eventually is furnished derive from experience. This supremely important word, 'experience', is not defined but is used as a synonym for 'observation'. "Our observation employed either about external sensible objects, or about the internal operations of our minds, perceived and reflected on by ourselves, is that which supplies our understandings with all the materials of thinking."[1] This sentence abounds in metaphors: the mind is something that performs "internal operations"; these, and also "external sensible objects," are "perceived" by "our observation"; in this way our understandings are "supplied" with "materials of thinking." The mind is being conceived of as a factory that receives raw material; thinking is the performing of operations on these materials. The working-up of these raw materials is, furthermore, a process that is itself observed—by "ourselves"—as foremen in the factory keep watch over the productive processes. Although speaking of the mind in this way is perhaps unavoidable, it can be misleading. A little thought should convince us that the mind is not in any literal sense a mill, and thinking is not much like an industrial process. The most dangerous of all the metaphors, though, is implicit in the little word 'in': the mind-as-container model and its ramifications, such as the notion that I can witness the ideas in my mind but not those in yours, derive from this innocent-seeming monosyllable.

The senses "convey into the mind several distinct perceptions of things, according to those various ways wherein those objects do affect them."[2] Or more exactly, Locke held that they "convey into the mind what produces those perceptions."[3] Impulses from the air strike the eardrum, light rays stimulate the retina; these are not the perceptions but are what produce "those ideas we have of yellow, white, heat, cold, soft, hard, bitter, sweet, and all those which we call sensible qualities."[4] Note that this list contains one noun, heat; the rest are adjectives, which are names of qualities. Qualities are powers in things to produce ideas. Yet we perceive ideas, not qualities, much less the things that have the qualities. The idea we have is not itself a quality, it is *of* the quality (say) yellow, which in its turn is a quality of a yellow buttercup or egg yolk. In perceiving we are thus twice removed from the buttercup. This is the official Lockean teaching—though often he talks, like the rest of us, about the *things* we perceive.

Locke in almost the same passage[5] gives another list of ideas, composed of nouns: "men have in their mind several ideas, such as are those expressed by the words whiteness, hardness, sweetness, thinking, motion, man, elephant, army, drunkenness, and others." Of these man, elephant, and army seem substantial enough; we shall be told that they are complex ideas of substances. Elephant is made up of gray, large, mobile, solid, and so on, which are simple ideas not distinguishable into different ones; simple ideas are all of qualities named by adjectives or by nouns (such as 'whiteness') derived from adjectives. This point, we shall see, is of great importance, not only for Locke's philosophy but for nearly all that is subsequent to him.

The mind can neither create nor destroy any simple idea. All come from experience. They form the basis of all our knowledge. However, few of them have names. By way of example, Locke discusses solidity. He defines this term operationally, as we should say nowadays. It is the same as resistance, and "If anyone ask me what this solidity is? I send him to his sense to inform him; let him put a flint or a football between his hands and then endeavor to join them, and he will know."[6]

Besides those that come from sensation there are simple ideas of reflection, which the mind derives from observing "its own actions." Perception and willing are the two most important ones. Some simple ideas have, curiously, a double source in both sensation and reflection; pleasure does, we are told, existence, and above all, power. It is an idea of reflection because we observe ourselves moving our muscles, thereby exerting power, and of sensation because we likewise observe the effects "that natural bodies are able to produce in one another."

The ideas are in us. They are the immediate objects with which our minds deal. How, then, can they give us any knowledge of the world out there? This is the principal problem that any inside-out or Cartesian philosophy such as Locke's must face. Locke made it difficult for himself by admitting right off that most ideas have no "likeness" to "something existing without us." The qualities of objects are their powers to produce ideas in us. A snowball has the power by communicating motion to our sense organs to produce in us the ideas of white, cold, and round. Our idea, round, is like the quality, round, in the snowball; roundness (or in general, figure) is therefore said to be a *primary quality* of body. Not so white and cold. These ideas are produced by "the operation of insensible particles on our senses"[7]; the qualities in the snowball that produce them are nothing like the ideas. White and cold are *secondary qualities*. Solidity, extension, figure, motion or rest, and number are primary; colors, sounds, smells, and tastes are secondary— "in truth nothing in the objects themselves, but powers to produce various sensations in us by their primary qualities."[8] Modern physics explains the red color of the tomato in terms of the resonant frequency of vibration of bonds in the molecules that make up the tomato's surface; that is, the color, a secondary quality, is explained as an effect of motion and extension, which are primary qualities. Locke did not know these details, but he anticipated the form of the explanation— as Hobbes had done already—when he wrote that "the different motions and figures, bulk and number of [insensibly small] particles, affecting the several organs of our senses, produce in us those different sensations, which we have from the colours and smells of bodies."[9]

Here arises an issue which, though verbal, has had the profoundest influence on the subsequent history of philosophy. Certainly when you look at a tomato there is an experience, quality of consciousness, or whatever you want to call it, that is the ground for your judgment that the tomato is red; and there is in the tomato some physical structure that affects the surrounding medium, and at last your eye, in such a way that you have this experience and not some other. Locke calls your experience the sensation of an idea; he calls the cause—in the tomato—of the idea the quality (of the tomato). But which of these is the color red? It was open to Locke to say that the word 'red' names the quality in the tomato that produces in us this particular idea; then he could have gone ahead to talk about how the insensible parts affect us, concluding with some such remark as ". . . and that is what red color is." If he had done so, he would have been on the side of ordinary usage—which in all languages ascribes colors to objects, not to our consciousness. But he did not do that. Instead, he decided that the word 'red' really is the name of the idea in the mind; and since neither this nor anything resembling it can be conceived to be in the tomato, all humanity has hitherto been mistaken in calling tomatoes red. Red color is no more in the tomato "than sickness or pain is in manna. Take away the sensation . . . ; let not the eyes see light or colours, nor the ears hear sounds; let the palate not taste, nor the nose smell; and all colours, tastes, odours, and sounds, as they are such particular ideas, vanish and cease, and are reduced to their causes, i.e. bulk, figure, and motions of parts."[10]

This move, which is really an ill-advised terminological decision but purports to be a discovery in physics or metaphysics, had been made previously by Hobbes and others. But it was Locke who made it with authoritative and catastrophic finality.

The mind is passive when it receives the simple ideas. It exerts power over them in three operations: putting them together to form complex ideas, comparing them to note their relations, and separating them from their accompaniments by abstraction to make general ideas. As Locke notes explicitly, these operations are analogous to processes of manufacture. "Man's power, and its way of operation, [is] much-what the same in the material and intellectual world: for the materials in both being such as he has no power over, either to make or destroy, all that man can do is either to unite them together, or to set them by one another, or wholly separate them."[11] Here the metaphor has misled the philosopher. He supposes that the first stage in acquiring knowledge is that of gathering simple ideas (raw materials) and the second that of forming them into complex ideas (finished products). Actually, however, the mental life of the infant consists in apprehending complex and distinguishable entities all together; learning is mainly a process of making finer and finer discriminations. At first all moving objects are "mama"; only later are they sorted out into mama, papa, uncle, Mrs. Robinson, and kitty. This sorting is not the same as abstraction, a still more sophisticated "operation," which Locke describes rather obscurely as follows.

> The mind makes the particular ideas, received from particular objects, to become general; which is done by considering them as they are in the mind such appearances, separate from all other existences, and the circumstances of real existence, as time, place, or any other concomitant ideas. This is called *abstraction*, whereby ideas, taken from particular beings, become general representatives of all of the same kind, and their names general names, applicable to whatever exists conformable to such abstract ideas.[12]

Whenever I see a triangle it is some particular thing: a drawing, say, two feet long, made in white chalk against a green background, in such and such a classroom. I form the abstract idea 'triangle'—according to Locke—by ignoring the color, size, location, time of day, everything but the shape. So far so good. Unfortunately, as Berkeley (1685–1753; see Chapter 38) was to point out, the shape I retain in mind after I subtract the context is still the particular shape of the particular triangle on the chalkboard. But my abstract idea of triangle is not that of an isosceles any more than of a right or scalene triangle; so the alleged abstract idea is not abstract at all but just as particular as any other idea, though simpler. This difficulty is insurmountable as long as words are held to be "outward marks of our internal ideas" and ideas are held to be mental pictures. But the fact is that my idea of a triangle is neither scalene nor isosceles, simply because it is not a picture at all. Thinking need not be, usually is not, and at least in many instances plainly cannot be carried on in pictures: what 'images' constitute the content of "The first and fundamental positive law of all commonwealths is the establishing of the legislative power," to take an example from Locke's political treatise?

The idea of Power is supposed to be got by reflecting on the constancy of certain kinds of changes: whenever sugar is put into water it dissolves; we conclude that water, besides its sensible properties, has also the Power to dissolve sugar. This is an active power, a power to bring about a change in sugar. The sugar for its part has a passive power to be dissolved in water. Though it may seem strange to talk of "passive power," we need some such term to mark the difference between sugar and (say) marble in this respect. Our clearest idea of active power comes, we are told, from "God and spirits," and our own thinking and willing; for when we are engaged in these activities, we are directly acquainted with power as it resides in us.

Substance

Besides primary and secondary qualities, which are powers of objects to produce ideas in us, Locke writes of tertiary qualities, powers of bodies to affect other bodies—such as the sun's power to bleach. Now since we possess ideas of all these qualities and there cannot be qualities without things that have the qualities, we must also have ideas of things—substances.

This straightforward reasoning was assented to by nearly all philosophers from Aristotle to Hobbes. Locke accepts it too, but then he notices how ill it fits into the "new way of ideas." What we find in the mind, he declares, is "a great number of simple ideas." We notice that

> a certain number of these simple ideas go constantly together; which being presumed to belong to one thing, and words being suited to common apprehensions, and made use of for quick dispatch, are called, so united in one subject, by one name; which, by inadvertency, we are apt afterward to talk of, and consider as one simple idea, which indeed is a complication of many ideas together: because, as I have said, not imagining how these simple ideas can subsist by themselves, we accustom ourselves to suppose some *substratum* wherein they do subsist, and from which they do result, which therefore we call *substance*.[13]

For example we encounter these simple ideas: red, round, smooth, juicy, squishy, subacid. We notice that they go constantly together. We presume—note the choice of the word: we do not know nor even conjecture, but *presume*—these ideas "belong to one thing"; to save time we call the whole set 'tomato', and "by inadvertency" talk about it as "one simple idea." We compound our inadvertency by a failure of imagination, and allow ourselves to *suppose*—again note the word—that the idea-set 'tomato' subsists in a *substance*.

Why does Locke speak of substance in this reluctant, vacillating, and inconsistent manner? (Observe that here he writes of ideas as being in *things*, though his official teaching is that they are in *minds* only.) The reason is inherent in the inside-out philosophy; Locke is simply more candid than Descartes, who postulated an "understanding" that with the help of God could miraculously make up for the limitations of the "imagination." Ideas, and the qualities to which they correspond, are denoted by adjectives, as we have seen. Adjectives are the parts of speech whose particular function is to describe things. It seems to the philosopher, then, that he can give a complete description of anything using only adjectives. But if the thing is completely described, evidently there can be nothing left over to say about it; the noun, he deems, has been rendered superfluous, reduced to a string of adjectives. Metaphysically, he supposes furthermore, qualities are what adjectives are the names of; nouns name substances. The conclusion looms ahead: there are no substances, really, there are only qualities.

But this conclusion was to be drawn only in the following generation. Locke could not bring himself to desubstantialize the world so radically. His solution (if it can be called that) to the problem was to affirm that we have an idea of substance, but in his famous phrase it is only an idea of "something, I know not what." The noun, or rather the pronoun, is thus allowed back into the language. A tomato is a round, red, juicy, squishy, subacid *something*.

This description states the "nominal essence" of tomato; that is, it is an enumeration of those ideas, caused in us by the tomato as we perceive it, which together constitute our reason for assigning the *name* 'tomato'. Since we have not included in it all the products of all the powers of tomatoes, the nominal essence is inadequate as expressing the nature of the tomato. The real essence of the tomato, the tomato as it is in itself, is "the constitution of the insensible parts of that body, on which those qualities and all the other properties . . . depend."[14] Locke says flatly of real essences that "we know them not," and compares us to peasants gaping at the famous Strasburg clock, not knowing of the wheels and springs within. Perhaps Locke would admit that chemistry and physics in our day have attained some knowledge of real essences. However, he declared the connection between secondary and primary qualities to be not merely hidden but "undiscoverable." And even if we could discover it, he lamented, we still would be hopelessly baffled by the further connection of secondary quality and idea.

> We can by no means conceive how any size, figure, or motion of any particles, can possibly produce in us the idea of any colour, taste, or sound whatsoever; there is no conceivable connexion between the one and the other.[15]

Knowledge

In accordance with his conception of thought as the observation of ideas, Locke declares knowledge "to be nothing but the perception of the connexion or agreement, or disagreement and repugnancy of any of our ideas."[16] Our most certain knowledge is intuitive; in this way we know, by a "clear light," that white is not black and that $1 + 2 = 3$. We also have intuitive knowledge of our own existence (*Cogito!*). The next lower degree is demonstrative, as in geometrical proof, where we have a succession of intuitions. We know demonstratively mathematics and the existence of God (because there must be a First Cause). Inferior to these in certainty, yet deserving the name of knowledge, is "sensitive knowledge of particular existence." To the skeptic who asks how we can be sure the world is not just our dream, Locke replies

> he may please to dream that I make him this answer: 1. That it is no great matter whether I remove his scruple or no: where all is but dream, reasoning and argument are of no use, truth and knowledge nothing. 2. That I believe he will allow a very manifest difference between dreaming of being in the fire, and being actually in it. But yet if he be resolved to appear so sceptical as to maintain, that what I call being actually in the fire is nothing but a dream, and we cannot thereby certainly know that any such thing as fire actually exists without us, I answer, that we certainly finding that pleasure or pain follows upon the application of certain objects to us, whose existence we perceive, or dream that we perceive, by our senses; this certainty is as great as our happiness or misery, beyond which we have no concernment to know, or to be.[17]

It is doubtful, to say the least, whether this is an answer to the skeptic. But Locke, consistently with his definition of knowledge, can do no better. He writes that "wherever we perceive the agreement or disagreement of any of our ideas, there is certain knowledge: and wherever we are sure those ideas agree with the reality of things, there is certain real knowledge."[18] But he is not entitled to. For "the reality of things"—being expressly distinguished from ideas—cannot be something we observe, hence cannot be one term of a comparison made by us. Locke's only serious attempts to meet this objection consisted in arguing first that simple ideas must agree with things, because the mind cannot make a new simple idea, and second, that we know by observing our organs of sense that our perceptions are produced by exterior causes. But these arguments beg the question.

The tension and inconsistency in Locke's theory of knowledge are generated by his desire to be at once Cartesian and commonsensical. Following Descartes he takes it as indubitable that what we are directly and immediately aware of is always an idea in our mind, never a thing out there. But common sense takes it as equally indubitable that not only is there an external world of things producing our ideas, we *know* there is such a world—and know that it contains solid, extended, figured, mobile objects. We must know this, moreover, in some more direct way than *via* the grace of God. But when Locke tries to show how on his Cartesian premises we have knowledge, he can do no more than pound the table, exclaiming "This certainty is as great as our condition needs."

To the questions that generated the *Essay*, the answers are: The origin of our knowledge is experience, which is sensation, which is observation of our ideas and reflection on them. The extent of our knowledge is (1) intuition of our own existence and of some relations of ideas, (2) demonstration of mathematical (and a few ethical) truths and of God's existence, and (3) sensitive knowledge of the existence of bodies. Our knowledge does not extend to the connections of primary with secondary qualities or of secondary qualities with each other, or with our ideas, or of the powers and operations of spirits.

Political Philosophy

Locke earned his passage from Holland back to England by his two *Treatises of Civil Government*, which justified the Glorious Revolution of 1688 that deposed James II and enthroned William and Mary. Nobody denied that James had a flawless hereditary claim to the throne, but nearly everybody agreed that it was intolerable to have an actively proselytizing Catholic king of a mostly Protestant country. Locke's polemical purpose was thus to show that inheritance, or more broadly tradition, does not confer sovereignty unconditionally but that in certain circumstances (such as existed in 1688) it is permissible or even obligatory to depose the hereditary monarch.

The first treatise is a detailed and tiresome refutation of the argument of Sir Robert Filmer, in his *Patriarcha*, that kings ought to be obeyed in everything because they are the fathers of their people, possessing an unlimited paternal right really or "reputedly" inherited from Adam. Filmer in his book had some less silly things to say: "the people" without a sovereign are a headless mob, do not constitute a community, and hence cannot create a sovereign; social contract is mere myth, but even if it had taken place it could have had no effect; and there is no reason to suppose that wisdom dwells always with majorities. These more serious points Locke passes over.

Locke's enduring reputation as a political philosopher rests on the second treatise, entitled *An Essay Concerning the True Original Extent and End of Civil Government*. This is Locke's reply to *Leviathan*, although in it Hobbes is not mentioned by name. Locke reasserts the teaching common to the medieval theorists that power in society is held and exercised legitimately only in furtherance of community interests and must be subject to moral restraints. To Hobbes' contention that sovereignty must be absolute, Locke replies crushingly

> As if when men, quitting the state of nature, entered into society, they agreed that all of them but one should be under the restraint of laws; but that he should still retain all the liberty of the state of nature, increased with power, and made licentious by impunity. This is to think that men are so foolish that they take care to avoid what mischiefs may be done them by polecats or foxes, but are content, nay, think it safety, to be devoured by lions.[19]

Locke's starting point was the state of nature, which, he insisted, must have been a historical actuality. His picture of it is pleasanter than Hobbes'. "Men living together according to reason without a common superior on earth"[20] are not, we are assured, in a state of war. God in creating them as rational beings acquainted them with the law of nature, which enjoins them to be helpful and well-disposed to one another. Thus they already form a community. Being equal, they recognize the right of each to be secure in life, health, liberty, and possessions. Only exceptionally will some malicious individual invade these rights. Whoever does breaks the law of nature, and the injured party has the right to punish the evildoer.

Property exists in the state of nature. The earth and its fruits are common to all, but a man has property in his own labor; when he "mixes" that labor with objects, they become likewise his. No one owns the plums on the wild plum tree in the beginning, but they are yours once you take the trouble to pick them. And the person who ploughs the wasteland, plants plum seeds in it, and cultivates an orchard acquires title to the land thereby. No injustice is done, because there is plenty of land for every industrious person to make use of.

If you pick more plums than you and your family can eat, you may use the extras to trade for my surplus acorns. Neither of us is entitled, however, to hoard foodstuffs till they rot. It is advantageous, therefore, to barter some perishable necessities for bright stones, bits of metal, and the like, which we put a fancy on and which are in no danger of spoiling. Money, thus created, has its value set not intrinsically but by our consent.

Money admittedly works against natural equality, but Locke deems this an advantage: if we could lay nothing up, there would be no incentive to hard work. In this way Locke avoided drawing the leveling conclusions to which his labor theory of value and of right to property seemed to point. However, it is still hard to see what Lockean justification there could be for inherited income. And while we may agree that back when the land rush began there was enough for all, no one can maintain that nowadays—or even in Locke's time—every baby has an equal start. These problems Locke did not discuss.

In the state of nature there are, however, "inconveniences." The punishment of criminals is uncertain—they may be stronger than the victims—and inequitable, for no one ought to be prosecutor, judge, and executioner all at once. To remove these inconveniences and to provide settled rules and procedures of enforcement, people find it expedient to set up a civil society. For the preservation of their life, liberty, and estate they band together, consenting to observe the laws made by a duly constituted legislature and to aid another person, the executive, in the administration and enforcement of these laws. The social contract in Locke's version entails no surrender of natural rights, only the securing and enhancement of rights that existed already. Property rights being prior to government, indeed even to community, they can never be justly taken away without consent.

In a settled civil society the executive ought to be separate from the legislature; otherwise the wielders of power would be under no restraint of law, and "wherever law ends, tyranny begins."[21] If the constitution provides checks and balances, it should be possible to stave off absolutism. If, however, in spite of precautions the sovereign power acts arbitrarily, its force is unjust and unlawful (that is, contrary to Natural Law), and may be justly opposed in the only way left, an "appeal to heaven," a revolution.

> If a long train of abuses, prevarications, and artifices, all tending the same way, make the design visible to the people, and they cannot but feel what they lie under, and see whither they are going, 'tis not to be wondered that they should then rouse themselves, and endeavour to put the rule into such hands which may secure to them the ends for which government was at first erected, and without which, ancient names and specious forms are so far from being better, that they are much worse than the state of Nature or pure anarchy; the inconveniences being all as great and as near, but the remedy farther off and more difficult.[22]

This defense of the Glorious Revolution was liberally drawn on by Thomas Jefferson, four score and six years later.

Religion

In the latter seventeenth century and through the eighteenth, the religious attitude called Deism spread widely among advanced thinkers in Europe and even America, but especially in England. Deists held that the existence of God is certain, as proved by the First Cause and Design arguments; but they rejected miracles, revelations, and whatever dogmas they judged to be contrary to reason.

Many Deists claimed to derive inspiration from Locke. Locke was not himself a Deist; he accepted the trustworthiness and authority of the Holy Scriptures, including the accounts of miracles. However, his study of the Bible convinced him that many Christian dogmas, including even those of the Trinity and predestination, were devoid of Scriptural support. He came to the same conclusion that Hobbes had reached: that acceptance of Jesus as the Messiah was the only belief absolutely required of a Christian.

In his celebrated *Letter Concerning Toleration*, Locke presented the same sorts of arguments that Spinoza had urged. He pointed out that force could do no more than coerce outward conformity, not inward conviction; that State and Church have altogether different functions, the one to protect life, liberty, and estate—for which force is necessary—the other to insure salvation, for which force is of no use; and that domestic tranquillity does not require uniformity of religious belief or observance among the inhabitants of a country. Locke thought that toleration should not be extended to Roman Catholics because they owed allegiance to the Papacy, a foreign power hostile to England. Nor to atheists, because they could not sincerely take oaths, which (so he asserted) are indispensable for holding society together. There is no excuse for atheism; the First Cause argument is so clear and conclusive that an atheist must be irrational.

Locke's Influence

Locke's religious and political philosophies are only loosely connected with his theory of knowledge. In some respects the departments do not appear to be altogether consistent with each other; for instance, the alleged comprehension of the Law of Nature by natural men seems to clash with the impassioned rejection of innate principles.

Nevertheless, the opinion was current in Locke's day (as it is in ours too) that his liberal social philosophy was somehow founded on his theory of knowledge, and that therefore anyone who aspired to be an advanced social thinker was under obligation to follow the "new way of ideas" in pure philosophy. It was also supposed that Locke, the personal friend of "the incomparable Mr. Newton," had worked out the philosophy appropriate to Newtonian natural science. These notions helped give Locke's philosophy an almost official status in England, its Cartesian affronts to common sense going mostly unnoticed. On the Continent, especially in France, admirers of English liberty such as Voltaire (1694–1778) gave Locke great prominence in their propaganda against despotism and religious obscurantism.

Although Locke was the principal producer of English ideas for export to France, if we inquire after the original of his most crucial idea—that whatsoever is the object of the understanding when a man thinks is an idea—the historical plain method leads us back to France and the *Meditations* of René Descartes.

37

Leibniz

GOTTFRIED WILHELM LEIBNIZ WAS born in Leipzig in 1646, two years before the end of the Thirty Years' War in whose opening campaigns Descartes had taken part. His father, a lawyer and professor of moral philosophy, died when Gottfried was a child of six, and he was left to do as he pleased. What he mainly pleased to do was to read in his father's large library. When at length he entered the University, he obtained the degree Doctor of Jurisprudence at the age of 20; he was also offered a professorship, which he declined.

He chose instead to pursue a career in the great world, entering first the service of the Elector of Mainz, for whom he attempted to reorganize the legal system. When twenty-six years old he went to Paris, where he remained for four years as the Elector's special representative. His principal mission, in which he was not successful, was to persuade Louis XIV to conquer Egypt instead of southwestern Germany.

Concurrently with his legal and diplomatic affairs, Leibniz never ceased to pursue science and philosophy. In Paris he studied mathematics with the great Dutch scientist Christian Huyghens, to such effect that he discovered the infinitesimal calculus, which ranks with Descartes's analytic geometry as the most significant breakthrough in mathematics since antiquity.

In 1676 Leibniz left Paris. After a brief stay in England he visited Holland, where for two months he talked philosophy almost daily with Spinoza. The two had corresponded before, but Spinoza—who with good reason tended to be suspicious of strangers—had been reluctant to let him see the manuscript of the *Ethics*.

Leibniz spent the remaining 40 years of his life as librarian, historian, legal counselor, and general adviser to the Elector of Hanover. His motto was "As often as an hour is lost, a part of life perishes." It is not likely that he ever lost an hour. He designed for himself a desk at which he could not only do his work but also (as we are delicately told) peform all the necessary functions. In this manner he carried on his official duties while corresponding with more than a thousand persons and keeping up an awesome flow of philosophical papers, vast numbers of which are still in the library of Hanover, unpublished but now available on microfilm.

For all his staggering production, Leibniz wrote hardly any books: only the *Theodicy*, a defense of the goodness of God against the objections brought from the existence of evil; a *Discourse on Metaphysics*; and the *New Essays Concerning*

Human Understanding, which since it comments on Locke's *Essay* section by section is more like an extremely long review. For the rest, Leibniz wrote his views in letters and papers, most only a few pages long, published (if at all) in the learned journals that were a new feature of intellectual life in his time. The founder of modern German philosophy wrote almost always in Latin or French.

Leibniz' last years were lonely, mainly as the result of a deplorable controversy over priority in discovery of the calculus. Newton and Leibniz worked out the conception independently. Newton did so first (as we now know), but delayed publication until after Leibniz's version was already known. Friends of Newton thereupon accused Leibniz of having plagiarized the idea; Leibniz' supporters replied with countercharges. National passions were aroused, and this unseemly scientific squabble became entangled with the burning question of the Hanoverian succession. As a result of principles established at the time of the Glorious Revolution, on the death of Queen Anne the British throne was to go to the Elector of Hanover, a distant relative but a Protestant; the remaining Stuarts were all debarred as Catholics. Dissatisfaction at this arrangement was great. So when in 1714 the Elector succeeded as George I, he understandably declined to allow old Leibniz to accompany him to London. Leibniz was left at the deserted court of Hanover, where two years later he died. The outcast Spinoza's coffin was followed to the grave by eight carriages bearing important personages; Leibniz, the diplomat and courtier, was buried almost without ceremony.

Logic

Leibniz occupied himself with projects to reconcile Protestants and Catholics, Frenchmen and Germans. The diplomatic approach is also dominant in his philosophy. Like Descartes, he strove to harmonize the new science with traditional religion. Instead of separating the combatants, however, he aimed to fuse teleology and mechanism, mind and matter, into a unity.

Leibniz held—in common with almost all logicians before the present century—that every statement is, or can be rewritten as, a subject term and a predicate term joined by 'is' or 'are'. 'Socrates is mortal' predicates mortality of the subject Socrates. 'Socrates refuted Thrasymachus' can be rewritten as the subject-predicate statement 'Socrates is a-refuter-of-Thrasymachus-at-a-time-in-the-past'.

Now consider the statement 'Triangles are three-sided'. This is true by definition. If we set out explicitly the definition of triangle, "plane figure having just three straight sides," we see that the predicate 'three-sided' is contained in this analysis of the subject term. We therefore call this statement an *analytic* truth: its predicate concept is contained in its subject concept. All analytic truths are true by the principle of identity: a thing is what it is, A is A. No appeal to experience is required for discerning the truth of analytic statements; we need only know what the terms mean—that is, be able to define them, which is to analyze them (take them apart) into their simpler constituent concepts. This independence of experience is indicated by calling them *a priori* truths, knowable prior to experience. (This is related to, but not the same as, the medieval sense of the phrase, which signifies an inference from what is "prior by nature" in Aristotle's sense.) Such truths are, moreover, *necessary* truths. Triangles could not be other than three-sided; the denial of the statement is a contradiction in terms.

In mathematics we can analyze complex concepts such as triangle into their simple component concepts, hence determine whether statements in which they occur are analytic. Leibniz, like so many other mathematician-philosophers, hoped to extend the precision of mathematics to other realms of knowledge. His scheme for doing so envisioned the analysis of *all* concepts: if we had a vocabulary of all the simple notions from which the others must be compounded, we could find out by purely logical manipulations whether the sentences in which they occur are likewise analytic (therefore true). This project of a "universal characteristic" was the beginning of a development that in our day has led to the creation of the artificial and precise languages used, for example, in computer programming.

On the other hand, "Socrates refuted Thrasymachus" is not, apparently, true by definition; it rather expresses a fact that we happen to know, but only by experience, *a posteriori*. Most philosophers—but, as we shall see, not Leibniz—hold that instead of the predicate being part of the analysis of the subject, it adds something to the subject. The statement puts the subject and predicate together, it is *synthetic*. Its truth is *contingent*, not necessary. It depended on Socrates' encountering Thrasymachus, having his wits about him, choosing to speak, and an indefinite number of other circumstances that, for all we know, might have been otherwise.

Whenever a contingent statement is true, there is some *sufficient reason* why it is true; no fact can be simply a brute fact, isolated and unintelligible. This is a fundamental assumption that Leibniz formulates as the Principle of Sufficient Reason: "Nothing happens without its being possible for him who should sufficiently understand things, to give a reason sufficient to determine why it is so and not otherwise."[1] As we have seen, this assumption played its usually tacit part in scientific and philosophical reasoning all the way back to Anaximander.

The sufficient reason may be a mechanical cause, as one motion is the reason for another, or as in the example it may be the choice of a rational being. Choices and their motives explain some of the behavior of human beings and other spirits. We see, after we have chosen to do something, that we had a sufficient reason for doing it. But we did not have to do it, we were not compelled or necessitated. "Motives incline without necessitating."[2] In this way Leibniz sought to provide for free will in his system and to avoid the deterministic conclusions of Hobbes and Spinoza.

The Existence of God

In Leibniz' hands the principle of sufficient reason is a powerful tool. With its aid he elegantly proves the existence of God. For we can ask: Why is there a universe? Why is there something rather than nothing? The sufficient reason cannot be found *in* the universe—that is, in the series of contingent things—for each of these must have its own sufficient reason, ad infinitum; moreover, the series as a whole needs a sufficient reason for being *this* series and not some other. Therefore, the sufficient reason for the existence of the universe must be a non-contingent, that is, a necessary being, that is, God. Now we find in the world power, knowledge, and will. The Being Who is a sufficient reason for these must also be endowed with these attributes and in the highest degree, hence must be a Person.

The Best of All Possible Worlds

To choose is to select one alternative and reject the others. If the choice is real, all the alternatives must be really possible. Leibniz, siding with common sense against Hobbes and Spinoza, held that not everything possible is actual. The possible he defined as that in the conception of which there is no contradiction. A golden mountain is then possible, for there is nothing in the conception of being golden that is incompatible with the conception of being a mountain. But there is not, and need never be, an actual golden mountain. (This is the notion or kind of possibility now referred to as "logical possibility.")

There are more possible mountains than actual mountains, and while there is only one actual world there are an infinity of possible worlds. For there is no contradiction in the conception of a world containing mermaids, or a Moscow Stock Exchange, or indeed containing nothing at all. Hence, by the principle of sufficient reason there must be an explanation of why just this world is actual. Even if it has existed from eternity, the demand for a sufficient reason persists: why *this* eternal series rather than some other?

As we have seen, the sufficient reason for the universe must be God, the Necessary Being. But in what way is He the sufficient reason? We must suppose that this world is actual because God chose it, but His choice could not have been random or arbitrary; even He had to have a sufficient reason. A nonarbitrary and rational choice must be always a choice of the best of the alternatives presented. Since God's intellect is infinite, He must have been aware of all the possible worlds; since His power is infinite, He must have been able to actualize any one of them. It follows that God chose the best one and made it actual.

So "All is for the best in the best of all possible worlds." This provoked the derision of Voltaire and led him to caricature Leibniz as "Doctor Pangloss" of *Candide*. The statement may be ridiculous, but only atheists or believers in a less than perfect God—and Voltaire was neither—have a right to laugh. If an infinitely powerful, wise, and good Being exists, then this has to be the best of all possible worlds; if it is not, then God, thus defined, cannot exist. These conclusions are logically inescapable.

Plotinus, Augustine, and other thinkers who have found the existence of evil embarrassing to their philosophies have tried to get rid of it by the device of defining evil as privation or negation, therefore nonbeing, therefore nonexistent. Leibniz was more straightforward. Though still conceiving of evil as essentially negative, he admitted and insisted that there really is evil in the world. But, he maintained, it must exist so that goodness can be maximized. It is "for the best."

God could have created a world with no evil in it; He could have made a world without sentient beings, or even one containing nothing at all, hence no evil. But neither of these would have been the best of all possible worlds, which is not the evil-less world, but the one with the greatest surplus of good over evil. Now in general, satisfactions, which are goods, cannot exist without preceding states of need, which are pains or at least uneases, evils. A world with no hunger would have to lack the gustatory delights. More crucially, a world without sin, which is the greatest evil, would have to be a world without free will, which is the greatest good. That people should be persons and not zombies is so great a good that whatever the price in necessary evils, it is worth paying.

Seen in the light of his actual treatment of the problem of evil, the pronouncement that so amused Voltaire turns out to be perhaps more poignant than fatuously optimistic; and the Dervish's (that is, Voltaire's) answer to the question "Why is there evil in the world?"—"When the Sultan undertakes a voyage from Cairo to Constantinople, does he concern himself with the comfort of the mice aboard the ship?"—not entirely un-Leibnizian.

Teleology

Leibniz specified the respects in which the plan of the world is the best possible.

> The greatest variety together with the greatest order; the best arranged ground, place, time; the most results produced in the most simple ways; the most of power, knowledge, happiness and goodness in the creatures that the universe could permit.[3]

The world is what it is neither as the result of random motions, as the atomists maintained, nor because all possibilities are realized, as Hobbes, Spinoza, and—according to Leibniz—even Descartes said, but as the consequence of God's reasoned choice of the best. The ultimate explanation of things is therefore teleological. What is more, the particular features that the best world has, such as "the most results produced in the most simple ways"—Leibniz was thinking of the astonishingly simple laws of gravitation and of motion that govern the paths of falling leaves and of planets—are accounted for in terms of purpose. The whole is purposively harmonized; and indeed, as we shall see, the events that happen in the career not only of a person but of a stone are to be understood ultimately in terms of the teleological notion of effort. Leibniz never tired of quoting, with enthusiasm, the speech of Socrates in the *Phaedo* where he castigated Anaxagoras for neglecting Mind in explaining particular occurrences. (See pages 77–8.)

Yet this reintroduction of purpose into the worldview did not lead Leibniz to reject the validity or relevance of mechanical explanations. Particular happenings ought to be accounted for mechanically—here Leibniz is really on the side of Anaxagoras; teleology comes in only when we raise the question why the mechanical order is as it is. Nevertheless, Voltaire's travesty—"noses are made to carry spectacles"—does not entirely miss the mark.

Substance

Let us now consider what this superlatively excellent world consists of. Bodies in motion, minds thinking thoughts, all of these interacting with one another—this familiar view of things is true, but it is not fundamental. Bodies need explanation. Leibniz is an analyzing philosopher; explanation for him entails reduction of the complex to the simple. Now anything extended is essentially complex and plural; however tiny it is, it can in principle be cut into tinier bits. Atomism declares that there is in fact an end to divisibility. Leibniz could not accept this, for it violated the principle of sufficient reason: why should divisibility stop at one size rather than another? No reason could be given; therefore, there could be no such limit. Leibniz also had a physical argument for denying that atoms could be simple bodies: if they rebound from one another, as the theory requires, they must be elastic. But elasticity implies internal motion, hence complexity.

If there are simple substances, then, they cannot be bodies. Nor can extension even be an attribute of a simple substance. But there *must* be simple substances: plurality presupposes unity. Mind or soul—which Descartes taught the world to conceive as unitary unextended substance—suggests itself as a candidate for the role, though it may be hard to conceive how a table could be composed of souls.

Motion, the other fundamental fact of physics, requires explanation in terms of its cause, which is force. Leibniz defines force as "that which, in the present, bears with it a change for the future." Force, physics teaches, is conserved. Thus it has at least one of the requisites for being substance, in that it is neither increased nor diminished, unless by God's omnipotence.

We experience force directly in ourselves, as that effort or endeavor which according to Spinoza is the very essence of man. Force, effort, will is that which initiates action. What we are conscious of in ourselves we are entitled to ascribe also to the rest of nature; we must suppose that other existence differs from our own only in degree.

The Monads

Consider your mind or soul. It is unextended. It can in no way be separated into self-subsisting parts. Therefore, it is a unity. Yet it is full of diversity: a vast multitude of thoughts, perceptions, feelings—all different, all complex. The mind supplies us with the unique model for diversity in unity. Therefore, a mind is a simple substance, and the only possible simple substance is a mind or something mind-like.

Leibniz calls a simple substance a monad, from the Greek word for unity. We find in a monad "perceptions (that is, representations of the compound, or of what is external, in the simple) and appetitions (that is, tendencies from one perception to another), which are the principles of change."[4] When I look at the tomato, what is out there and compound—the tomato, extended, round, red, soft—is represented in the monad that is my soul, which itself does not have any of these properties. If I am hungry I have a tendency to advance to a perception of the juiciness and subacid flavor of the tomato, that is to say, I have an appetition to eat it. Life, the being of the monad, consists of the succession of such perceptions and appetitions.

Your soul is different from my soul. Even if we are very close together, looking at the same tomato, our points of view are not quite the same. Perhaps I am hungry and you are not, or I like tomatoes and you do not; then there are appetitive differences as well. Every monad "mirrors the universe from its own point of view," and no two monads are exactly alike. Monads differ also in the clarity of their perceptions. You and I perceive the tomato clearly; God perceives it more clearly still; the caterpillar crawling on its surface has only a confused perception—only a sort of hardly differentiated feeling; while the perception by the dish on which the tomato reposes is below the level of consciousness altogether. It may seem fantastic to speak of the dish as "perceiving" the tomato; but a dish is altered, however slightly, by the presence of a tomato on it. And according to Leibniz, alterations differ in degree only, not kind.

The Monads Are Windowless

Physics teaches that every body in the universe affects every other body. Leibniz interprets this to mean just that whenever there is a change in any body (or monad), there is a corresponding change in every other body (or monad). But, he insists, no monad exercises metaphysical action on any other monad. The monad is a series of perceptions and appetitions; it develops according to its inner nature alone. "The monads have no windows." If it were otherwise, the monad could not be a substance, for its being would depend on that of some other thing.

To understand this crucial point we must return to Leibniz' logic. The ordinary view that in a contingent statement the predicate is added on to the subject, of whose concept it is not an essential part, was rejected by Leibniz. There has to be a sufficient reason why the predicate 'visiting Paris' applies to Leibniz; and ultimately this sufficient reason cannot be anything other than that the predicate is, after all, part of the subject concept 'Leibniz'. The connection between subject and predicate must be logical—anything less would be arbitrary and fortuitous, merely a brute fact, and hence ruled out by the principle of sufficient reason. But inclusion of one in another is the only way, really, in which concepts can be logically related. Therefore, the predicate must be included in the subject; "Leibniz went to Paris" turns out to be an analytic statement after all. The principle of sufficient reason requires that all true propositions be analytic. "A complete or perfect concept of an individual substance involves all its predicates past, present and future."[5] The distinction between necessary and contingent truths reduces to this: necessary truths are true in all possible worlds and can be demonstrated by analysis of concepts in a finite number of steps. Contingent truths, on the other hand, hold only of the actual world, which depends for its reality on God's choice of the best. Only God could demonstrate them by *a priori* analysis, for the process is infinite. The difference is like that between the square root of 9, which is 3, and the square root of 3, which begins 1.732 . . . and proceeds to infinity; only God can know its exact value.

The Preestablished Harmony

The Cartesians had the problem, which they did not solve, of making comprehensible the interaction of mind and body. One hypothesis, Occasionalism, was to the effect that God had so arranged the physical and mental series that on the occasion of the occurrence of an event in one, for example a volition, an appropriately corresponding event such as a muscular motion would take place in the other. The series were compared to two clocks that being made and adjusted by the same clockmaker, seem to interact without really doing so.

Leibniz adopted this line of thought, multiplying from two harmonized substances to the infinity of monads. No monad affects any other; if however they seem to, if my perceptions when I am in the same room with you are rather like yours, that is because God in His wisdom created the monads in accordance with a Preestablished Harmony. You and I live our lives in our windowless cells. However, on one wall of my cell is projected a television picture of your cell, while simultaneously on the wall of your cell there is a picture of mine. The effect (if we limit ourselves to the senses of sight and hearing) will then be as if there were no wall at all, as if we were really communicating.

Bodies

Now we can return to the question: How can complex substances, which are extended, be composed of simple substances, which are not? For no aggregate of nonextensions can make an extension. The answer is that bodies, and all extension and motion, are "really appearances like rainbows."[6] The rainbow is, in a way, an illusion, but not a mere illusion. There is something out there, namely refracted light; the illusion consists in our mistaking it for a thing, like a painted arch. Similarly, the apparent interaction of things is not mere illusion, for it is grounded in something real, the preestablished harmony; there is illusion only if we take it for direct influence of one thing on another. Bodies are appearances, but "well-founded appearances."

Perhaps this can be understood with the help of another photographic analogy. The metaphor is suggested by Leibniz himself, who says that the perceptions in different monads "vary like different perspective drawings of the same town seen from different points."[7]

The crown jewels are on display. For security reasons they are in a circular strong box with 16 peepholes.

Robbers come. Before heisting the jewels, they take color photos through each peephole. These 16 pictures they then paste up in position inside the box. If they work cleverly enough the theft may go undetected, for to visual inspection everything will be as it was when the jewels were really there.

That is what God does for the monads. Strictly and literally, the monads are nowhere, for space itself is only a well-founded appearance; in reality there exist only the points of view of the monads, which can be ordered in a three-dimensional array.

Perhaps this suggests that Leibniz' God is the same as Descartes' deceiving demon. But Leibniz would protest that the crown jewels really do exist: every possible point of view is occupied, so there are jewel monads that in a low-grade manner are staring back at the spectator (or, we should rather say, at photos of the spectators). When there are jewel perceptions in the spectators, there are harmonized spectator perceptions in the jewels. The principal difference between jewels and spectators is that jewels cannot remember their perceptions. Matter is mind without memory.

Solipsism

Leibniz was an outside-in philosopher. The starting point of his philosophy is the world, not his own consciousness. Cartesian doubt he rejected out of hand, declaring that "if ever it could justly be raised, it would be absolutely insuperable." Nor did he assume at the outset, as Locke did, that the immediate objects of our understanding are mental and private to us. Nevertheless, he did come to this conclusion, which he derived from the analysis of a proposition that to him was self-evident: there are simple substances.

The objection is sometimes raised to Leibniz' philosophy that if the monads are windowless, there can be no way for one monad to know that any other monads exist. The monad's dream—as some people call the unfolding monadal consciousness—would be the same if there were no other monads at all, or if they dreamed quite unconnected dreams. But this objection overlooks the fact that

Leibniz proved the existence of God without assuming a plurality of monads; the plurality then follows from goodness of God. (Leibniz did assume, with all European philosophers before Schopenhauer, that the more existence there is, the better.) So Leibniz' position is at least as tenable as Descartes' who likewise based the rejection of solipsism on divine *bona fides*.

Free Will Again

More formidable dangers lurk at the bottom of Leibniz' doctrine, in the principles that every true proposition is analytic and that "A complete or perfect concept of an individual substance involves all its predicates past, present and future." If the complete concept of Judas involves the predicate 'betraying-his-Lord', must it not then be inevitable that Judas will betray his Lord? And how can he be held responsible for the sin, if he could not avoid it? Leibniz held that Judas' motive "inclined without necessitating," and that Judas could have remained loyal. He did not explain, however, in what sense one could do what was incompatible with one's complete concept. In any case, he protested, Judas' act was free—it followed from Judas' own nature and not from any external compulsion. This would be so, however, only because monads are not, metaphysically, affected by anything at all outside themselves. The result would then be that all actions whatsoever are free, including those you perform at gun point or when totally under the physical—and even mental—control of another person. But it is as unacceptable to hold persons responsible for everything they do, as for nothing they do.

Waiving this point, Leibniz would still have on his hands the task of avoiding the imputation of Judas' guilt to God. For God knew that Judas would sin; nevertheless, He went ahead and created him. And then He damned him for having sinned. How could this be just? Leibniz replied that God chose to create Judas, who would be damned—not that God chose to damn Judas. But this seems to be a distinction without a difference.

Compossibility

To believe that only what is actual is possible, Leibniz warned the world, is to start on the road to atheism. For if that were so, everything would happen by necessity, and God—a personal God, working good deeds and avoiding bad ones—would be superfluous. But it is hard to see how Leibniz' own philosophy could be kept from leading to the same unwanted conclusion.

By aid of the notion of compossibility, Leibniz sought to show that the possible is wider than the actual. Compossibility is a common-sense notion: things possible in isolation are yet impossible in some contexts. It is possible to have a swimming pool in my back yard, or a tennis court, but given its size they are not compossible. It is possible that the next President will die of old age and it is possible that the assassin of the next President has already been born, but these are not compossibilities.

A possible world is any set of compossible monads. Some things are compossible with many other things and some with only a few, as everyone knows who has ever arranged furniture. Since Leibniz held that the more being there is, the better, he concluded that the best of all possible worlds is the set of monads of maximal compossibility. This may be taken as a technical formulation of what he meant by "the greatest variety together with the greatest order; . . . the most results produced in the most simple ways." But this idea raises two problems.

First, it is not clear that any monad could be incompatible with any other. For if a monad, as maintained, is just a series of perceptions and appetitions, why could not any monad coexist with any other—as different movie houses may simultaneously show any films they choose to? Perhaps if the monads are to "mirror the universe," that is, if there is to be Preestablished Harmony between them, their compatibilities must be limited. But this is doubtful. For it seems if anything at all is possible, it must be possible also to "mirror" it.

Second, granting the validity and applicability of the notion of compossibility, if God must choose the best or maximally compossible world, in what sense can the excluded worlds be said to be possible at all? This difficulty is in fact independent of the notion of compossibility. If there is a sufficient reason uniquely determining one world to be the best of all possible ones, and that one must be chosen, then the others, it seems, are impossible after all. So there is only one possible world, and that is Spinozism. The reply seems unsatisfying that the rest are still possible in the defined sense of not internally self-contradictory.

Leibniz' Influence

After Leibniz, philosophy in Germany fell into the hands of professors, where it has remained to this day. It happened that the man of greatest influence in German eighteenth-century university teaching of philosophy was Christian Wolff (1679–1754), a follower of Leibniz. Thus down to the era of Kant, a modified version of Leibniz' philosophy was the dominant tradition in Germany.

Outside Germany Leibniz never was influential. However, at the present time more books seem to be published about Leibniz than almost any other of the great philosophers. No doubt there are several sufficient reasons for this attention, one of them being that the chaotic state in which Leibniz left his papers affords exceptional opportunities for the exercise of scholarship. But interest in his work is genuine. Leibniz had perhaps the most comprehensive philosophical mind since Aristotle. If his system lacks intuitive plausibility, admiration for its ingenuity and rigor increases with familiarity. Leibniz was a philosopher's philosopher.

38

Berkeley

EIGHT CENTURIES AFTER JOHN Scotus Erigena, another philosopher arose in Ireland. George Berkeley was born to Anglo-Irish parents in Kilkenny, 1685, and educated at Trinity college, Dublin, where later he taught Greek, divinity, and Hebrew for fifteen years. Most of the distinctive ideas for his philosophical writings came to him and were written down in notebooks while he was still a teenage undergraduate. The publications on which his reputation rests were all completed before his thirtieth year.

Berkeley had extraordinary gifts of persuasion. Having conceived the project of founding a college in Bermuda for the higher education of American colonists and savages, single-handed he induced Parliament to authorize a grant of twenty thousand pounds for the purpose. In his elation he composed these verses.

AMERICA, OR THE MUSES REFUGE: A PROPHECY

> The Muse, disgusted at an Age and Clime
>   Barren of every glorious Theme,
> In distant Lands now waits a better Time,
>   Producing Subjects worthy Fame:
>
> In happy climes, where from the genial Sun
>   And virgin Earth such Scenes ensue,
> The Force of Art by Nature seems outdone,
>   And fancied Beauties by the true:
>
> In happy Climes the Seat of Innocence,
>   Where Nature guides and Virtue rules,
> Where Men shall not impose for Truth and Sense,
>   The Pedantry of Courts and Schools:
>
> There shall be sung another golden Age,
>   The rise of Empire and of Arts,
> The Good and Great inspiring epic Rage,
>   The wisest Heads and noblest Hearts.
>
> Not such as *Europe* breeds in her decay;
>   Such as she bred when fresh and young,
> When heav'nly Flame did animate her Clay,
>   By future Poets shall be sung.

> Westward the Course of Empire takes its Way;
> The four first Acts already past,
> A fifth shall close the Drama with the Day;
> Time's noblest Offspring is the last.

This poem—especially the last stanza—is the reason why Berkeley, the seat of the University of California, is so named.

In 1728 Berkeley married, and sailed with his bride and a few professors to Rhode Island, there to begin organizing the college and to await the final appropriation of the parliamentary grant. Three years later no money had come, and it was clear that the Prime Minister did not intend to provide any. Berkeley returned to England.

In 1734 he was appointed (Anglican) Bishop of Cloyne, which post he held for eighteen years. Later in life he became an enthusiast for tar-water, a remedy he had learned of from the American Indians. It was an infusion of the pitch exuded from pine trees. The Bishop prescribed it to the faithful of his diocese for all ailments. To spread the good news he wrote *Siris: A Chain of Philosophical Reflexions and Inquiries Concerning the Virtues of Tar-Water, and Divers Other Subjects* (1744). This was the only one of his books to be successful on publication: it went through six printings in the first year.

In 1752 Berkeley and his wife retired to Oxford to be near their son, who was an undergraduate. They had been there only a year when the philosopher died, suddenly and peacefully. His will provided that his body was not to be buried "until it grow offensive by the cadaverous Smell."

The Task

By the early eighteenth century, the spectacular triumphs of science were well-known to all educated men. The Copernican system was no longer seriously questioned. Newton had demonstrated how the motions of the planets, described by Kepler, and of falling bodies on the earth's surface, as studied by Galileo, are all of the same kind and exemplify a few elegantly simple laws. *Newtonianism for the Ladies* was the title of a best-seller. Perhaps even more impressive in the public mind was Halley's verified prediction of the return in 1682 of the comet that had appeared before in 1607 and 1531. There were no more portents in the sky, only algebraic equations. One fact sums up the advance of the rational outlook: at the beginning of the seventeenth century most educated people believed in the reality of witchcraft; at its close the belief had receded to such backwoods as Scotland and Massachusetts.

Some people in England contemplated with anxiety the effects of the new science on religion. The mechanical philosophy was suspected of fostering infidelity. The defense dwelt on the sublime conception of God to be derived from the majestic, inexorable, harmonious system of nature—God's creation—revealed by Science. Newton himself was induced to parry criticism of his philosophy as godless by adding at the end of the third edition of the *Mathematical Principles of Natural Philosophy* a discourse on God, emphasizing the design evident in the heavens.

> This most beautiful system of the sun, planets, and comets, could only proceed
> from the counsel and dominion of an intelligent and powerful Being . . . We know
> him only by his most wise and excellent contrivances of things, and final causes . . .
> Blind metaphysical necessity, which is certainly the same always and every where,
> could produce no variety of things. All that diversity of natural things which we find
> suited to different times and places could arise from nothing but the ideas and will of
> a Being necessarily existing.

In previous ages the occurrence of miracles had provided proof of the existence, power, intelligence, and goodness of God. Now the nonexistence of exceptions to the order of nature proved the existence, power, intelligence, and goodness of God.

These expressions of piety were sufficiently reassuring to make astronomy, physics, chemistry, and mathematics respectable. Alexander Pope (1688–1744) hardly exaggerated British opinion in his famous couplet

> Nature and Nature's Law lay hid in Night:
> GOD said, Let Newton be; and all was Light.

Still, some there were who perceived that at best science lent support to Deism, not to Christianity; and that the only room it left for God was as First Cause and Designer back at the beginning. An awesome Being, no doubt, worthy of reverence and respect, but not a Providence—a Being with a day-to-day interest in the welfare of His creatures, a Father (or Son) to whom one could pray. Religion cannot shrink itself into a theory about the beginning of things. That can have no hold on any powerful emotions nor any influence on conduct. Besides, as a theory of the beginning, religion would find itself in competition with other simpler theories, such as the self-sufficiency and eternity of matter. Deism was not really a religion. Physics led to materialism and atheism.

George Berkeley the teenager, studying divinity and reading Newton and Locke in his rooms in Dublin, hit on a strategy to rescue religion. Materialism was the enemy to be destroyed. It would not be difficult to cast doubt on purported knowledge of matter. Locke had shown how our immediate knowledge is only of our own ideas, and our inferences to their causes in a material substance are hazardous, our very conception of matter confused. However, Berkeley saw that dwelling merely on this point would at best produce skepticism: the contention that there is a reality but it is unknowable to us. Skepticism had been used in defense of religion, but it was an unreliable weapon. Instead of making the desired inference "Science is uncertain and requires faith, so I might as well believe Christianity," a person might instead conclude that if even science was open to doubt, revealed religion must be altogether indefensible. Besides, Berkeley was temperamentally antiskeptical.

His plan was audacious. He would argue not just that we do not know that material substance exists, but that we *do* know that it does *not* exist. Thus the materialist would be utterly undone, his support having vanished; the skeptic likewise, for there would be no hidden reality to be skeptical about. There would be left only our minds and their ideas, and their Cause, who could be none other than God. No longer a remote Cause; ideas, being fleeting, must be caused at every moment anew. God as Providence would be vindicated.

Outline of Berkeley's Argument

Berkeley argues this way.

1. All the philosophers agree that besides God, reality consists of mental substance, or material substance, or both.
2. But we cannot know that there is any such thing as material substance. Berkeley's argument here is a vigorous development of Locke's and Descartes' worries on the subject. If his philosophy stopped here it would be Skepticism. But
3. Moreover, the supposition that there is material substance is entirely useless. It does not explain anything.
4. And further, the notion of material substance is not even logically coherent, since matter is supposed to be both like and unlike ideas.
5. Therefore, reality is wholly mental.
6. Therefore, reality consists of minds and their ideas. Since ideas cannot just float around, they must inhere in something: mental substances or minds.
7. The coherence of our ideas, some of them at least, and their agreement with ideas in other minds, proves that they have an external cause. This cause must be God, Who by His power and goodness arranges that our ideas are, so to speak, synchronized.
8. The totality of all ideas, and of the spirits in which they inhere, is the universe. God eternally perceives the whole. In this perception (by God or other spirits) does all reality consist.

The argument was first published in the *Principles of Human Knowledge* (1710). Berkeley was pained when it was derided by the few who paid any attention to it; for, he protested, he was only setting out in systematic form what was really implicit in common-sense notions and attacking the extravagant pretensions of the philosophers. "In all things I side with the mob," he had written in his notebook.

In 1713 he published *Three Dialogues between Hylas and Philonous*, in an attempt to present his thoughts in more popular form and in such a way as to win a more favorable reception by making the denial of matter appear less paradoxical. This hope was in vain also.

Berkeley on Ideas

The *Principles* begins thus.

> It is evident to anyone who takes a survey of the *objects* of human knowledge that they are either ideas actually imprinted on the senses, or else such as are perceived by attending to the passions and operations of the mind, or lastly, ideas forged by help of memory and imagination.

Berkeley thus accepts without comment, as his starting point, Locke's New Way of Ideas—according to which our awareness is strictly speaking of the contents of our mind, only loosely speaking (at best) of the things those contents are caused by. In the *Dialogues*, however, which were aimed at a less sophisticated audience, considerable space is devoted at the beginning to expounding and advocating this doctrine. We shall scrutinize the argument in some detail.

The convention in dialogue writing was to assign Greek names to the characters, who in Berkeley's dialogues nevertheless are supposed to be British college students talking before breakfast. Philonous means Mind-Lover and represents Berkeley; Hylas, a proper name often found in Greek poetry, was chosen because of its similarity to *hyle*, Greek for matter.

After some introductory remarks in which Hylas speaks disparagingly of "skeptics" who "deny the real existence of sensible things, or pretend to know nothing of them," Philonous asks: "What mean you by 'sensible things'?" Hylas replies: "Those things which are perceived by the senses."

Neither Hylas nor Philonous offers any examples of "things which are perceived by the senses." Instead, Philonous at once suggests a distinction between "perceive immediately" and "perceive mediately." When you read, the letters on the page are perceived immediately; "but mediately, or by means of these, are suggested to one's mind the notions of God, virtue, truth, etc." This is not, as it purports to be, a distinction between two kinds of perception but between perception and suggestion.

Philonous wants to establish that we perceive our ideas immediately but only infer their causes. Hylas admits that it would be absurd to suppose that God or virtue are sensible things; whereupon Philonous immediately asks "Does it not follow from this that, though I see one part of the sky red, and another blue, and that my reason does thence evidently conclude there must be some cause of that diversity of colors, yet that cause cannot be said to be a sensible thing or perceived by the sense of seeing?" Hylas answers "It does." But it does not follow, and it is not even true. The cause may be the setting sun or the glow of neon lights, which are "sensible things"—at this point we have been given no reason to doubt that they are "things which can be perceived immediately by sense."

Philonous, however, continues: "In like manner, though I hear variety of sounds, yet I cannot be said to hear the causes of those sounds"—as if I could hear a bang or a chime, but never an explosion or a bell. After making similarly dubious points about heat and weight, Hylas not only ratifies all his unnecessary admissions about causes but even goes beyond to a further surrender: "To prevent any more questions of this kind, I tell you once for all that by 'sensible things' I mean those only which are perceived by sense, and that in truth the senses perceive nothing which they do not perceive immediately, for they make no inferences. The deducing therefore of causes or occasions from effects and appearances, which alone are perceived by sense, entirely relates to reason."

A new word, 'appearances', has here been introduced. "Appearances . . . alone are perceived by sense." We never see a tomato, we see only an appearance of a tomato. We never taste a lemon, only the appearance of a lemon. But this phrase "taste an appearance," introduced (by implication in the phrase "perceive appearances") by Hylas—supposedly the representative of naive common sense uncorrupted by philosophy—has no meaning in ordinary English.

Even the phrase "see an appearance of a tomato" is of doubtful intelligibility. You might say "I saw something in the refrigerator that appeared to be a tomato" or "The vegetable has the appearance of a tomato"; but you would not report a glimpse into the refrigerator by saying "I saw the appearance of a tomato." Hylas, however, has conceded that all seeing is the seeing of appearances. What this means has not been explained. Hylas at this point is talking nonsense, though Berkeley, one of the great English prose stylists, has so arranged things that we do not immediately perceive the fact.

Philonous presses on: "You will further inform me whether we immediately perceive by sight anything besides light and colours and figures; or by hearing, anything but sounds; by the palate, anything besides tastes; by the smell, besides odours, or by the touch, more than tangible qualities. Hylas: "We do not."

Hylas has surrendered unconditionally. Although all the passages so far quoted occur in two pages near the beginning of a hundred page work, the remainder is only the making explicit of the implications in these admissions.

If you are asked "Can you hear anything but sounds?"—just like that—you might be inclined to answer "No, nothing else." You would feel that you had been tricked, though, if you were then told that you had admitted the impossibility of hearing a bell—"in truth and strictness," as the qualification is phrased later in the *Dialogues*. For "I hear a sound" no more excludes "I hear a bell" than "I struck a blow" rules out "I struck him on the chin," or "I am reading words" precludes "I am reading *Hamlet*," or "I am climbing a rope" precludes "I am climbing Mount Shasta." To strike a chin *is* to strike a blow; to read *Hamlet is* to read words; to climb Mount Shasta *is* (in part) to climb ropes. These are not either-ors, they are both-ands. To hear a bell is to hear a sound, though it does not follow that a bell is a sound. To see a buttercup is to see a yellow shape, though a buttercup is not (merely) a yellow shape.

Philonous, however, insists on misinterpreting the structure of language (specifically and technically, he ignores the existence of internal accusatives to verbs of perceiving) in order to draw the conclusion that the object of perception is never a thing, a substance, but always a "sensible quality." The "sensible thing" is reduced to a sum of sensible qualities by the argument "If you take away all sensible qualities, there remains nothing sensible. Sensible things therefore are nothing else but so many sensible qualities, or combinations of sensible qualities." This argument is fallacious, as is easily seen by comparing it with "If you take away all lovable qualities, there remains nothing lovable. Lovable persons therefore are nothing else but so many lovable qualities, or combinations of lovable qualities."

The Secondary Qualities

The rest of the first *Dialogue* is devoted to showing that "the reality of sensible things consists in being perceived," which in turn is said to entail the existence of sensible things only "in the mind." The "secondary qualities" are taken up one by one. Berkeley does not differ in his conclusions here from Galileo, Descartes, and Locke.

Philonous begins with heat, which is argued to be "in the mind" because pains and pleasures admittedly are in the mind, and at least certain degrees of heat are inseparable, indeed indistinguishable, from pain and pleasure. It then becomes implausible to try to rejoin (as Hylas halfheartedly does) that at least moderate heat may be "without the mind."

Philonous reinforces the conclusion with a famous experiment. If you soak one hand in hot water and the other in cold, then put them both into tepid water, the water will seem cold to the one and hot to the other. But since the same water cannot be both hot and cold, it must be neither. So the heat and cold are not in the water but in the mind.

Throughout the discussion of heat and of all the other qualities, Philonous reiterates that by a quality he means a "sensible quality," and a sensible quality is a perceived quality. But then he goes on to identify the perceived quality with the sensation; for instance, ". . . you should not judge the sensation occasioned by the fire, or anything like it, to be in the fire." Hylas: ". . . I . . . acknowledge that heat and cold are only sensations existing in our minds."

That sensations are "in the mind," and that no sensation "or anything like it" is in the fire, will be granted. There is a temptation to say that heat and other quality words are ambiguous: heat means both the sensation we have when (for example) we stick a hand in the fire and the quality in the fire that produces the sensation. We may suspect that Philonous is taking advantage of this ambiguity. Berkeley recognizes and answers this criticism. Heat, he maintains, is not an ambiguous word. If it ever referred to something not a sensation, we could know nothing of what is intended, since our knowledge is of sensations only. Berkeley is right in denying ambiguity; but to the contrary of what he held, the word 'heat' is never the name of a sensation. For sensations do not have names at all. Rather, we describe them in terms of their typical causes: "There is a prickly feeling in the big toe"—that is, the kind of feeling you would have if you stepped on a porcupine; "I feel hot"—I feel as one normally feels when in proximity to a source of heat. If our sensations did have names, as opposed to descriptions by causes, we could never communicate with each other about them because I could never know what you were talking about.

The section concludes with Hylas saying "I frankly own, Philonous, that it is in vain to stand out any longer. Colours, sounds, tastes, in a word, all those termed 'secondary qualities', have certainly no existence without the mind. . . . This is no more than several philosophers maintain . . ." He means Galileo, Descartes, and especially Locke; and he is inaccurate, inasmuch as Locke put secondary qualities in things. Only the ideas of them, which he distinguished from the qualities themselves, did he assert to be in the mind. Nevertheless, Berkeley was right in spirit; Locke, as we have seen, did suppose that quality *words* are names of ideas. And he was prone to such alarmist declarations as "Take away the sensation of them; let not the eyes see light or colours, . . . and all colours . . . vanish and cease." Why did he, and other eminent men, talk this way? Let us consider the matter with respect to sound.

The nature of sound as a physical occurrence was understood from the time of Aristotle at least. Some vibrating object moves the air, which "striking on the drum of the ear, causes a vibration which by the auditory nerves being communicated to the brain, the soul is thereupon affected." What is out there is air in motion. Therefore sound, considered as an external happening, is air in motion. It sets the eardrum to vibrating, and the auditory nerve to responding. As a mysterious consequence of these events, we experience a certain kind of sensation. So went the doctrine, innocently enough, from Aristotle to Galileo.

But then the question arises: What is the sensation? And what is it to be called? This is where the physics ends and the philosophy begins. If, as was universally held, the sensation is a real *thing* but also obviously not moving air or eardrum or nerve, then it must be a nonphysical thing, a mental thing, "in the soul."

Now the philosopher is moved to ask: What has happened to the *sound?* For he has been told by physicist and physiologist that all there is in the surrounding atmosphere and in the interior of the skull is a succession of motions. But (the philosopher thinks) motions cannot be sounds—sounds are heard, while motions are seen or felt. So what has become of the sound? Then he remembers that the sensation, which doesn't seem to be a physical process, is all that is left. It, then, must *be* the sound. The philosopher then announces his conclusion in this misleading way: "There are no sounds in the physical world; sound is something mental, an affection of the soul." Common people who go on talking about "the explosion being heard for miles around" are cautioned that they are speaking loosely or even ignorantly.

Similar reasoning about colors, tastes, and odors—combined with the dogma that "strictly speaking we do not see tomatoes and sunsets, we see only red color"—led to the curious conclusion that the real world must be soundless, colorless, tasteless, and odorless. The scientists had tried to explain the qualities, but the philosophers interpreted them as explaining them *away.*

The Primary Qualities

Locke and the others held, however, that the qualities of extension, figure, solidity, gravity, motion, and rest have archetypes in objects; that is to say, pennies look round and are round, although their copper color is a phenomenon "in the mind" caused by real qualities in the penny but not resembling any real property of it. The grooves in the phonograph record cause but do not resemble (are not "archetypes" of) the sound made by a pianist playing the Moonlight Sonata.

Berkeley proceeds to attack this distinction. His method is to show that "the same arguments which are brought against secondary qualities will hold good against these also." He begins with extension and figure. As color was deemed not in objects because the apparent colors of things vary with the condition and location of the perceiver, so (we are told) also figure and extension vary with the perceiver: things look big when we are close to them, little when we are at a distance. Consequently, size cannot be "in" an "external unthinking substance." In the discussion there is no reference to the method whereby we establish the size and shape of objects, namely, comparison with standards. Philonous seems to take for granted that we have no means of determining whether anything is a yard long other than just seeing whether it looks a yard long (no yardsticks allowed) and that our answer will (or ought to) vary for the same object at different distances.

Hylas, gathering his wits for a moment, remarks "I have somewhere heard of a distinction between *absolute* and *sensible* extension. Now though it be acknowledged that *great* and *small*, consisting merely in the relation which other extended beings have to the parts of our own bodies, do not really inhere in the substances themselves, yet nothing obliges us to hold the same with regard to *absolute* extension, which is something abstracted from *great* and *small*, from this or that particular magnitude or figure." But the very words used to signify the distinction—with their suggestion that every object has two extensions, one of which is "sensible" and the other not, as well as the unfortunate, unnecessary, and incorrect addition that absolute extension is "something abstracted from great and small"—make it easy for Philonous to dispose of this feeble attempt to rescue the objectivity of primary qualities while ignoring the real issue raised. Philonous embarks on a polemic against Lockean abstract ideas which, whatever its merits may be, is irrelevant at this point. There is nothing abstract about measuring a trout with a footrule. And as extension is dealt with as if there were no such things as yard-sticks, so the disputants treat motion in all innocence of clocks.

The arguments that Berkeley inherited and used to show the subjectivity of secondary qualities are so bad that it is a hard question whether his original ones against primary qualities are any worse. But while Descartes and Locke fell victims to confusion in holding the ideas of secondary qualities to be "in the mind," it is confusion compounded when Berkeley puts the secondary qualities themselves there and stuffs the primary qualities in along with them. However, Berkeley does not really depend on the arguments about how what is perceived varies with the condition of the perceiver. His main argument, applying indifferently to all quali-ties, is based on the admissions extracted from Hylas at the beginning: that a sensible thing is nothing but a collection of sensible qualities, sensible qualities are sensations, and sensations are "in the mind."

This argument, odd as it is, really does follow from premises granted by the philosophers. Locke was inconsistent in trying to hold both that the immediate objects of perception are our own ideas and that we somehow know that objects independent of our ideas somehow contain archetypes of some of our ideas.

Near the end of the first *Dialogue*, Philonous introduces another version of the main argument against the materialists. Hylas concedes: "Properly and immedi-ately nothing can be perceived but ideas. All material things, therefore, are in themselves insensible and to be perceived only by their ideas." To this Philonous objects: "Ideas then are sensible, and their archetypes or originals insensible? . . . But how can that which is sensible be like that which is insensible? Can a real thing, in itself *invisible*, be like a *colour*, or a real thing which is not *audible* be like a *sound*? In a word, can anything be like a sensation or idea, but another sensation or idea?" To paraphrase:

1. If an idea *I* is like its material cause *M*, then it must be possible to compare *I* with *M* and observe the likeness.
2. But if *I* is to be compared with *M*, we must be able to observe both *I* and *M*.
3. But *M* (Descartes and Locke must concede) is not observable.
4. Therefore there is not, nor can there be, any ground for the claim that *I* is like *M*. Or to put it more strongly, we do not know what we are talking about when we suggest that *I* is like *M*.

This is a valid refutation of Descartes and Locke and anyone else who holds that though the causes of our ideas are unperceivable, they are nonetheless like ideas. It is such an obvious argument that we wonder why Descartes and Locke did not anticipate it. Perhaps the answer is something like this: Descartes thought it was just an unfortunate fact about us that we can inspect only our own states of consciousness—we are shut up inside our minds. The physical piece of wax, "naked," is forever unperceivable by us—we only receive messages from it, like prisoners in solitary who know of the outside world only through letters. But God can perceive the "naked" wax—He is not shut up. So after all the wax is in a sense perceivable. Put less theologically: Descartes and Locke, in speculating about what material objects are like in themselves, had in the backs of their minds a notion that the real nature of the object would be apparent to a being who somehow transcended human limitations and could perceive the object "immediately" or "directly" in a way somehow like that in which we directly perceive our own ideas. Berkeley exposed the inconsistency in this mode of thinking. Since (it was granted) the only notion we have of perception is the one formed from our own experience, which is inspection of the idea "in our minds," it follows that to suppose that even God could perceive something not in any mind (not even His) is to fall into contradiction.

Refutation of Skepticism

Philonous: "Well then, are you at length satisfied that no sensible things have a real existence, and that you are in truth an arrant *skeptic?*" Hylas: "It is too plain to be denied."

Hylas at this point is in a condition like that of Descartes at the close of the first *Meditation.* Having reviewed their reasons for supposing that their knowledge extended beyond the immediate data of consciousness and having found those reasons insufficient, both were in the trough of skepticism or solipsism. However, Hylas is worse off than Descartes, who was able to escape with the help of God and the assumption that it is *possible* for there to be material objects that cause ideas resembling them. This route is closed to Hylas, who has already admitted the force of the argument that nothing but an idea can be like an idea. Since Hylas in addition supposes that ideas have no "real existence," they are "only ideas," the solipsism seems invincible.

Philonous proceeds now to deliver the longest speech in the *Dialogues,* to the effect that skepticism is absurd because the universe is so vast and marvelous. This prefaces a short argument.

1. "Sensible things cannot exist otherwise than in a mind or spirit."
2. Sensible things "depend not on my thought" but "have existence distinct from being perceived by me."
3. Therefore, *"There must be some other mind wherein they exist."*
4. "As sure, therefore, as the sensible world really exists, so sure is there an infinite omnipresent Spirit, who contains and supports it."

Crudely put, the argument is that Berkeley's philosophy leads to absurdity (solipsism) unless God exists. Therefore, God exists.

Descartes, in availing himself of God in order to rescue himself from solipsism, made a decent pretense of proving God's existence from premises that would be granted by any reasonable person. Berkeley merely appeals to prejudice, as is shown by Hylas' remark immediately following: "What! this is no more than I and all Christians hold."

Consider the second premise: "Sensible things depend not on my thought but have an existence distinct from being perceived by me." No doubt; but how does Berkeley know? If you manage to raise, seriously, the question whether the furniture in the office continues to exist after the custodian has locked up for the night, how are you going to prove that it does? Will it do to sneak back in the middle of the night, quickly thrust open the door and switch on the light? Hardly. We cannot be assured of the continued existence of unperceived entities by perceiving them.

Philonous, nevertheless, stoutly maintains that sensible things "have an existence exterior to my mind, since I find them by experience to be independent of it." His reasoning, which takes us rather far from "experience," is this: "I know myself not to be the author [of the things I perceive], it being out of my power to determine at pleasure what particular ideas I shall be affected with upon opening my eyes or ears." That is to say

1. Things are ideas.
2. Ideas are produced.
3. *I* do not produce them.
4. But some mind produces them. "How can any idea or sensation . . . be produced by anything but a mind or spirit? This indeed is inconceivable."
5. Therefore, God produces them.

What are the grounds for the third premise? Berkeley is relying on "experience" for the distinction between ideas of imagination, which he can "determine at pleasure," and those that strike him when he opens his eyes or ears. If we concede for the sake of argument that both of these are species of "ideas," still the victim of hallucination and the dreamer cannot "determine at pleasure" what they are going to hallucinate and dream; yet no one would want to say that their "ideas" therefore must be externally produced. Hence, Berkeley is not entitled to conclude that those ideas he has that are independent of his will are "produced" by some other mind—certainly he cannot so conclude "from experience." As far as his principles take him, the universe may consist simply of Berkeley's consciousness, divided into two parts—a relatively coherent part called "waking" and an incoherent part called "dreaming."

Moreover, the argument hinges on the word "produce," which is synonymous with "cause," and is not explained. Its use in this passage is unintelligible, even if we know what 'produce' ordinarily means. Berkeley is maintaining that only minds can produce ideas. Perhaps this is all right, if imagining is taken to be a case of "producing ideas." But Berkeley is trying to account for the origin of those ideas that are precisely not our imaginations; and what he says is that our minds do not produce them, therefore some other mind must produce them in our minds. However, with the doubtful exception of telepathy (in any case unknown to Berkeley), we have no experience of one mind "producing" an idea in another mind, and hence—on Berkeley's own principles—no conception of what the phrase means.

Why do ideas need to be "produced" at all? Because they are "things altogether passive and inert." This we are to take as obvious. We may ask, then, for an instance of something that is active: a stone hitting us on the head? Not so, we are told: "Matter, in the common current acceptation of the word, signifies an extended, solid, movable, unthinking, inactive substance." We might suspect that Berkeley's account of the "common current acceptation of the word" is somewhat strained. It is plausible to suppose that those who believe that fire is matter in motion believe also that it is capable of doing something. But Berkeley is driven into the position of having to claim inactivity for part of the common meaning of the word, because otherwise he would not be able to ask the rhetorical question "And though it should be allowed to exist, yet how can that which is *inactive* be a *cause*?" That is to say, if anyone should think, rightly or wrongly, that matter is active, then that person would think that matter might be a cause. Consequently, the hypothesis that matter exists could be invoked to explain various phenomena, perhaps including ideas.

Viewed in this light, Dr. Johnson's refutation of Berkeley, which historians of philosophy unanimously laugh at, does not appear to be so misguided.

> After we came out of the church, we stood talking for some time together of Bishop Berkeley's ingenious sophistry to prove the non-existence of matter, and that every thing in the universe is merely ideal. I observed, that though we are satisfied his doctrine is not true, it is impossible to refute it. I never shall forget the alacrity with which Johnson answered, striking his foot with mighty force against a large stone, *till he rebounded from it* [emphasis supplied],—"I refute it *thus*."[1]

But to return to Philonous. Having shown to his satisfaction that matter could not be a cause even if it existed and that ideas cannot be causes, he can enunciate the doctrine on which the whole proof of God and refutation of solipsism depend.

> Now I desire to know in the first place, whether you can conceive any action besides volition; and, in the second place, whether to say something and conceive nothing be not to talk nonsense; and, lastly, whether, having considered the premises, you do not perceive that to suppose any efficient or active cause of our ideas other than *spirit* is highly absurd and unreasonable? [Hylas:] I give up the point entirely.

The doctrine is that we cannot conceive of anything being done except as the result of an act of willing. This is a dubious teaching. Even if it were clear what sort of entity an "act of will" or "volition" is, it would remain a mystery what the connection is between such things and muscular motions. It is shocking, moreover, to find primitive animism thus revived in the Age of Enlightenment: animism which, when it explains our ideas as caused by a Great Spirit without material intermediaries, is simply magic.

At the end of the second *Dialogue*, Hylas is forced into admitting that "it is possible we might perceive all things just as we do now, though there was no matter in the world; neither can I conceive, if there be matter, how it should produce any idea in our minds." Philonous can then point out that really Hylas has no conception of matter at all, the word is but empty noise.

And so it would be if we perceived nothing but our own ideas; if those ideas were inert; if we knew they had causes; and if we were clear about how one mind can produce an idea in another mind, or indeed how a mind can produce an idea at all, or even what "the mind produces ideas" means.

The Third Dialogue

In the concluding *Dialogue*, Berkeley replies to various objections to immaterialism. Philonous presents himself as the defender of common sense, as one who is "obliged to think like other folks," against the materialists who are only a "few philosophers." To the obvious objection that folks do talk about matter, Philonous concedes that in a sense there is such a thing: "If by material substance is meant only sensible body, that which is seen and felt (and the unphilosophical part of the world, I dare say, mean no more), then I am more certain of matter's existence than you or any other philosopher pretend to be."

Hylas points out that "according to your own way of thinking, and in consequence of your own principles, it should follow that you are only a system of floating ideas without any substance to support them." For mental substance is just as unperceivable, hence as nonexistent, as material. Berkeley replies that "the being of my self, that is, my own soul, mind, or thinking principle, I evidently know by reflection. . . . I have a notion of spirit, though I have not, strictly speaking, an idea of it." The "reflection" in question seems to be the argument that ideas, being passive and inert, stand in want of causes. At any rate, this is the most charitable conjecture to make; for what Philonous says is mere table-thumping: "How often must I repeat that I know or am conscious of my own being, and that *I myself* am not my ideas, but somewhat else, a thinking, active principle that perceives, knows, wills, and operates about ideas. . . . I know what I mean when I affirm that there is a spiritual substance or support of ideas, that is, that a spirit knows and perceives ideas."

Berkeley reserves for his climax the "mighty difficulty" of reconciling his philosophy with the Biblical account of creation. Since any philosophy according to which reality is mind-dependent will be faced with the problem of giving some plausible interpretation to such sentences as "Before there was any life on earth the atmosphere consisted mainly of ammonia and methane," this objection cannot be dismissed as no longer of interest. In the form in which Hylas puts it, it is this. All things are eternally in God's mind. There was not a time when God began to think of the earth. Creation, then, could not consist in there coming to be ideas in God's mind that were not there previously. It seems, then, that if things are ideas, creation must mean making them to be perceived by other, that is finite, minds. But *Genesis* states explicitly that the earth and heavens—things other than minds—were created not only before Adam but prior to all sentient beings.

Philonous first replies that there might have been other created intelligences, namely angels, in existence before the world. Evidently sensing this answer to be lame, he makes a concession that effectively undermines the philosophy: "I imagine that if I had been present at the creation, I should have seen things produced into being—that is, become perceptible. . . . We may conceive the creation as we should at this time a parcel of plants or vegetables of all sorts produced by an invisible power in a desert where nobody was present." Evidently "To be is to be perceived" has been abandoned in favor of "To be is to be perceptible"—an altogether different doctrine.

Comparison of Berkeley and Leibniz

Berkeley was not very familiar with Leibniz' thought; the published writings were meager and Berkeley was not in the circle of Leibniz' correspondents. Leibniz on his part, when he was told that a man in Ireland had purported to prove the nonexistence of matter, snorted that some fellows will stop at nothing to attract attention. Yet their metaphysical conclusions are in striking coincidence. Both hold that nothing really exists but minds with their perceptions and volitions; that the series of perceptions in individual minds are established by God and adjusted to all the other series, so that there is a common subjectivity that amounts to objectivity; and that all causation is volition.

The routes by which they reached these positions were, however, distinct. Leibniz proceeded by the application of rigorous logic to the conception of simple substance and to the assumption that the world is a rational whole. Berkeley did little but seize on the opportunity presented by Locke's vacillations on the topic of substance. There is a legend that Berkeley is irrefutable. On the contrary, a little attention to his arguments shows them to be shot through with irrelevances, quibbles, incoherencies, unwarranted assumptions, and miscellaneous sophisms. The standard of argumentative cogency in many great philosophers is not so high as one might wish, but Berkeley's is below the modest norm. He was arguing, moreover, from a brief: not merely in defense of religion, nor even of Christianity, but (like Parson Thwackum in *Tom Jones*) specifically of Anglican Christianity.

Narrowness of purpose in Berkeley goes with narrowness of scope. Not every great philosopher has treated every department of philosophy, but most have been men of broad interests. But Berkeley's whole philosophical endeavor was concentrated on the one tenet of theory of knowledge, that what we perceive immediately must be an idea. To be sure, Berkeley has also some reputation as a philosopher of mathematics—inasmuch as he exposed certain logical difficulties in the assumptions about infinitesimals that were made by the mathematical analysts of his day. This too, however, was part of his ax grinding; he was concerned to show that the "infidel mathematicians" had no right to reject as incomprehensible the mysteries of the Church of England when the calculus required similar feats of faith.

Berkeley was not taken seriously as a philosopher in his own day except by the Rankenian Club, an undergraduate group at the University of Edinburgh, and by Samuel Johnson (not *the* Samuel Johnson but) the first President of King's College in New York (now Columbia University). Because nineteenth-century German historians of philosophy saw Berkeley as a transitional figure between Locke and Hume, and because there had to be exactly three "British Empiricists" to match the three "Continental Rationalists," he got into the history books; once in, he is hard to dislodge. There is, furthermore, the natural fascination attaching to anyone with the audacity to espouse so violent a paradox as the unreality of matter. One thing has led to another, until a recent editor of Berkeley's writings[2] can report that editions of his writings are proliferating almost exponentially.

But the authentic Berkeleyan note rings in his advertisement for tar-water: "A cure for foulness of blood, ulceration of bowels, lungs, consumptive coughs, pleurisy, peripneumony, erysipelas, asthma, indigestion, cachectic and hysteric cases, gravel, dropsy, and all inflammations; of great use in the gout; cures a gangrene as well as erysipelas, the scurvy, and all hypochondriac maladies; is particularly recommended to seafaring persons, ladies, and men of studious and sedentary lives." Berkeley's place is in the company of the great British eccentrics.

39

Hume

"OUR DAVIE'S A FINE good-natured crater [creature], but uncommon wake-minded." Thus the widow Hume spoke of her son David when he refused to become a lawyer.

Born in Edinburgh in 1711, he left Edinburgh University at the age of fifteen to pursue for eight years his own course of reading in literature and philosophy. In 1734 he almost collapsed from overwork. For a few months he abandoned study for employment in a merchant's office. Finding a business career intolerable, he went to France and lived in seclusion for three years on meager funds. In this time he wrote the three volumes of his *Treatise of Human Nature*, the book he had planned when in his teens. In 1738, when he was 27, the first two volumes were published. "Never literary attempt was more unfortunate," he later wrote. "It fell *deadborn from the press*, without such distinction as even to excite a murmur among the zealots." It had appeared at a time when there were few in Britain capable of understanding and appreciating so abstruse and unusual a work. "But being naturally of a cheerful and sanguine temper," Hume continued, "I very soon recovered the blow and prosecuted with great ardour my studies in the country. In 1742, I printed at Edinburgh the first part of my essays; the work was favourably received, and soon made me entirely forget my former disappointment."

For a year, when he was 34, Hume was tutor and guardian to the mad Marquis of Annandale. Afterwards he was aide-de-camp to General St. Clair during a raid on the French coast, and accompanied him on an embassy to Austria and Italy. During this interlude Hume rewrote the first book of his *Treatise* in smoother style, and published it under the title *Philosophical Essays* (later *Enquiry*) *Concerning Human Understanding*. This version also failed to attract attention. A volume of *Political Discourses*, however, sold well and began to bring Hume literary fame—the love of which, he confessed, was his ruling passion. But disappointments did not cease: the *Enquiry Concerning the Principles of Morals*, a revision of the third book of the *Treatise* that Hume judged "incomparably the best" of all his writings, also came unnoticed into the world. Only when the Bishop of Gloucester attacked him did he begin to feel that his books were "esteemed in good company." The Bishop wrote to Hume's publisher: "You have often told me of this man's moral virtues. He may have many, for aught I know; but let me observe to you, there are vices of the mind as well as of the body; and I think a wickeder mind, and more obstinately bent on public mischief, I never knew."[1]

Even the Bishop did not know the full extent of Hume's wickedness. About this time he was writing his *Dialogues Concerning Natural Religion*, demolishing

Allan Ramsay, David Hume, *1766. Oil. National Galleries of Scotland, Edinburgh.*

the argument from design, which Newton had endorsed as providing scientific support for religion. These *Dialogues* Hume did not attempt to publish in his lifetime. Nor would his usual publishers bring them out after his death. A brave and loyal nephew obeyed the injunction in Hume's will and saw to their printing in 1779.

Hume applied for the post of Professor of Moral Philosophy in Edinburgh University but was unsuccessful on account of opposition from influential preachers. In 1752 he obtained appointment as Librarian to the Faculty of Advocates. Now he had the leisure and resources in books to carry out another longstanding plan for a *History of England.* The first volume came out in 1754. "Miserable was my disappointment: I was assailed by one cry of reproach, disapprobation, and even detestation; English, Scotch, and Irish, Whig and Tory, Churchman and Sectary, Free-thinker and Religionist, Patriot and Courtier united in their rage." Perhaps Hume exaggerated the number of denunciations; the book sold only 45 copies in its first year. But, as usual, he was not daunted, and went ahead to write two more volumes. They were better received. The work eventually became the standard history. Hume's writings after unpromising beginnings made such advances "that the copy-money given me by the bookseller much exceeded anything formerly known in England; I was become not only independent, but opulent." By 1769 he enjoyed the enormous income of a thousand pounds a year.

In 1761 Hume, who disliked Englishmen, retired to Scotland with the intention of remaining there. Two years later, however, he was persuaded to accept an invitation—from a man he had never met—to be First Secretary of the British Embassy in Paris. He was lionized by the French intellectuals on account of his political essays. After three years of this life he returned to Edinburgh. His connections, however, soon took him to London as Undersecretary of State for Scotland. He occupied this office for two years. At the age of 58 he at last retired permanently to Edinburgh.

In 1775 it became apparent that he was afflicted by stomach cancer. He knew that the disease was mortal, but it gave him little pain. In the spring of 1776 he wrote a short autobiography in which he declared that he "never suffered a moment's abatement of my spirits, insomuch that were I to name the period of my life which I should most choose to pass over again, I might be tempted to point to this later period. I possess the same ardour as ever in study, and the same gaiety in company. I consider, besides, that a man of sixty-five, by dying, cuts off only a few years of infirmities." Three months later he was dead, after having scandalized his countryman James Boswell by his calm deathbed denial of hope for an afterlife.

Hume concluded his autobiography with a sketch of his own character.

> I was a man of mild dispositions, of command of temper, of an open, social, and cheerful humour, capable of attachment, but little susceptible of enmity, and of great moderation in all my passions. Even my love of literary fame, my ruling passion, never soured my temper, notwithstanding my frequent disappointments. My company was not unacceptable to the young and careless, as well as to the studious and literary; and as I took a particular pleasure in the company of modest women, I had no reason to be displeased with the reception I met with from them. In a word, though most men anywise eminent have found reason to complain of calumny, I never was touched or even attached by her baleful tooth; and though I wantonly exposed myself to the rage of both civil and religious factions, they seemed to be disarmed in my behalf of their wonted fury. My friends never had occasion to vindicate any one circumstance of my character and conduct; not but that the zealots, we may well suppose, would have been glad to invent and propagate any story to my disadvantage, but they could never find any which they thought would wear the face of probability. I cannot say there is no vanity in making this funeral oration of myself, but I hope it is not a misplaced one; and this is a matter of fact which is easily cleared and ascertained.

Hume's Purpose

Hume disarmingly states his reasons for doing philosophy.

> At the time . . . that I am tir'd with amusement and company, and have indulg'd a *reverie* in my chamber, or in a solitary walk by a river-side, I feel my mind all collected within itself, and am naturally *inclin'd* to carry my view into all those subjects, about which I have met with so many disputes in the course of my reading and conversation. I cannot forbear having a curiosity to be acquainted with the principles of moral good and evil, the nature and foundation of government, and the cause of those several passions and inclination, which actuate and govern me. I am uneasy to think I approve of one object, and disapprove of another; call one thing beautiful, and another

deform'd; decide concerning truth and falsehood, reason and folly, without knowing upon what principles I proceed. I am concern'd for the condition of the learned world, which lies under such a deplorable ignorance in all these particulars. I feel an ambition to arise in me of contributing to the instruction of mankind, and of acquiring a name by my inventions and discoveries. These sentiments spring up naturally in my present disposition; and shou'd I endeavour to banish them, by attaching myself to any other business or diversion, I *feel* I shou'd be a loser in point of pleasure; and this is the origin of my philosophy.[2]

The ignorance the learned world lies under in these particulars, we are told elsewhere, fosters superstition. Theologians lay down abstruse metaphysical principles, by which they overawe the laity into supposing that they possess some profound knowledge upon which they found their "airy sciences."

> The only method of freeing learning at once from these abstruse questions is to enquire seriously into the nature of human understanding and show, from an exact analysis of its powers and capacity, that it is by no means fitted for such remote and abstruse subjects. We must submit to this fatigue in order to live at ease ever after, and must cultivate true metaphysics with some care in order to destroy the false and adulterated.[3]

Hume like Locke says that he is going to investigate the nature of human understanding in order to discover what questions it is capable of answering. We shall find, however, that in the end Hume does not conclude that certain questions are unanswerable, so much as that the alleged questions are really nonsense.

The Structure of Hume's Philosophy

Hume felt himself under no constraint to reach edifying conclusions. Although in a few instances he expurgated his text to avoid giving offense, he never added anything that he did not believe. And since he had an extraordinarily clear and powerful intellect, he accomplished what Descartes and Locke did not: he drew the logical conclusions from the initial premise of the Cartesian philosophy.

That premise, the *Cogito*, requires philosophy to be inside-out. What alone we are sure of, what therefore we have to begin with, is our immediate knowledge of our own mental states. Descartes, Locke, and Berkeley justify the transition from the stream of consciousness to an external reality by various arguments, all of which appeal to a principle of causality: everything, including our ideas, must have a cause. Hume is the first to subject this allegedly self-evident truth to critical scrutiny. Causality he finds to be not a necessity of logic but a human habit of expecting things to go on as usual. Belief in an external world cannot then be justified by appeal to the reasoning faculty. *De facto* we cannot help believing, but proof is impossible. There are no solipsists, but if there were, they could not be refuted.

Hume's philosophy is Leibniz' minus the principle of sufficient reason. Hume and Leibniz agree that pure reason can establish only analytic truths, for reason can do nothing by itself beyond deciding whether one concept is included in another. To Leibniz the principle of sufficient reason happily guarantees that every truth is ultimately analytic, so that everything is rationally connected with everything else. To give up the principle is to make every fact a brute fact; nothing is left but the actual succession of perceptions and appetitions in the monad. Hume does not shrink from this conclusion.

Or does he? Hume held: (1) We are directly aware of the existence of perceptions only. (2) No inference from the existence of a perception to the existence of anything else can be rationally guaranteed—not even an inference to the existence of another perception. (3) We make inferences from our perceptions, and we are animals that cannot do otherwise. Sometimes Hume emphasizes (3). In this mood he lends himself to the interpretation that he is only pointing out the fact that the presuppositions of all our reasoning are indeed presuppositions; that is, they cannot be proved—to do so we should require pre-presuppositions and so on in a vicious regress. We must take for granted the existence of bodies and the regularity of nature. Bodies *do* exist, nature *is* regular. These fundamental truths, however, cannot be derived from any more prior truths—there are none. This interpretation we shall call the *soft* Hume. But in other passages he dwells on (2), to the extent of reproaching us (and himself) for believing in a world of merely imaginary entities which we invent to put regularity into experience that does not really possess it, and which we continue to believe in despite clear proofs that there can be no such things. Hume's philosophy interpreted in this way, as skepticism seriously meant, we shall call the *hard* Hume.

These two aspects of Hume pose between them a dilemma. The soft Hume is ineffective for deflating the airy sciences of metaphysics and theology. If Hume's message is that we may justifiably believe whatever as a matter of psychological fact we have to believe, then the theologian need only affirm that he cannot help believing in his theology. The hard Hume can forestall this move; but no one, not even Hume, is capable of accepting all the conclusions of *that* philosophy.

Impressions and Ideas

Hume's *Treatise* begins "All the perceptions of the human mind resolve themselves into two distinct kinds, which I shall call IMPRESSIONS and IDEAS. The difference betwixt these consists in the degrees of force and liveliness with which they strike upon the mind, and make their way into our thought or consciousness." Examples of impressions include seeing a tomato, the pain of excessive heat, the feelings of anger and love. To remember any of these, or to imagine them, is in Hume's terms to have an idea.

The inside-out orientation of his philosophy is thus established at the very beginning, and Hume, unlike Locke, maintains it with rigor. Whatever I know, he says to himself, must be in my consciousness. What is there? He introspects and discovers sensations, feelings, remembrances, and imaginings. At this point there is naturally a temptation to distinguish the sensations from the rest by reference to external causation. To see a tomato is to be affected through the eyes by something out there; to sit in the dark and remember what a tomato looks like is to generate an internal image. Hume recognizes, however, that to proceed this way would be to beg the question of the external world. He says therefore that the sensations arise "from unknown causes," and continues his introspective analysis.

Ideas, he finds, are exact though faint copies of impressions. To see Mount Shasta at high noon on a clear day is to have an impression of considerable force and vivacity. To remember having seen Mount Shasta is to have—literally—a picture of Mount Shasta in the mind which, however, is relatively dim and hard to make out. Remembering is picturing, and picturing is looking at an internal picture.

Despite initial plausibility, this model for remembering is beset with difficulties that Hume did not face. "When I shut my eyes and think of my chamber, the ideas I form are exact representations of the impressions I felt," he declares.[4] If that is so, you should be able to answer any question about your chamber—such as how many boards there are in the floor—simply by attending to your idea of it. Or if you cannot, your disability must be due to the "faintness" of the idea. But something seems to be wrong here. If the lighting in your room is poor, you can at least strain to make out details, and so also if you are looking at a grainy photograph. It is not clear, however, what it would be like to strain to count the ideas of floor-boards in the idea of your chamber. The model is even less appealing with reference to the other senses. Remembering the smell of Limburger cheese is hardly like getting a faint whiff of Limburger. Nor is remembering or imagining a toothache the same as having a slight twinge in the tooth. On Hume's account, moreover, the remembrance of how the band sounded when it played fortissimo ought to be impossible to distinguish from actually hearing it playing pianissimo. In fact, however, we never fall into such confusions. The reason can hardly be what Hume says it is—that "the most lively thought is still inferior to the dullest sensation"[5]—for the degrees of sensation diminish continuously to zero. There is no room in the continuum to insert the ideas. Nor does this model allow for the distinction that we plainly can make between remembering passages in the music *as* fortissimo and *as* pianissimo.

Hume next distinguishes ideas into the simple and complex, as Locke had done, and lays down the principle that every simple idea is derived from an antecedent impression which it exactly resembles. We can imagine complexes we have not seen, but "That idea of red, which we form in the dark, and that impression, which strikes our eyes in sun-shine, differ only in degree, not in nature."[6] This principle, equivalent to Locke's denial of innate ideas, is to be used also as Locke used it: to eliminate nonsense. "When we entertain . . . any suspicion that a philosophical term is employed without any meaning or idea (as is but too frequent), we need but inquire, *from what impression is that supposed idea derived?* And if it be impossible to assign any, this will serve to confirm our suspicion."[7] Here and elsewhere Hume equates meaning with idea: the word 'tomato' means the mental picture you have of a round red fruit; 'love' means the faint stirring of that emotion in you. Since every mental image is particular, there are no universals, not even "in the mind"; there are only particulars that stand for all members of a collection indifferently.

The difficulty of maintaining coherence in the inside-out philosophy is illustrated in the principle that all ideas are derived from impressions. We (including Hume) can hardly avoid thinking of impressions as externally caused (hence the reference to striking our eyes in sunshine). When we do, the proposition that ideas are copies of impressions becomes "We can't remember what we haven't seen" and is plausible in the highest degree. But if we think strictly in accordance with Hume's official definitions, the principle in question conveys instead the thesis that every weak simple perception has been preceded by a strong resembling one. This, however, seems arbitrary; no reason is apparent why there should not be exceptions to it, the weaker sometimes coming first. So how can it be invoked to eliminate spurious ideas? Moreover, it is hard to see how on Hume's other principles we could know or even suspect the truth of the doctrine. For if we conclude from experience that every weak perception has been preceded by a strong one, our basis can only be our memory of the strong perceptions. But memory of a strong perception is itself a weak perception; how can inspection of the reminiscence reveal that its original was forceful and lively?

Hume next notes that in our thinking, even in our reveries, ideas do not succeed each other at random but are joined with a certain regularity. They tend to be associated according to three types of relations: resemblance (pictures make us think of what they are pictures of), contiguity (the idea of Staten Island leads to the idea of Manhattan), and cause and effect (smoke and fire). "Here is a kind of *Attraction*, which in the mental world will be found to have as extraordinary effects as in the natural."[8] The principle of association was not new, Hobbes having had much to say about it; but Hume, as we shall see, made more use of it than did his predecessors. He hoped to be the Newton of psychology.

In summary, Hume's notion of the human mind is this: it is an assemblage of perceptions that vary in degree of liveliness and are divisible into two great groups: one of superior liveliness, denominated impressions—the other fainter, denominated ideas. Simple ideas (those that are incapable of analysis into other ideas) are all copies of impressions. The ideas that are memories, though complex, are also copies. Complex ideas of imagination (such as mermaids) may correspond to no impression, but the constituent simple parts must. Perceptions arise from unknown causes; all are distinct, and any one may exist without any other. The tendency, however, is for them to occur in clusters, such as the yellow-heavy-malleable that we call gold; and they are usually followed by ideas related to them by contiguity, resemblance, or cause and effect.

Perceptions are, furthermore, all we know of existence, or can even conceive of it. "Let us fix our attention out of ourselves as much as possible: Let us chace our imagination to the heavens, or to the utmost limits of the universe; we never really advance a step beyond ourselves, nor can conceive any kind of existence, but those perceptions, which have appear'd in that narrow compass."[9] Thus at any rate the hard Hume.

With this economy of materials and machinery, he constructs the theory of human knowledge.

Cause and Effect

By simple inspection of our ideas we can determine whether they resemble each other or are contrary, how they compare with each other with respect to degrees of some quality, and (when they are subject to quantitative treatment) their numerical relationships. In these matters then, and in these alone, where we need consider only *relations of ideas*, we can attain to certainty. It is certain that wet is contrary to dry, that scarlet is not pink and is darker in hue, and that $7 + 5 = 12$. Algebra and arithmetic, being concerned solely with quantitative relations, are sciences that yield certainty, barring mistakes in our reasoning. Geometry does not have quite that status, for its foundations rest on appearances: of equality of lines and coincidences of figures, for example, which are subject to error. How can we be sure, Hume asks, that two lines intersecting at a very small angle have only one point in common?

Identity (as distinguished from equality) is a relation about which only experience can inform us. That the book you are now reading is the same one you read yesterday, and not another copy, is a proposition that can be established only by investigations in the world. It is, if true, true as a *matter of fact*. Relations in space and time, and the relation of cause to effect, likewise concern matters of fact. These are all the relations there are in which things can stand to one another.

Only by means of the cause-effect relation can we make inferences concerning matters of fact that go beyond the present data of perception and memory. Since nearly all our reasonings about the world come down to establishing causal relations, the notion of cause evidently deserves close philosophical scrutiny. Almost all philosophers before Hume passed it by with a few words, perhaps a definition such as Hobbes' "The aggregate of all the accidents both of the agents how many soever they be, and of the patient, put together; which when they are all supposed to be present, it cannot be understood but that the effect is produced at the same instant; and if any one of them be wanting, it cannot be understood but that the effect is not produced."[10] But what are we to understand by the phrase "it cannot be understood but"? Hobbes evidently meant that, for example, if Socrates drinks a massive dose of hemlock and it stays down, "it cannot be understood but" that he dies: he *must* die, where 'must' has the same sense as in "Socrates must be mortal, for he is a man, and all men are mortal."

This Hume denied. If a causal statement expressed a relation of ideas, that is, if it were a necessary truth, its denial would be self-contradictory. But the cause and the effect are two events, or two perceptions, that are distinguishable and therefore (what amounts to the same thing) separable, at least in thought. So to say of anything, X, that it came into existence, and to say that Y was the cause of X's coming into existence, is to make two separate statements. The first could be true when the second was false. "X came into existence and there was nothing that caused it" is a statement that, though perhaps always false, is at least conceivable. We can imagine what it would be like for a golf ball or a hippopotamus to appear suddenly in front of us, nothing whatever having produced it. By trick photography we can even make it seem to happen. But we cannot imagine anything really self-contradictory, such as a round-cubical golf ball, or an invertebrate hippopotamus.

Since the causal principle, "whatever begins to exist must have a cause of existence," is not a statement of relations of ideas but of matter of fact, our knowledge of its truth must come from experience. How? Hume ponders the more particular question, "Why we conclude, that such particular causes must necessarily have such particular effects, and why we form an inference from one to another?"[11] In any instance of this relation we find that the cause and effect are "contiguous," in contact. At any rate, if they are separated (the voice in New York moving the telephone diaphragm in San Francisco) we find or assume action through a medium (the telephone wire or radio waves). The cause is also prior in time to the effect—but only just prior; otherwise there are (or are assumed to be) intermediate stages. Contiguity in space and succession in time, therefore, are component parts of our conception of causality. Clearly they are not all of it, however. We have also the idea that the cause is *necessarily connected* to its effect.

From what impression can this idea be derived? In a single instance we can observe nothing but the contiguity and succession. But cause-effect relations are in their nature repeatable. We observe not merely that Socrates drank hemlock and died, but that many others did too, and none recovered. We have discovered here the relation of *constant conjunction*. Where we find contiguity, succession, and constant conjunction, "without any farther ceremony, we call the one *cause* and the other *effect*, and infer the existence of the one from that of the other."[12] But still we may be dissatisfied that we have not found the necessary connection, which we suppose to be more than merely *de facto* togetherness. We want to know why they *must* be constantly conjoined.

If we attend to our situation, Hume avers, we will find one and only one further circumstance that is altered when we have observed not one but a number of instances of *C* followed by *E*. It comes about that when we perceive *C* we expect *E*; that is, we form a "lively idea" of *E* with the belief that *E* is in the offing—the belief being not an additional idea but only the superior degree of liveliness. A habit of association has been developed; the impression of *C* now generates the idea of *E*. Since this expectation is the only impression in the situation besides the others we have noticed, it has to be the source of the idea of necessary connection! "The necessary connexion betwixt causes and effects is the foundation of our inference from one to the other. The foundation of our inference is the transition arising from the accustom'd union. These are, therefore, the same."[13]

> I am sensible, that of all the paradoxes, which I have had, or shall hereafter have occasion to advance in the course of this treatise, the present one is the most violent, and that 'tis merely by dint of solid proof and reasoning I can ever hope it will have admission, and overcome the inveterate prejudices of mankind. Before we are reconcil'd to this doctrine, how often must we repeat to ourselves, *that* the simple view of any two objects or actions, however related, can never give us any idea of power, or of a connexion betwixt them: *that* this idea arises from the repetition of their union: *that* the repetition neither discovers nor causes any thing in the objects, but has an influence only on the mind, by that customary transition it produces: *that* this customary transition is, therefore, the same with the power and necessity; which are consequently qualities of perceptions, not of objects, and are internally felt by the soul, and not perceiv'd externally in bodies?[14]

Cause, then, can be defined in two ways. On the side of objects it is "An object precedent and contiguous to another, and where all the objects resembling the former are plac'd in like relations of precedency and contiguity to those objects, that resemble the latter." From our side "A CAUSE is an object precedent and contiguous to another, and so united with it, that the idea of the one determines the mind to form the idea of the other, and the impression of the one to form a more lively idea of the other."

Contrary to Locke, we have no idea of a productive power in objects. If we had, it would have to be a copy of some impression of some sensible quality; but there are no sensible qualities of objects save their admittedly inefficacious colors, sounds, odors, tastes, and textures. Contrary to Leibniz and Berkeley, we do not derive the idea of power from our own experience of effort. Granted that we have an impression of volition, the connection between volition and muscular movement is just as inexplicable as any other; we observe only that volitions are precedent, contiguous, and (more or less) constantly conjoined to exertions.

Causal Inference

> The necessity, which makes two times two equal to four, . . . lies only in the act of the understanding, by which we consider and compare these ideas; in like manner the necessity or power, which unites causes and effects, lies in the determination of the mind to pass from the one to the other.[15]

In arithmetic we are determined to our conclusions by reason; is the same true in causal thinking? If I affirm that Socrates and a thousand others have died after drinking hemlock, therefore if I drink it I too shall die—is my argument valid? Not as it stands, surely, for it is conceivable that its one premise might be true and its conclusion false. The conclusion does not contradict the premise; I can form a clear conception of what it would be like to be the first survivor of hemlock drinking. We need another premise, to the effect "that instances, of which we have had no experience, must resemble those, of which we have had experience, and that the course of nature continues always uniformly the same."[16] This Principle of the Uniformity of Nature or of Induction (as it is usually called now—Hume does not use the word 'induction'), if added to the argument, makes it valid. For

1. In the course of nature so far, everybody who has drunk hemlock has died;
2. The course of nature continues always uniformly the same;

logically entail the conclusion

3. The next person to drink hemlock will die.

So the question whether we argue validly from past to future reduces to the question "What reason have we to accept the principle of uniformity of nature?"

Hume observes that this principle, like that of causality, is not guaranteed to be true by mere comparison of ideas. For "we can at least conceive a change in the course of nature; which sufficiently proves, that such a change is not absolutely impossible."[17] He means 'possible' in Leibniz' sense, "logically" possible: we can intelligibly describe a situation in which the sun no longer rises and heavy objects fall upwards, so there is no self-contradiction involved. Therefore, the principle must be validated by reasoning from experience.

It looks as if it would be easy to do so. For our whole experience of nature is that it has continued uniformly the same. However, what we want is not assurance of what has happened but of what will happen. The argument "Nature in the past always continued uniformly the same; therefore, nature tomorrow will continue uniformly the same" is incomplete. We need another premise, which can only be one to the effect that what has always happened will continue to happen—and that is precisely what we are trying to prove!

Thus the uniformity of nature can be demonstrated neither by reason nor by experience, neither *a priori* nor *a posteriori*. We in fact expect it to continue the same; this habit of expectation has in fact been set up in our minds. But there is no possibility of an external justification for it.

It gets us nowhere, Hume points out, to argue that past experience gives us a reason to infer a productive power in things distinct from their sensible qualities. Grant for the sake of argument that we are right in concluding from past experience with hemlock that it has a power to poison. We know, then, that the power to poison has so far always been found in conjunction with the particular color, taste, odor, and so forth of hemlock. We still are unable to conclude that this power will continue to be associated with these sensible qualities unless we know that past connections will go on holding in future—the principle, again, that we are trying to prove.

> Thus all probable reasoning is nothing but a species of sensation. 'Tis not solely in poetry and music, we must follow our taste and sentiment, but likewise in philosophy [including natural science]. When I am convinc'd of any principle, 'tis only an idea, which strikes more strongly upon me. When I give the preference to one set of arguments above another, I do nothing but decide from my feeling concerning the superiority of their influence. Objects have no discoverable connexion together; nor is it from any other principle but custom operating upon the imagination, that we can draw any inference from the appearance of one to the existence of another.[18]

> If we believe, that fire warms, or water refreshes, 'tis only because it costs us too much pains to think otherwise.[19]

Thus Hume at his hardest. The soft Hume, however, frequently reassures us. He speaks, for instance, of "proofs, those arguments, which are deriv'd from the relation of cause and effect, and which are entirely free from doubt and uncertainty,"[20] citing tomorrow's sunrise and the mortality of all men as instances of provable propositions. In the *Treatise*, after the passage in which necessary connection is declared to be nothing but a habit of expectation, the next section is headed "Rules by which to judge of causes and effects." There we are told not to introspect and determine whether we have a habit of expectation, but to note such points as that "the difference in the effects of two resembling objects must proceed from that particular, in which they differ."[21]

Criticism of Hume on Causation

Hume was right in what he said about causation; but it is important to attend carefully to what he said. He said that objects have no discoverable connection together, and the whole doctrine of causality follows from that pronouncement. If cause and effect are distinct objects, then plainly they cannot stand in any relations other than contiguity and succession. But what did Hume mean by 'object'? A sensible quality or set of them. "We know that, in fact, heat is a constant attendant of flame; but what is the connexion between them, we have no room so much as to conjecture or imagine."[22] Quite so. Why a flickering light should produce heat, we do not know. But in fact, a flickering light does *not* produce heat. A certain redistribution of energy and restructuring of molecules manifests itself to vision as light, to the thermal sense as heat. At the micro level where these transactions occur, talk of "objects" that are "contiguous" and "successive" would be irrelevant. When Hume lamented that "Our senses inform us of the colour, weight, and consistency of bread, but neither sense nor reason can ever inform us of those qualities which fit it for the nourishment and support of the human body,"[23] he was too pessimistic. Neither sense nor reason had informed the eighteenth century of the metabolism of proteins, but nutritional science in the twentieth does inform *us*. As for the worry, if it is a worry, that the course of nature might change so that beginning tomorrow afternoon flames will cool us but bread will be poisonous, we should note that any such catastrophe would not be a matter of "objects" suddenly altering their accustomed behavior—as kind persons may suddenly become cruel—but a total annihilation of nature and the substitution of something else. It is not the case that burning is accompanied by oxidation accompanied by the release of energy in the visible spectrum plus the release of energy in the infrared—four "objects"; burning *is* oxidation which *is* (among other things) the release of energy in the visible and the infrared spectra. Against the total annihilation of nature there is, presumably, no charm, philosophical or other.

These remarks are intended as objections not to Hume, whose account of prescientific causal beliefs is largely correct, but to those philosophers of the present day who suppose they are being tough-minded when they assume that the Humean account is applicable to the physics of the present century.

Two different and apparently incompatible conceptions of causation are to be found in Hume's writings. One, the official doctrine, has just been described. But often there are remarks about "unknown causes," which at least by the second definition of cause—that to be a cause is to be an occurrence such that the impression or idea of it determines the mind to form a lively idea of the effect—could not exist. For example,

> We are placed in this world, as in a great theatre, where the true springs and causes of every event are entirely concealed from us . . . We hang in perpetual suspense between life and death, health and sickness, plenty and want; which are distributed amongst the human species by secret and unknown causes, whose operation is oft unexpected, and always unaccountable. These *unknown causes*, then, become the constant object of our hope and fear . . . Could men anatomize nature, according to the most probable, at least the most intelligible philosophy, they would find, that these causes are nothing but the particular fabric and structure of the minute parts of their own bodies and of external objects, and that, by a regular and constant machinery, all the events are produced, about which they are so much concerned.[24]

Here—and there are many such passages—Hume's position seems to be materialist, the same as that which Locke adopted with respect to the distinction between nominal and real essences. We know that there must be real active powers in things. But because they are associated with the microstructure of bodies, to which our senses cannot penetrate, they are and (so Hume believed) will forever remain hidden from us.

The External World

This view of things, however, seems irreconcilable not only with the official account of causation but also with the official philosophy of body. Hard Humean skepticism flatly denies the possibility of knowledge of an external world—a world of things other than perceptions.

The soft Hume writes the preface to the discussion. We are soothed to hear that although "we may well ask, *What causes induce us to believe in the existence of body?* [yet] 'tis in vain to ask, *Whether there be body or not?* That is a point, which we must take for granted in all our reasonings."[25] However, we do not proceed many pages before the hard Hume takes over, and we hear much of "the fiction of a continu'd existence."[26]

The question why we believe in the existence of body is quickly reduced to "why we attribute *continu'd* existence to objects."[27] Because our senses tell us? Since in Hume's terminology objects are not different from perceptions, it would be a plain contradiction to say that we know through the senses of the continued existence of what is not being sensed. Our reason, then? Reason instead informs us that—contrary to the opinions of ordinary people—shapes, colors, and pains are all perceptions on the same footing: interrupted and dependent on the mind. The belief in continued existence, then, "as it is entirely unreasonable, must proceed from some other faculty than the understanding."[28] The imagination is the culprit; by association of ideas we are led to mistake resemblance for identity. The book you read yesterday and the one you are reading today are distinct, separate perceptions, and therefore distinct existences; but they are so resembling that the mind falls into the error of identifying them.

Plain people believe (so Hume tells us) that what they perceive—the impression—persists, just as it is perceived, when out of attention. Philosophers know that this cannot be so. Perceptions, they realize, are dependent on the mind. In order to have something independent of mind, they invent the theory of a double existence. Besides the perception, "an internal and perishing existence,"[29] there is supposed to be a distinct object, external and persistent, which is the cause of the perception. But this theory, Hume argues, is against reason. It maintains that perceptions, of which alone we can be aware, are effects of objects themselves never perceived. The analysis of cause and effect has shown, however, that this relation holds only between objects known by perception to be constantly conjoined. Nor, Hume tells us, is the theory even imaginatively plausible.

The Self

So much for the external world. There is nothing of which we have any awareness or knowledge that is not dependent on the mind. But what is the mind that has such knowledge as there may be of internal and perishing existence? The mind, philosophers say, is a substance. Hume remarks that if by substance is meant that which is capable of existing by itself, then every perception is a substance. But if the word 'substance' is supposed to signify the self, that which underlies perceptions without itself being a perception, the word is meaningless; there can be no idea of anything of which there can be no impression.

> For my part, when I enter most intimately into what I call *myself*, I always stumble on some particular perception or other, of heat or cold, light or shade, love or hatred, pain or pleasure. I never can catch *myself* at any time without a perception, and never can observe any thing but the perception. When my perceptions are remov'd for any time, as by sound sleep; so long am I insensible of *myself*, and may truly be said not to exist. And were all my perceptions remov'd by death, and cou'd I neither think, nor feel, nor see, nor love, nor hate after the dissolution of my body, I shou'd be entirely annihilated, nor do I conceive what is farther requisite to make me a perfect non-entity. If any one upon serious and unprejudic'd reflexion, thinks he has a different notion of *himself*, I must confess I can reason no longer with him. All I can allow him is, that he may be in the right as well as I, and that we are essentially different in this particular. He may, perhaps, perceive something simple and continu'd, which he calls *himself*; tho' I am certain there is no such principle in me.

But setting aside some metaphysicians of this kind, I may venture to affirm of the rest of mankind, that they are nothing but a bundle or collection of different perceptions, which succeed each other with an inconceivable rapidity, and are in a perpetual flux and movement. Our eyes cannot turn in their sockets without varying our perceptions. Our thought is still more variable than our sight; and all our other senses and faculties contribute to this change; nor is there any single power of the soul, which remains unalterably the same, perhaps for one moment. The mind is a kind of theatre, where several perceptions successively make their appearance; pass, re-pass, glide away, and mingle in an infinite variety of postures and situations. There is properly no *simplicity* in it at one time, nor *identity* in different; whatever natural propension we may have to imagine that simplicity and identity. The comparison of the theatre must not mislead us. They are the successive perceptions only, that constitute the mind; nor have we the most distant notion of the place, where these scenes are represented, or of the materials of which it is compos'd.[30]

But this extreme hardness in philosophy was too much even for Hume. In a postscript added to the third volume of the *Treatise*, he confessed that there must be a principle of connection binding together a bundle of perceptions to constitute the identity of a person, but that on his philosophical principles he could not give a satisfactory account of what it might be. In the rewritten version entitled the *Enquiry*, the whole subject of personal identity was ignored.

Hume presented the odd spectacle of a philosopher recommending "carelessness and in-attention"[31] as the proper remedy for his own philosophy. Following his own prescription,

I dine, I play a game of back-gammon, I converse, and am merry with my friends; and when after three or four hours' amusement, I wou'd return to these speculations, they appear so cold, and strain'd, and ridiculous, that I cannot find in my heart to enter into them farther.[32]

He was convinced, nevertheless, that he had accomplished what he set out to do. The concluding paragraph to the *Enquiry concerning Human Understanding* goes

When we run over libraries, persuaded of these principles, what havoc must we make? If we take in our hand any volume—of divinity or school metaphysics, for instance—let us ask, *Does it contain any abstract reasoning concerning quantity or number?* No. *Does it contain any experimental reasoning concerning matter of fact and existence?* No. Commit it then to the flames, for it can contain nothing but sophistry and illusion.

Popular Religion

The religion actually preached in the churches and believed, or professed, by all but a few "refined and philosophical theists" was to Hume an object of contempt and loathing. It was mere superstition, so obviously absurd as to be beneath the dignity of refutation. In his *Natural History of Religion*, he traced its origin from the hopes and fears of men confronted with the overwhelming power of a nature that brought both goods and disasters. Our ignorant ancestors inevitably interpreted natural events as analogous to the consequences of human volitions, and invented not one but a great number of invisible intelligent powers to preside over the various divisions of the world and human interests. The gods being conceived on the analogy of human tyrants, religious observances took on all the repulsive aspects of flattery appropriate thereto. When Hume contemplated the spectacle of a congregation singing the praises of the infinite goodness of a being who, according to their doctrines, would consign the majority of souls to torments infinitely exceeding the worst that the most monstrous mere human being could wish to inflict, he could scarcely preserve his philosophical calm. "Examine the religious principles, which have, in fact, prevailed in the world. You will scarcely be persuaded, that they are any thing but sick men's dreams."[33] Their effects on the moral and intellectual faculties are equally pernicious.

Hume condescended to examine the question of miracles, in an essay omitted from the *Treatise* in a vain attempt to placate Joseph Butler, Bishop of Bristol, but included in the *Enquiry*. A miracle is a violation of a law of nature; a law of nature is a regularity established by uniform experience which "amounts to a proof." Human testimony, therefore, could never be "sufficient to establish a miracle unless the testimony be of such a kind that its falsehood would be more miraculous than the fact which it endeavours to establish. And even in that case there is a mutual destruction of arguments."[34] It is hardly possible that any human testimony could meet this condition. "But if the spirit of religion join itself to the love of wonder, there is an end of common sense, and human testimony in these circumstances loses all pretensions to authority."[35] Stories of miracles, offered in support of religion, come from barbarous times and places, and are related by interested parties; furthermore, the miracles of every religion conflict with those of every other. The same considerations apply to prophecies, which are only a particular kind of miracle.

For almost the last time in European literature, Hume inserted the disclaimers—customary in medieval writings on theologically sensitive topics—that this argument was concerned only with natural knowledge and was not to be construed as telling against revelation. He professed to be defending the Bible against "pretended Christians" who, failing to realize that "our most holy religion is founded on *faith*, not on reason," treat it "not as the word or testimony of God himself, but as the production of a mere human writer and historian." This transparent irony was dropped in the mordant concluding sentences.

> So that, upon the whole, we may conclude that the Christian religion not only was at first attended with miracles, but even at this day cannot be believed by any reasonable person without one. Mere reason is insufficient to convince us of its veracity. And whoever is moved by *faith* to assent to it, is conscious of a continued miracle in his own person, which subverts all the principles of his understanding and gives him a determination to believe what is most contrary to custom and experience.

Natural Religion

Hume dealt more circumspectly but no less devastatingly with philosophical theology or "natural religion," as it was called: the propositions of religion insofar as they are capable of being established by reason unaided by revelation.

The *Dialogues Concerning Natural Religion* are conversations (sometimes orations) between three characters: Demea, who is conservative and orthodox; Cleanthes, who urges the allegedly scientific argument for theism—many of his speeches were in fact lifted almost word for word from popular books by George

Cheyne and Colin Maclaurin, two Scottish Newtonians; and the skeptical Philo, who is Hume. Their talk is ostensibly about the nature of God, not about His existence, which even Philo pronounces to be an "unquestionable and self-evident truth." The distinction, however, seems to be largely ignored in the proceedings.

The argument from the necessity of a first cause, or from the contingency of the world—which was the principal rational support for theism from Aristotle to Leibniz—is treated only briefly. There can be no *a priori* proof for the existence of any being, for we can conceive the nonexistence of any being whatsoever; therefore, its nonexistence cannot involve self-contradiction. "The words, therefore, *necessary existence* have no meaning."[36] If that point were waived, there would still be no reason for denying that the material world might be the necessarily existing being. To the Aristotelian and Leibnizian contention that even a world without a beginning in time would have to have a cause—in the sense of a reason why the series should be this one and not some other—the significant reply is made that one may legitimately demand an explanation for each member of a collection, in terms of other members; but to extend the demand to the whole collection, considered as a unity, would be senseless. The unity is a fiction.

> Did I show you the particular causes of each individual in a collection of twenty particles of matter, I should think it very unreasonable should you afterwards ask me what was the cause of the whole twenty. This is sufficiently explained in explaining the cause of the parts.[37]

Except for this passage, the *Dialogues* are devoted entirely to discussion of the argument from design. Cleanthes states it thus.

> Look round the world, contemplate the whole and every part of it: you will find it to be nothing but one great machine, subdivided into an infinite number of lesser machines, which again admit of subdivision to a degree beyond what human sense and faculties can trace and explain. All these various machines, and even their most minute parts, are adjusted to each other with an accuracy which ravishes into admiration all men who have ever contemplated them. The curious adapting of means to ends, throughout all nature, resembles exactly, though it much exceeds, the productions of human contrivance—of human design, thought, wisdom, and intelligence. Since therefore the effects resemble each other, we are led to infer, by all the rules of analogy, that the causes also resemble, and that the Author of nature is somewhat similar to the mind of man, though possessed of much larger faculties, proportioned to the grandeur of the work which he has executed. By this argument *a posteriori*, and by this argument alone, do we prove at once the existence of a Deity and his similarity to human mind and intelligence.[38]

Skeptical Philo and orthodox Demea join in objecting that the analogy between a house or watch as product of human intelligence, and the world as product of a superhuman intellect, is weak; that to make "this little agitation of the brain which we call *thought* . . . the model of the whole universe"[39] is hasty; and that as we have no experience of the production of a world, or anything much like one, we have no basis in experience for concluding what the cause of one must be like. To explain the material order as the effect of an order of thoughts is only to generate the further problem "What is the cause of that order of thoughts?" For we have no experience of an order of thoughts not associated with the material structure of a brain. If we insist that, nevertheless, thoughts have the power of ordering themselves, what is to keep us from ascribing a similar power to material particles in a crystal or an embryo?

Granting all the premises of the design argument, it can never prove the infinity of any divine attribute, since the evidence is limited to experience of the finite. Nor perfection, since the world is not perfect. Anyway, in human productions an ingenious and complicated device may be found to have been made by a "stupid mechanic" who followed instructions by rote. Nor divine unity, for houses and ships are the products of many craftsmen and designers. Nor even immortality, as the house may survive the architect.

> In a word, Cleanthes, a man who follows your hypothesis is able, perhaps, to assert or conjecture that the universe sometime arose from something like design; but beyond that position he cannot ascertain one single circumstance, and is left afterwards to fix every point of his theology by the utmost license of fancy and hypothesis. This world, for aught he knows, is very faulty and imperfect, compared to a superior standard, and was only the first rude essay of some infant deity who afterwards abandoned it, ashamed of his lame performance; it is the work only of some dependent, inferior deity, and is the object of derision to his superiors; it is the production of old age and dotage in some superannuated deity, and ever since his death has run on at adventures from the first impulse and active force which it received from him. You justly give signs of horror, Demea, at these strange suppositions; but these, and a thousand more of the same kind, are Cleanthes' suppositions, not mine. From the moment the attributes of the Deity are supposed finite, all these have place.[40]

Further, the world is as much like an animal (the Stoic model) or even a vegetable as it is like a machine; we should then infer that it arose from generation or vegetation. Nor, as far as reasoning from experience goes, can we rule out the Epicurean hypothesis of a fortuitous concourse of atoms that settled of themselves into a relatively stable pattern.

If experience thus fails to support the theistic theory of the infinite perfection of God's intellectual attributes, it is at least consistent with that view. Not so with the moral qualities ascribed to God. The religious sentiments have their origin in the experience of misery more than in anything else: in the hope and demand that the ultimate Power of the universe is kindly disposed to us, inflicts suffering only for a purpose, and will make up for it in another existence. But experience shows us that

> the whole earth . . . is cursed and polluted. . . . All the goods of life united would not make a very happy man, but all the ills united would make a wretch indeed; and any one of them almost (and who can be free from every one?), nay, often the absence of one good (and who can possess all?) is sufficient to render life ineligible. . . . Epicurus' old questions are yet unanswered. Is he willing to prevent evil, but not able? Then is he impotent. Is he able, but not willing? Then is he malevolent. Is he both able and willing? Whence then is evil?[41]

The best we can say, viewing the world as it is, is that its cause is not malevolent but indifferent to suffering.

> The whole presents nothing but the idea of a blind nature, impregnated by a great vivifying principle, and pouring forth from her lap, without discernment or parental care, her maimed and abortive children![42]

Nevertheless, at the conclusion of the *Dialogues*, the skeptical Philo is represented as conceding that "the works of nature bear a great analogy to the productions of art" and suggesting that the controversy whether the Cause of the universe should be called a mind or intelligence is merely verbal.

> If the whole of natural theology . . . resolves itself into one simple, though somewhat ambiguous, . . . proposition, *That the cause or causes of order in the universe probably bear some remote analogy to human intelligence*—if this proposition be not capable of extension, variation, or more particular explication, if it affords no inference that affects human life, or can be the source of any action or forbearance, and if the analogy, imperfect as it is, can be carried no further than to the human intelligence, and cannot be transferred, with any appearance of probability, to the other qualities of the mind, if this really be the case, what can the most inquisitive, contemplative, and religious man do more than give a plain, philosophical assent to the proposition, as often as it occurs, and believe that the arguments on which it is established exceed the objections which lie against it?[43]

Hume set out in his *Dialogues* not to demolish "religion" altogether, but to accomplish a definite and limited task: to show that the inference from the alleged design in nature to an infinitely wise, powerful, and good Author of nature is invalid. He achieved his goal. It is true that William Paley (1743–1805), a generation after Hume, stated the design argument in its most popular form—the watch discovered on the desert island—and that in the years from 1833 to 1840 eight eminent British men of science published books under the auspices of the Royal Society expatiating on design in nature, for which service each scientist received a thousand pounds from the estate of the eighth Earl of Bridgwater. And versions of the argument are still found from time to time in *The Reader's Digest*. Nevertheless, few philosophers or even theologians in the past century have defended it. Hume was not the sole cause of the collapse; Darwin, in providing an alternative hypothesis to explain the curious adaptation of means to ends in nature, had enormous psychological effect. But for all that, Hume can be credited with what is rare in philosophy: a definitive refutation.

Ethics

As we might expect after his denial of rational supports for our beliefs in causal efficacy and independent existence of bodies, Hume denies that moral distinctions are derived from reason. Many philosophers before Hume had made moral judgments dependent ultimately on feelings, but Hume's arguments for this position are vigorous and original.

Morality, like truth, is apprehended by the reason, some philosophers such as Plato and St. Thomas Aquinas have claimed. But this cannot be so, Hume says, inasmuch as our moral beliefs influence our actions, while reason—that by which we discover truth or falsehood—is "perfectly inert, and can never either prevent or produce any action or affection."[44] The mere comprehension of what is the case can never of itself be an incentive to action. By reason employed arithmetically I may discover that my debts exceed my resources. Thereupon I take action: I go to the bank and borrow some money, or I stage a holdup. It was not reason that impelled me to either course, it was fear or greed or hunger—some emotion or desire, 'passion' in Hume's terminology. The passions are "impressions," but they are not copies or representations of anything else; hence they are incapable of being true or false, reasonable or unreasonable. "'Tis not contrary to reason to prefer the destruction of the whole world to the scratching of my finger. 'Tis not contrary to reason for me to chuse my total ruin, to prevent the least uneasiness of an Indian or person wholly unknown to me."[45] A passion can be said to be unreasonable only in two derivative senses: if directed toward a nonexistent object or one of a different character from what we suppose, for example if I worship Zeus or crawl toward a mirage or drool over plastic fruit, or if the means selected for obtaining the desired object are inadequate, as if I try to cure my cold by eating garlic or do in my enemies by sticking pins into dolls made to resemble them. Means may be well or ill chosen, thus reasonable or unreasonable; but ends are simply desired. "Reason is, and ought only to be the slave of the passions, and can never pretend to any other office than to serve and obey them."[46] If this is not obvious, it is because so many of our activities are motivated by the "calm passions" such as benevolence or desire for self-preservation, which resemble reason and are easily mistaken for it.

If the propositions of morality could be demonstrated *a priori*, they would have to consist in assertions concerning one or another of four relations—resemblance, contrariety, degrees of quality, and proportions in quantity—for these alone are the relations in which ideas can stand. But these relations hold between material and even inanimate objects. Consequently, if morality were reducible to them, virtue and vice could be attributed to dogs and stones. Nor can morality consist in the matter of fact relations of space and time, identity, and causality, for similar reasons. If the viciousness of parent murder consisted simply in the causal relation of killer to victim combined in a certain way with that of parent to child, the sapling that grows up next to its parent tree and overtops it and kills it by depriving it of sunlight would be guilty of murder. Incest in animals would be blameworthy. In general, all animals would be equally capable of virtue and vice with men. Their ignorance would not absolve them, for on this theory the turpitude would still be there even if the beasts did not recognize it. Therefore, morality is discovered by reason in neither of its Humean senses: comparison of ideas or discovery of matter of fact.

What then is a moral judgment? It is an expression of a feeling of a certain kind. "When you pronounce any action or character to be vicious, you mean nothing, but that from the constitution of your nature you have a feeling or sentiment of blame from the contemplation of it."[47] "We do not infer a character to be virtuous, because it pleases: But in feeling that it pleases after such a particular manner, we in effect feel that it is virtuous."[48]

We have met this kind of theory before, for instance in Hobbes and Spinoza. Those philosophers, however, had claimed to find a single source for all actions and attitudes: concern for one's own well-being. But in the meantime Joseph Butler (1692–1752, the relatively enlightened Bishop whom the young Hume had striven to please with his *Treatise*) had argued convincingly that the selfish system rested on a confusion between "If I satisfy my desire, I shall get pleasure," which is true, and "I cannot really desire anything but my own pleasure," which is false. Anything can be an object of desire; in particular, another person's well-being can. Benevolence is not selfishness in disguise. Butler it was who made the illuminating if tautological remark "Everything is what it is, and not another thing."

Hume, in explaining our moral sentiments, does not try to derive them all from self-love. Humanity and sympathy are their basis. We approve what is useful, what contributes to the happiness of society. Hume's proof consists of examining the virtues one by one to show that virtuous conduct is in fact socially beneficial. The "monkish virtues" of celibacy, fasting, penance, mortification, self-denial, humility, silence, and solitude serve no purpose, but they are not counterinstances; they are "everywhere rejected by men of sense" and transferred to "the opposite column."[49]

Hume discusses justice at length. He declares this to be an artificial virtue, regarded as a good only in certain conditions. We can imagine a world of universal plenty in which all goods that anyone wanted could be procured instantly and without effort. We should then not concern ourselves with distribution; justice, because useless, would not be a virtue. The case would be the same if benevolence reigned to the extent that consideration for others was always the overriding motive of action. Also in the opposite condition of scarcity, as in a city under siege, justice has no place; anyone may be called upon to sacrifice property or even life, and it would be positively a vice to insist on niceties of compensation. But in normal conditions, rules for apportionment of goods, meticulously observed, are indispensable for the smooth functioning of society. Hence our feeling—even the feeling that justice ought to be done in particular cases where we recognize that the consequences may be harmful, as in bestowing an estate on an unworthy but legal heir. For the overriding social advantage lies in having regular procedures settled beforehand.

To the question raised by Thrasymachus so long ago—Why should I be moral, why should I do the right thing when it is against my interest—Hume replies that if anyone should raise that question in all seriousness,

> it would be difficult to find [an answer] which will to him appear satisfactory and convincing. If his heart rebel not against such pernicious maxims, if he feel no reluctance to the thoughts of villainy or baseness, he has indeed lost a considerable motive to virtue; and we may expect that his practice will be answerable to his speculation. But in all ingenuous natures, the antipathy to treachery and roguery is too strong to be counterbalanced by any views of profit or pecuniary advantage. Inward peace of mind, consciousness of integrity, a satisfactory review of our own conduct; these are circumstances, very requisite to happiness, and will be cherished and cultivated by every honest man, who feels the importance of them.[50]

Anyway, real virtue, based on utility, is not irksome.

> The dismal dress falls off, with which many divines, and some philosophers, have covered her; and nothing appears but gentleness, humanity, beneficence, affability; nay, even at proper intervals, play, frolic, and gaiety. She talks not of useless austerities and rigours, suffering and self-denial. She declares that her sole purpose is to make her votaries and all mankind, during every instant of their existence, if possible, cheerful and happy; nor does she ever willingly part with any pleasure but in hopes of ample compensation in some other period of their lives. The sole trouble which she demands, is that of just calculation, and a steady preference of the greater happiness.[51]

Reid

The even temper on which Hume prided himself was much tried by the tiresome rant of outraged divines who, besides being nuisances, kept him from obtaining any academic appointment. There were few with whom he could carry on calm and serious discussion of his philosophical ideas: one was his friend Adam

Smith (1723–1790), eminent as a philosopher though better remembered as a political economist; another, his distant relation Henry Home, Lord Kames, a judge with a taste for logic and aesthetics.

Almost the only man who understood him, disagreed with him, and published competent criticism of his philosophy during his lifetime was his countryman Thomas Reid (1710–1796), who read the *Treatise* on its first appearance nearly a quarter of a century before he published his reflections on it. Reid was Professor of Philosophy at Aberdeen, but did not receive the appointment until he was 42; before that he had been a country parson. Consequently, Hume was suspicious when through a mutual friend Reid submitted parts of the manuscript of his *Inquiry into the Human Mind* to him for criticism. However, Hume recognized his ability, sincerity, and freedom from bigotry. The correspondence between the two was polite, even cordial.

Reid's *Inquiry*, which was an attempt at a positive philosophy of mind as well as a polemic against the ideal theory, was successful on publication in 1764 and secured its author the chair of philosophy at Glasgow vacated by the resignation of Adam Smith. More than twenty years later Reid published *Essays on the Intellectual Powers of Man*, an expanded restatement of the *Inquiry*, and *Essays on the Active Powers of the Human Mind*, on the subjects of the second and third books of Hume's *Treatise*.

Reid was by no means the philosophical genius that Hume was, but he was canny enough to see that effective criticism of Hume's philosophy would have to begin at the beginning. He had once been an adherent of the new way of ideas; in youth he had even subscribed to Berkeley's immaterialism. But the writings of Hume awakened him, as they were later to awaken Kant, though to a different dawn. He perceived that once ideas were interposed between the mind and the thing, there was no stopping short of complete skepticism—the denial not only of matter but of mind and all knowledge. In his *Essays* he paid a sort of tribute to Hume.

> A system of consequences, however absurd, acutely and justly drawn from a few principles, in very abstract matters, is of real utility in science, and may be made subservient to real knowledge. This merit Mr. Hume's metaphysical writings have in a great degree.[52]

There was nothing wrong with Hume's logic; therefore, Hume's first premises must have been mistaken. Those premises presented the mind as the passive receptacle for ideas. What had gone wrong?

Reid was one of the first philosophers to lay emphasis on the structure of language as relevant to philosophical conclusions. All languages, he observed, use active verbs to refer to the operations of the mind, implying that mankind universally think of the mind as active. All languages, furthermore, make a threefold distinction between the process of perceiving, the mind which perceives, and the object perceived. None has a word for a fourth entity, the "idea"—this is a philosophers' invention. Introduced by Descartes and Locke as the supposed representation of objects that is the immediate object in perception, in Berkeley and Hume it successively swallowed up first the matter it was supposed to represent, then the mind that was supposed to contemplate it.

Hume was able to wreak this havoc only because on his first page he tossed sensations, passions, emotions, remembrances, perceptions, pains, and imaginations—between which ordinary language makes sharp distinctions—into a single bin labeled "perceptions." "He might as well speak of the hearing of sight, or of the smelling of touch; for, surely, hearing is not more different from sight, or smelling from touch, than perceiving is from remembering, or imagining."[53] We do not say that we "perceive" pain; we "feel" it or "are conscious" of it. We reserve the word 'perception' for apprehension of external objects.

These usages, found in all languages, create at least a presumption that the mind deals in several ways with several kinds of entities, none of which is the "idea" of the philosophers. What evidence is there for the existence of this strange entity? Reid finds only one serious argument, in Hume or elsewhere: the argument from perspective.

> The table, which we see, seems to diminish as we remove farther from it: but the real table, which exists independent of us, suffers no alteration. It was, therefore, nothing but its image which was present to the mind.[54]

Reid calls attention to the distinction between real magnitude, measured in linear units, and apparent magnitude, measured in degrees (of the angle in the visual field filled by the object). Apparent magnitude, despite the name, is not an appearance of real magnitude; it is something altogether different.

> Let us suppose, for a moment, that it is the real table we see: Must not this real table seem to diminish as we remove farther from it? It is demonstrable that it must. How then can this apparent diminution be an argument that it is not the real table? When that which must happen to the real table, as we remove farther from it, does actually happen to the table we see, it is absurd to conclude from this, that it is not the real table we see. It is evident, therefore, that this ingenious author has imposed upon himself by confounding real magnitude with apparent magnitude, and that his argument is a mere sophism.[55]

Concerning the question whether sensations do or do not resemble objects, Reid observes that they do not, but that ordinary people never suppose they do. They do not suppose that the sensations in their fingers, when they are grasping a ball, are anything like roundness, or that there is anything in a fire the least like their sensation of heat. By the words 'roundness' and 'heat', they signify whatever it is out there that causes the typical sensations. Sensations resemble things no more than words do; in both cases the relation is that of signification. Sensations constitute a natural language for interpreting the world, as words do a conventional one.

It is a disappointment, however, to find that after these able criticisms of the basis of the ideal theory, when Reid passes to defense of the reality of the external world, personal identity, other minds, uniformity of nature, and the existence of God, he simply lays them down as "first principles," ascribes them to "the inspiration of the Almighty," and declares that they constitute "common sense." They cannot be proved but they need no proof. Anyone who really doubted them would be mad.

A Note on Classification

Readers of this book should be aware that Locke, Berkeley, and Hume are referred to in other modern histories of philosophy as The British Empiricists and contrasted to the Continental Rationalists, who are Descartes, Spinoza, and Leibniz. Some apology is perhaps required for not adopting this terminology.

The term "empirical," if taken as signifying recommendation and practice of experimentation, is not accurately applied to the three Britons. Here, to be sure, the "British Empiricists" are partly at fault. All of them praised "experience" as the only source of knowledge of matter of fact. Part of the marathon subtitle of Berkeley's *Three Dialogues* is: "Also to Open a Method for Rendering the Sciences More Easy, Useful, and Compendious." The subtitle of Hume's *Treatise* in full is: "Being An Attempt to Introduce the Experimental Method of Reasoning into Moral Subjects." But these are misleading. The principles of all three philosophers are just as *a priori* as anything on the Continent: Ideas are whatever are the objects of mind when a man thinks; Causes cannot be sensible things; All the perceptions of the human mind resolve themselves into impressions and ideas. These, and other propositions of similar abstract generality, are the starting points, and no evidence, certainly no experimental evidence, is offered for them. In all the principal writings of the "Empiricists" only three experiments are reported—Berkeley one, Hume two—and these are thought experiments. (This is not meant as a reproach to the philosophers. Philosophy cannot be empirical. If it were it would be just another natural science.)

Of more importance is the fact that the classification obscures connections that exist and insinuates some that do not. Locke follows Descartes far more closely than either Spinoza or Leibniz does; Berkeley is very much like Leibniz; Hume is Descartes carried to the logical conclusion. Descartes, Berkeley, and Hume are inside-out philosophers; that is, they believe the systematization of knowledge must begin with consideration of the mind's contents. Spinoza and Leibniz are outside-in. Locke vacillates. One could go on indefinitely listing important across-class similarities and within-class differences.

Is there then no question that all the rationalists would answer Yes to, all the empiricists No? The touchstone often suggested is the question "Are there innate ideas?" But five of the six answered this question "In a sense, yes; in another sense, no," either explicitly or in practice. For the sixth, Spinoza, who did not succumb to the box model of the mind, the question was without significance.

On the whole, the British Empiricist versus Continental Rationalist contrast is far more geographical than philosophical.

40

The Enlightenment in France

VOLTAIRE, TREMENDOUS FIGURE THAT he was, accomplished more as a popularizer and propagandist than as an original thinker in philosophy. The Age of Voltaire mirrored him in being more notable for extending, drawing out, implications than for founding. The mechanistic worldview was worked out to its logical conclusion—producing an illogical reaction.

Voltaire

François Marie Arouet (1694–1778), who invented the name Voltaire for himself, was like Descartes educated by the Jesuits. Unlike Descartes he spent his whole life harassing his teachers. Apparently the sting of his ridicule is still felt in that holy army nearly two centuries after his death. Frederick Copleston, S.J., who in his cool and judicious *History of Philosophy* seldom comments on personal characteristics, writes of Voltaire

> He had a strong dose of common sense; and his call for a reform in the administration of justice, together with his efforts, even if inspired by very mixed motives, to bring certain miscarriages of justice to public attention, show a certain amount of humane feeling. But, in general, his character was not particularly admirable. He was vain, revengeful, cynical and intellectually unscrupulous.[1]

Father Copleston here echoes an article by George Saintsbury in the eleventh edition of the *Encyclopaedia Britannica*. From neither do we learn the particulars of "certain miscarriages of justice," such as the case of Jean Calas, a Protestant merchant of Toulouse whose son hanged himself. Calas and his family were accused, on no evidence at all, of having strangled him to prevent him from turning Catholic. All members of the family were tortured; M. Calas was broken on the wheel (*i.e.* stretched over a large wheel and beaten with a sledgehammer until all his bones were broken) and then, still alive, burnt. Answering an appeal from the widow Calas, for three years Voltaire spent most of his time and energy arousing sentiment that at last pressured the King of France into annulling the sentence and paying an indemnity. In another case two 16-year-old boys of Amiens, prosecuted by the Bishop and convicted on perjured evidence of having mutilated a crucifix and sung insulting songs about the Virgin Mary, were sentenced to have their right hands cut off, their tongues torn out, and then be burnt. One boy escaped to the domains of Frederick the Great; the other's sentence was mercifully commuted to decapitation. Voltaire worked twelve years, without success, to obtain reversal of the sentence and pardon for the refugee. From what "very mixed motives" Voltaire exerted himself in these and numerous other cases, neither Saintsbury nor Copleston informs us.

After having spent some months in the Bastille, Voltaire made an extended visit to England, 1726–29. Here was the land of liberty and intelligence. In his *Letters on the English*, 1732, he praised English physics, philosophy, and political institutions, contrasting those of Louis XV's France so unfavorably that the government burnt the book. But the ideas could no longer be suppressed. In 1738 he published a popular exposition of Newton's philosophy, which was at last allowed to supersede Descartes'.

Insofar as he concerned himself with metaphysics, Voltaire was a theistic materialist. He relied on the authority of Locke for the proposition that it was not impossible for God to have made matter capable of thinking, and claimed to have been reliably informed that Newton had concurred.

Voltaire looked with disfavor on the agnosticism or atheism of most materialists. Despite his ridicule of final causes in *Candide*, he was convinced of the validity of the design argument. The regularity and sublimity of nature points unmistakably to an intelligent cause. But the evil in the world is not to be explained away. Voltaire solved the problem as Plato did: matter exists coeternally with God and limits His power. God tries to eliminate evil but, like a master craftsman working with shoddy materials, cannot do so completely.

The greatest of evils that afflict mankind in Voltaire's opinion, however, had little connection with matter as such. It was superstition, concentrated in the power of the Catholic Church. Hence his motto *Ecrasez l'infâme!* Once the infamous thing was crushed, Voltaire seemed to think, further reform would be hardly necessary or desirable. He wished to see the monarchy reformed—even strengthened, as it would be, once freed of popish influence. Despotism was not objectionable as long as it was enlightened, that is, permitted freedom of thought. Purified religion should limit itself to the furtherance of morality. Although Voltaire did not himself believe in the immortality of the soul, he approved of teaching the doctrine, which he regarded as indispensable for keeping the rabble in order.

La Mettrie

The man with the best claim to having founded French materialism is Julien Offray de La Mettrie (1709–1751). An army surgeon, he was struck by the way a bodily condition such as fever could entirely alter the dispositions of the mind. His researches on the material basis of mental phenomena were published as *The Natural History of the Soul*, 1745, as a result of which he had to flee from France. In Holland he wrote his best work, *Man a Machine* (*L'Homme Machine*, which should be rendered *Man a Mechanism*, but the mistranslation is traditional).[2] When it came out in 1748, the Dutch also began to persecute him. There was only one refuge left, the court of Frederick the Great, philosophical King of Prussia. La Mettrie was honorably received in Potsdam, where Voltaire was living at the time, and resumed the practice of medicine. But three years later he died suddenly; his enemies characteristically attributed his demise to gluttonous overindulgence in a meat pie. Frederick himself composed and delivered the funeral oration.

Man a Machine is a development from Cartesianism. Descartes, equating think-ing substance to the soul of theology, had to deny that animals other than men are conscious. They are stimulus-response mechanisms. La Mettrie reproached Descartes for having insincerely attempted thus to appease the theologians. Descartes should have held—and really did, La Mettrie suggests—that there is no sharp line between brutes and human beings. They are alike material structures, mechanisms that feel. "The human body is a mechanism which winds its own springs; . . . the soul is but a principle of motion or a material and sensible part of the brain." Matter is not inert, but has inherently the powers of motion and consciousness.

Physicians who are philosophers are alone qualified to speak on the subject of the soul. Only they have the experience and observations that confer the right to have opinions on these questions. And clearly the soul's character depends on bodily conditions. When the body is diseased, so is the soul; fever makes a genius into a temporary idiot. Opium, wine, and coffee alter thought. In old age the soul degenerates along with the body. Diet influences character: the custom of the English of eating red and bloody meat accounts for their savagery and their "pride, hatred, scorn of other nations, indocility and other degrading sentiments."

Comparative anatomy explains this dependence. Man is the most intelligent animal because he has the largest and most convoluted brain. But in the continuity of the animal world, the orangutan is so close to us that it ought to be possible to choose a young ape, "one with the most intelligent face," and teach him to speak. Then "he would no longer be a wild man, nor a defective man, but he would be a perfect man, a little gentleman, with as much matter or muscle as we have, for thinking and profiting by his education."

Like Hume, La Mettrie based morality on feeling. Here too, therefore, man has no reason to fancy a gap between himself and the other animals. Natural law is "a feeling that teaches us what we should not do, because we would not wish it to be done to us." It manifests itself in remorse, in a man's bad conscience and a dog's "crouching and downcast air." In sum, "man is not moulded from a costlier clay; nature has used but one dough, and has merely varied the leaven."

La Mettrie's remarks on religion strikingly anticipate Hume's views in the *Dia-logues Concerning Natural Religion*. Probably a supreme being exists, La Mettrie allows, but this is "a theoretic truth with very little practical value." Belief in it is far from ensuring moral conduct, just as disbelief does not make for wickedness. As for the design argument, there is no use piling up evidences of design in nature, for "either the mere structure of a finger, of an ear, of an eye, a single observation of Malpighi proves all, . . . or all the other evidences prove nothing." These facts may rule out the possibility of a chance universe, but the existence of a supreme being is not thereby proved, "since there may be some other thing which is neither chance nor God—I mean, nature." We know nothing of ultimate causes; the recourse to God is mere disguise for ignorance. "The weight of the universe therefore far from crushing a real atheist does not even shake him."

In contrast to Voltaire's remark that if God did not exist it would be necessary to invent Him, La Mettrie held atheism to be beneficial whether true or not. If there were no more religion, there would be no more religious wars.

> Nature, infected with a sacred poison, would regain its rights and its purity. Deaf to all other voices, tranquil mortals would follow only the spontaneous dictates of their own being, the only commands which can never be despised with impunity and which alone can lead us to happiness through the pleasant paths of virtue.

Diderot

Denis Diderot (1713–1784) was one of the first evolutionary thinkers. His own thought evolved generally parallel to that of French thought of the era. Beginning a Deist in the Voltairean manner, he ended an atheist and materialist, or "Spinozist." He was editor of the great *Encyclopedia of the Sciences and Crafts*, whose publication in 35 volumes, 1751–1776, impeded by government censorship, was the culminating event of the Enlightenment. Diderot himself wrote many articles on industrial and technical processes, studying them firsthand for this purpose. He gained thereby a genuine appreciation for practical and experimental knowledge that led him to urge the founding of scientific laboratories.

The notion of a natural hierarchy is at least as old as Aristotle. Leibniz asserted the continuity of animal creation and explained it metaphysically: there could be no Sufficient Reason for a gap in it. Diderot took this idea in the developed and observationally confirmed form it had in La Mettrie and gave it a twist new for the modern era, though actually harking all the way back to Anaximander: he suggested that the hierarchy was not static but resulted from continuous development through time. The simpler organisms came first, the more complex ones evolved from them in progressive stages. Earlier, La Mettrie had prefigured the conception of progress through a struggle for existence; "beings without wants are beings without mind," he had written. The idea of evolution was there already in the eighteenth century, although another hundred years were to elapse before its mechanism was explained plausibly.

Diderot, like all the French materialists, deemed thought and motion to be fundamental properties of matter. He was fascinated by Leibniz' conception of all things as being full of life. There are many diverse elements, he held; these can be divided down to minima, the molecules of the substance. Each molecule has a sort of consciousness; how else can the undoubted fact of consciousness in the complex organism be explained? Diderot saw, however, that to ascribe thought to each minute part of a human body was useless for explaining the unity of the human mind. But he had no solution to this problem.

Holbach

In France, since the middle ages, intellectual life has been concentrated in the capital. A peculiar importance attaches to the *salons*, the groups that meet more or less regularly in the houses of those with the means to entertain thinkers whose interest and viewpoint they share. In the eighteenth century the most important *salon* keeper for the radical intellectuals, the group associated with the *Encyclopedia*, was a naturalized German. Paul Heinrich Dietrich, Freiherr von Holbach (1723–1789) settled in Paris, styled himself Paul Henri Thyry, Baron d'Holbach, and devoted his large fortune to hospitality for the advanced thinkers. He was good-natured, friendly, witty, simple in his habits, devoted to his wife and family. His modesty precluded him from putting himself forward among his guests; he was to everybody the "*maître d'hôtel* of the philosophers." Hence even those who came every week to his dinner parties did not suspect the truth, that he was the author of *The System of Nature*, which shocked even the avant-garde when copies were smuggled in from Holland in 1770.

They should have suspected, for the book has German characteristics: it is very long and devoid of humor. It begins "Man is unhappy, just because he misunderstands nature." He invents phantoms to frighten himself, which kings and priests use to their advantage. Like Lucretius, Holbach believed that dissemination of knowledge of nature would free humanity from the prejudices and follies of religion, and thereby bring about the triumph of justice, goodwill, and peace.

There is nothing outside nature. Man is a part of it: natural influences determine his every action. Nature is matter in motion. Its course is the circulation of material particles, proceeding according to laws from attraction and repulsion that are fundamental properties of all matter. Consciousness is motion within the brain.

People give the name of order to the arrangements that they deem beneficial, and which they can easily grasp; the opposite they call disorder. But as everything in nature is equally necessary, there can be no objective distinction between order and disorder. Hence there can be no miracles; the very notion rests on the contrast.

Nonsuperstitious morality is to be based on rational recognition of the means to human happiness. We seek our own happiness but recognize, or should, that we cannot separate it from the happiness of others. Since there is no free will, there can be no guilt in any absolute sense. Criminals should be understood and helped; Holbach makes the original suggestion that criminality in many of its forms is simply a disease, to be treated and cured by medicine.

The second part of the book consists of a thorough refutation of arguments in favor of religion. Holbach shocked many of his own guests by combatting deism and pantheism no less than Christianity. But in the end he declared atheism to be essentially an aristocratic doctrine; the common people could not be expected to learn an entirely new way of looking at the universe.

Rousseau

Jean-Jacques Rousseau (1712–1778) belongs only chronologically to the Enlightenment, which bore him within itself as the seed of its own destruction. In the midst of his rather messy life—which besides secretarial work, music copying, and composition of operas included a twelve-year stint as kept man of a rustic baroness—Jean-Jacques heard one day that a learned society was offering a prize for the best essay on the question "Has the progress of the arts and sciences had a purifying effect on morals?" He decided to enter the contest with a defense of the affirmative; but a sophisticated friend persuaded him that the more paradoxical and sensational negative would stand a better chance of winning. This strategy was correct. Not only did Rousseau's essay win the prize, it made him famous overnight.

The *Discourse on the Arts and Sciences* is anti-intellectual in form and in content. It contains no argument, or even consecutive presentation of ideas, but only magnificently rhetorical reiteration of contrasts between the rough, unlettered, unadorned, vigorous, and virtuous Spartans, early Romans and Iranians, and North American Indians—and on the other hand the luxurious, learned, vicious, and flabby populaces of late Rome, Byzantium, and eighteenth-century France. No attempt is made to show that the arts and sciences are responsible for enervation and corruption, or even that individual learned men are more wicked than individual ignoramuses; it is enough for Rousseau that learning and vice coexist. He asperses the origins of the sciences too.

Astronomy was born of superstition, eloquence of ambition, hatred, falsehood, and flattery; geometry of avarice; physics of an idle curiosity; and even moral philosophy of human pride.[3]

And they are useless.

Tell me, then, illustrious philosophers, of whom we learn the ratios in which attraction acts *in vacuo*; and in the revolution of the planets, the relations of spaces traversed in equal times; by whom we are taught what curves have conjugate points, points of inflexion, and cusps; how the soul and body correspond, like two clocks, without actual communication; what planets may be inhabited; and what insects reproduce in an extraordinary manner. Answer me, I say, you from whom we receive all this sublime information, whether we should have been less numerous, worse governed, less formidable, less flourishing, or more perverse, supposing you had taught us none of all these fine things.[4]

He praises the Caliph Omar for having burnt the library of Alexandria.

Artificiality and debauchery had been raised to such a pitch in the eighteenth century that there was bound to be a revulsion in favor of plainness, sincerity, and natural decorum. Rousseau's discourse appeared at just the right time to articulate this feeling. Five years later, in 1755, he published a *Discourse on the Origin of Inequality* in which he advocated a return, not to utter savagery, but to the presumed transitional stage between the purely natural man, who did not even have language, and the civilized man. There were some who saw through Rousseau's sentimentality and scorned it, notably Voltaire, who when Rousseau sent him a copy of his book replied

I have received your new book against the human race, and thank you for it. Never was such cleverness used in the design of making us all stupid. One longs, in reading your book, to walk on all fours.

But as appeals to stop thinking and let feeling take over are perennially popular, Rousseau and his noble savage became a major fad.

In 1761 Rousseau published a novel, *The New Eloise*, again commending the simple life and sincere feelings. It is notable for a long passage on religion. Rousseau proclaimed himself the most religious of men; he *felt* that God exists, the will is free, the soul immortal.

The next year his two principal works appeared. The first was his treatise on education, *Emile*. The author advocated a natural and permissive approach to education. Children should not be forced by fear to memorize information that does not interest them; they are naturally curious and if let alone will at the proper time beg to be taught. This excellent book shows how little necessary experience is to wisdom: Jean-Jacques sired five bastards but raised none; all were sent to the orphanage as soon as possible after birth.

The other book of 1762, *The Social Contract*, is one of the most influential books ever written. If the claim that it caused the French Revolution is an exaggeration, it was at least an important factor, and gave the thinking (such as it was) of Robespierre and his colleagues much of its direction.

The book, which is a fragment from a larger work that the author did not finish, is unlike his other works on society: it is coherent and closely reasoned. We are not exhorted to burn our libraries and return to the forest; on the contrary,

Rousseau now agrees with Hobbes that association into civil society makes a "stupid and dull-witted animal" into an intelligent being, human in the full sense. The electrifying opening sentence "Man is born free; and everywhere he is in chains," can be misleading out of context. It looks like a call to anarchy, or at least bloody revolution, but it is not. Rousseau is concerned with legitimacy: assuming that there is such a thing as political obligation, what is it and on what does it rest? What can make the chains legitimate?

He shows first that mere force or conquest cannot create right; nor, contrary to Hobbes, can complete submission, even if voluntary. If I give up all my rights irrevocably to a sovereign and make myself his slave, he can then have no obligation to me. In consequence, I have none to him. Rousseau dismisses Hobbes' insistence that we must submit to obtain a peaceful life with the remark that "Tranquillity is found also in dungeons; but is that enough to make them desirable places to live in?" Moreover, even if one could enslave oneself, this act could not obligate one's children.

The problem as Rousseau sees it is this: "To find a form of association which will defend and protect with the whole common force the person and goods of each associate, and in which each, while uniting himself with all, may still obey himself alone, and remain as free as before."[5] Rousseau must assume that legitimacy implies some kind of contract, at least an implicit one; for if force and submission cannot create right, only consent is left. It looks, however, as if any kind of social contract would be a blank check, which no reasonable person could be deemed to have issued. This is a principal trouble with all consent theories of the State.

Rousseau thought to overcome this difficulty by making submission not to some other person or persons but to what he called the "general will." "Each of us puts his person and all his power in common under the supreme direction of the general will, and, in our corporate capacity, we receive each member as an indivisible part of the whole."[6] This compact creates a sovereign, but not a king or limited assembly—it is the Sovereign People. Sovereignty, the highest authority in the state, is nothing other than the exercise of the general will.

> The Sovereign, being formed wholly of the individuals who compose it, neither has nor can have any interest contrary to theirs; and consequently the sovereign power need give no guarantee to its subjects, because it is impossible for the body to wish to hurt all its members . . . The Sovereign, merely by virtue of what it is, is always what it should be.[7]

The Sovereign is always what it should be because it expresses the general will, which is always right. This would be an implausible claim if, as we might suppose, the general will were determined by the vote of the people. But Rousseau makes a distinction. What a vote determines is the will of all, and that is not the same thing. The general will expresses the public interest: the will of all, private interests as well. If the voters were fully informed of the issues and insulated from each other so as to prevent them from exerting any persuasions or pressures, then a vote would express the general will because (Rousseau held) the particular private interests would cancel out. (It is not clear why.) This condition perhaps cannot be satisfied. But to approximate it in a democracy, parties and pressure groups should be banned; if that cannot be done, then they should be multiplied so that they can neutralize one another.

What Rousseau intended by his distinction between general will and will of all is this. As an individual, it is natural for me to wish that I had all sorts of advantages and privileges. I wish that there were one law for me and another for the rest; that is my individual will. But as a university professor I have interests in common with others in the profession. All of us form a Professors' Association, agreeing to put ourselves, considered as professors, under the supreme direction of the general professorial will. What is the general will of professors is, however, only an individual will when confronting, say, the Association of University Administrators. Yet for certain purposes, professors and administrators may find it necessary to merge in pursuit of their yet more general will. Within each group, wide or narrow, I can claim no special privilege. Professors as a group may want, and even get, some advantage; but if so, the professorial general will dictates that it be shared impartially among all the professors. Now, the most inclusive group there is is the State. Considering myself as citizen, I recognize that the general will cannot play favorites. What makes the general will general is its impartiality. It is the will for those benefits that accrue to all citizens alike.

This does not mean that some groups or even individuals may not seem to derive special benefits. It might be an expression of the general will, for example, that churches should be exempt from taxation and clergymen from the draft—but only on the ground of a presumed benefit to every member of society.

It is not so grotesque, then, for Rousseau to claim that the general will is always right, that laws expressing it cannot be unjust, and that if I vote against it I am making a mistake about my own interest. Nor is it intolerable paradox when we are told that when the citizen who refuses to obey the general will is compelled to do so, he is only being "forced to be free."[8] However, though the theory is perhaps innocent enough, it is extraordinarily vulnerable to perversions. For whether intentionally or not, it sets up the State as an entity with a will of its own, over and above the citizens who compose it. From the claim that the State's will is always right, it follows that opposition to it is always wrong, either through ignorance or through malice. Hence there is no need to safeguard the rights of dissenters; they need rather to be "forced to be free." And since nothing so straightforward as a vote can determine what the general will is, the way is open for all sorts of parties and strong men and women to proclaim themselves its incarnation. In Rousseau's theory sovereignty, resting in the whole people, is inalienable; government officials, even kings and dictators, only have a commission from it, revocable at any time. Again, in practice this has proved difficult.

The government of Louis XV banned Rousseau's books of 1762 and issued a warrant for his arrest. He fled to his native Geneva, which however also outlawed him. He found, as everyone did in those days, refuge for a while in a territory under the control of Frederick the Great. Hume had offered him his protection, and in 1766 Rousseau accepted the invitation. In England Hume was warmly hospitable, the literary world honored Rousseau, and he even received a pension from George III's government! But his fears of persecution had become pathological. At length he accused Hume of plotting against him, and left England in 1770 after a bitter and unseemly quarrel which became public. He wandered around France—the government appeared no longer interested in prosecuting him—and died in 1778, in poverty and obscurity. In the same year Voltaire died, in the midst of the triumphs of his return to Paris.

41

Kant

IN HIS EIGHTY YEARS, Immanuel Kant never once left the environs of the city of Königsberg in East Prussia. (After World War II this area was annexed to the Soviet Union. The city is now called Kaliningrad.) He was born in 1724. His father, a harness maker, was a member of the sect of Pietists. Like the Methodists of the same time in England, these people deplored abstruse theology and formal religious observances, striving to return instead to an ideal early Christian condition of brotherly love. Kant's Pietistic upbringing and the influence of his mother are said to have been responsible for the deep moral earnestness that informs his writings on ethics, writings which exalt Duty to an extent surpassing even the emphasis given it by the Stoics. The excessive religiosity of some Pietists, however, produced in the young Kant a permanent abhorrence of public worship. In later life he never entered a church. When as Rector of the University he had the duty of leading the academic procession to a church service, he did so—but having reached the church he stood aside at the portal while the rest of the faculty marched in.

He entered the university in 1740 with the intention of becoming a pastor, but soon gave up theology for philosophy and natural science. Kant had scientific talents of the first order. When only thirty he published a *General Natural History and Theory of the Heavens*, in which he put forward the speculation that the sun and planets originated as condensations out of diffuse matter. This Nebular Hypothesis, which he supported with detailed mathematical reasoning, was thus propounded by Kant half a century before its enunciation by the French astronomer Laplace, who usually gets the credit.

Scientific eminence, however, brought neither money nor position in eighteenth-century East Prussia. Kant had to support himself with private tutoring and billiard playing for ten years before he was appointed *Privatdocent*. A German *Privatdocent* has the use of University classrooms and other facilities but no income other than the fees his students pay him directly. Kant, however, was an enormously popular lecturer, whose classes met five hours a day, six days a week, beginning at seven in the morning.

In 1770 he at last received appointment as Professor of Logic and Metaphysics, with a suitable stipend. About this time he began to write the *Critique of Pure Reason*, a work that can be said to be the fount of German philosophy in the way Locke's *Essay* is of British. This stupendous book was published in 1781 (in Riga, a city then as now under Russian dominion), and despite its difficulty made Kant at once the leading philosopher of Germany. Two years later he published *Prolegomena to Any Future Metaphysics*, a hundred-page exposition of the leading ideas of his great work. In 1785 appeared the *Foundation of the Metaphysics of Morals* that despite its brevity is generally regarded as Kant's most important contribution to ethics, taking precedence over the *Critique of Practical Reason* (1788), which suffers from awkward organization due to the author's desire to draw parallels with the argument of the first *Critique*. The third and last *Critique*, that *of Judgment*, appeared in 1790. Formally it is a scrutiny of the faculty by which we apply general principles to particular instances; its influence, however, has been greatest as a work in aesthetics, the principles of art criticism. A second edition, much rewritten, of the first *Critique* was published in 1787. During all this time Kant continued to lecture and to write treatises and essays—including a tract on *Perpetual Peace* (1795) in which he proposed a United Nations organization to settle international disputes, poignantly suggesting that princes might consult with philosophers in secret without compromising their dignity.

The regularity of Kant's life was celebrated. He got up at 4 (a.m.), had a breakfast consisting of a cup of tea, and prepared his lectures. After teaching from seven to noon, he entertained guests at the main meal of the day. He was a polished and lively conversationalist. He then read until four, when he left the house to walk up and down the square eight times. After a light supper he wrote for three hours, retiring to bed at nine. He died in 1804, unfortunately not before senility had affected his mental powers.

The *Critique of Pure Reason:* The Setting

Through most of the eighteenth century, philosophy in Germany was dominated by Christian Wolff (1679–1754), a disciple of Leibniz who made a world system from his master's passion for the *a priori*. It was this in particular, and more generally the clear-and-distinct-ideas tradition from Descartes on, that Kant referred to as "dogmatism." Until in his mid-forties, Kant did not doubt the adequacy of the intellect to penetrate to the core of metaphysical reality. From these "dogmatic slumbers" the reading of Hume awakened him. The essence of Dogmatism was the conviction that necessary connections between the things in the world can be apprehended, as they are in themselves, by our minds. This Hume challenged.

> For how is it possible, says that acute man, that when a concept is given me, I can go beyond it and connect with it another, which is not contained in it, in such a manner as if the latter necessarily belonged to the former? Nothing but experience can furnish us with such connections (thus he concluded from the difficulty which he took to be an impossibility), and all that vaunted necessity, or, what is the same thing, all cognition assumed to be *a priori*, is nothing but a long habit of accepting something as true, and hence of mistaking subjective necessity for objective.[1]

Kant seems to have first heard of Hume, and become convinced of his importance, by reading attempted refutations put out by the Scottish Common Sense philosophers. (Such is the usefulness of refutations.) Kant, once awakened, by no means became a convert to Humean skepticism; he was not moved to burn all the books in Königsberg containing neither abstract reasoning concerning quantity nor probable reasoning concerning matters of fact. But Hume, Kant recognized, had raised a serious question concerning the possibility of any metaphysical knowledge at all, that is, knowledge of how things must be. The question required an answer.

Synthetic A Priori Judgments

Plato began his argument against the skepticism and relativism of the Sophists by pointing out that there is undoubtedly such a thing as real knowledge: there is mathematics. Kant likewise was unattracted by skeptical doubts. Science *is* knowledge. We may ask how it can exist, but not whether it does. And like Plato he grounded his theory of knowledge on an analysis of geometry and arithmetic.

Hume admitted that arithmetic and (to some extent) geometry are exceptions to the rule that all we know is what we gather from experience—but only apparent exceptions, for their certainty is explained by their consisting entirely of "comparisons of ideas." By this obscure phrase he seems to have meant that (for example) our knowledge that seven and five are twelve is a consequence of our definitions of the terms seven, five, and, and twelve. Mathematics is a vast collection of statements to the effect that one symbol or set of symbols has been endowed, by us, with the same meaning as some other symbol set. Things in the world conform to mathematical statements about them, but this is not mysterious; it is no more surprising than that things do have the names we give them. In the Leibnizian terminology, all mathematical statements are analytical. As such they tell us nothing about how things are; they cannot state any matters of fact.

This is where Kant came to grips with Hume. On the contrary, Kant averred, mathematics consists entirely of "synthetical judgments," truly informative statements. In "7 + 5 = 12" the subject is "7 + 5," and we can never "by mere dissection" of this subject concept discover the predicate "= 12." In geometry the theorems are, to be sure, logical consequences of the axioms; but these axioms are synthetic judgments. "A straight line is the shortest distance between two points"; Kant maintained that there is nothing about the mere concept of being straight that includes the concept of being the shortest distance.

On this issue, who was right—Kant or Hume? The weight of opinion nowadays is in favor of Hume. Kant is reproached for having claimed eternal and exclusive validity for Euclidean geometry hardly a generation before the discovery of two non-Euclidean geometries, those of Lobatchevsky and Riemann—geometrical systems that are internally consistent but in which one of the axioms consists in the denial of the corresponding Euclidean axiom. (Euclid lays it down that through a point outside a line, one and only one line can be drawn parallel to the given line. Lobatchevsky allows more than one parallel, Riemann none.) Astrophysicists are said to have discovered that space is in fact Riemannian rather than Euclidean. Modern thinkers assent almost unanimously to the dictum attributed to Einstein: insofar as mathematics is certain, it is not about the world; insofar as it is about the world, it is not certain.

Perhaps victory should go to neither Hume nor Kant, on the grounds that the notion of "comparison of ideas" is unclear, whereas the distinction between analytical and synthetical judgments is clear, if at all, only in relation to a restricted class of sentences that by no means comprises all or even very many mathematical "judgments."

The issue between Kant and Hume can perhaps be put into more modern terms this way. We form the notion of an *uninterpreted system*. We set down certain marks and announce rules by which these marks may be allowably combined. Thus we may have the marks #, II, * and a rule that wherever we have the string of marks #*# we may replace it by the single mark II. This is arbitrary and tells us nothing about the world. But now we assign an *interpretation* to the marks. We let # be a one-pound weight, II a two-pound weight, and * the operation of putting weights into the same pan of an equal-arm balance without destroying the existing equilibrium. On this interpretation the replacement rule tells us that we may substitute two one-pound weights for one two-pound weight, and if the balance was in equilibrium it will remain so. This is a true statement about weights and balances. But we might have interpreted the symbols differently: let # be a one-liter volume of any fluid, II a two-liter volume, and * the operation of pouring fluids together. The substitution rule now tells us that if a liter of any fluid is mixed with a liter of another, the volume resulting will be two liters—and this is false in some cases, for example, alcohol and water.

The issue between Hume and Kant can now be put this way. Given a set of symbols, a consistent set of rules for their combination, and an interpretation of the symbols, can we ever know of any interpretation of any set, *a priori* (that is, otherwise than by trying and seeing), that the statements in the interpretation must be true? To this question Hume presumably would have answered No, Kant Yes. Yet before deciding in Hume's favor it should be noted that although there now exist alternative geometries, they differ in but one axiom (out of a dozen or so); so that the subset without this axiom seems still to describe any possible space, just as Kant claimed; while there are no alternative arithmetics at all. And there remains the fact that we do feel about some interpretations of some sets— for example, weighing is additive—a certainty not plausibly to be ascribed merely to generalization from trials. In any case, if the issue were to be decided entirely in Hume's favor, Kant's system would be weakened but not destroyed. If mathematical judgments are not synthetic *a priori*, there might still be synthetic *a priori* judgments of other sorts, though we might be less hopeful of finding them.

However that may be, Kant was convinced that mathematical judgments are all synthetic. That they are *a priori* was conceded by Hume. Therefore we have in mathematics genuine knowledge of how things must be, not generalized from experience; for experience can never produce knowledge that is universal (admitting of no exception) and necessary. The problem thus arises: How is this pure mathematical knowledge possible?

Kant's answer is audacious. Geometry is the science of space; our knowledge of geometry is not derived from experience; therefore, space itself is not something given in experience but is instead a contribution of the knower's mind. It is a "pure intuition *a priori*, a mere form of sensibility."

The Situation of the Knower

In order for there to be knowledge there must be minds that know and something independent of minds to be known. All knowledge begins with experience. Let us consider the simplest kind, that which Kant calls *intuition* (*Anschauung*; "intuition" as translation of this word is a technical term, not to be confused with its ordinary meanings). We are looking at, feeling, tasting a tomato.

We have a faculty of receiving intuitions—visual appearances, feels, tastes, smells, sounds—the *sensibility*. When the tomato comes into our attention, there arises in our sensibility one or more sensations or intuitions: something is "given."

This *given* is not to be identified with the tomato considered as an object independent of the mind. Nor is the given just a figment of the mind. It has a reality of its own, as a product of the tomato colliding, so to speak, with the sensibility. We can call it an appearance if we are careful not to prejudice the case by supposing that it is somehow mere.

Within this appearance we can make an important distinction. On the one hand there are the color, the juiciness, the shape, and all the other particular qualities that vary from experience to experience and whose characteristics we can become acquainted with only by having the appropriate experience. It is possible to go through life without ever seeing anything colored Chinese red or ever tasting a papaya. Such qualities as these, revealed only in experience, we call the *matter* of appearance. On the other hand, so Kant maintains, we can know in advance of any experience whatsoever that it will occur in time, will have some duration; and of all "outer" experiences—that is, all experiences except those that consist simply of noting our state of mind at the moment—we can know in advance that they will be spatial. These two, and only they, are characteristics that experiences must have simply in order to be experiences. They are, then, the "forms of sensibility."

It remains to be shown that the forms of sensibility—space and time—are contributions of the mind to experience, not appertaining to the object of experience itself. Of space, Kant argues that our concept cannot be derived from experiences of outerness; for, on the contrary, the perception or even imagination of anything as being outside me presupposes that I have this notion already—*a priori*. And although I can conceive of space with nothing in it, I cannot conceive of the absence of space. Nor is space a concept arrived at by generalizing from particular relations or spaces. Though we speak of "parts of space," space as a whole is one and unique; its "parts" are not constituents but particular locations in the one space. (We can imagine Egypt without the Pyramids, but we cannot imagine Egypt without the space currently occupied by the Pyramids.) Finally, we conceive of space as a given infinite extension, although experience can never give rise to a notion of infinity.

The fact that this form of outer intuition is prior to the objects of it shows that the intuition is a formal character of the subject only, the mind, not of the tomato by itself. Thus space represents no property of things in themselves, things as they are (or may be) apart from our experience of them; it is a concept meaningful only in connection with sensibility, that is, with actual and possible experiences.

The synthetic but *a priori* nature of geometry can now be explained. Any outer experience, to be an experience, must be spatial. *We* contribute the space—as it were, we see the world through space-colored glasses. Geometry is knowledge not of experience but of the spatial conditions of any possible experience. In setting forth the properties of space we are not getting out more than we—our minds—are putting in.

Kant argues in a similar way for the conclusion that time is the form of inner sense, and that temporal notions cannot be known to apply to things in themselves. This analysis of time is supposed to account for the synthetic *a priori* character of arithmetic, on the ground that arithmetic is the science of counting, and counting takes time.

This method of arguing from the existence of knowledge of a certain sort to the conditions that make that knowledge possible, Kant called "transcendental." The knowledge of the conditions for experience gained by application of this method is also called transcendental. It is strictly limited to the conditions of experience; there cannot be any knowledge of objects transcending experience, that is, outside all possible experience. The general problem of the *Critique*, How are synthetic judgments *a priori* possible?, is called the Transcendental Problem. Kant breaks this down into three subproblems; the first, How is pure mathematics possible?, we have just considered.

The Understanding and Its Concepts

The second part of the transcendental problem is, How is the pure science of nature possible? Nature, as Kant defines the word, is "the existence of things, so far as it is determined according to universal laws." But if nature as the object of scientific study were just the assemblage of things in themselves, we could never know nature's laws: neither *a priori* nor *a posteriori*. Kant agrees with Hume that no laws of nature, necessarily true of everything that there is, could be produced as generalizations from experience.

But, Kant maintains, we do have such laws—we do have a pure science of nature. We know such synthetic *a priori* truths as that substance is permanent and that "every event is determined by a cause according to constant laws." The question then, as before with mathematics, is, How is this knowledge possible?

Kant's answer, as presented in the *Prolegomena to Any Future Metaphysics*, begins by distinguishing between judgments of perception and judgments of experience. In a judgment of perception I merely report how things seem to me. The room is warm, the wine is sour, the flash came before the crash. Such things may seem otherwise to others, or even be really otherwise, without making me modify my judgments further than to substitute "seem" for "is." My perceptions are my perceptions; I cannot be argued out of them. They certainly are what they seem to be—but for me only. Knowledge of my perceptions is not knowledge of the world that is the same for all of us, objective knowledge, nor does it even claim to be.

But if on the other hand I say that the wine has turned sour because you left the bottle uncorked in the sunlight, I am making a claim about how things really are. Here real disagreement is possible, and only one side can be right. And whereas if challenged I can retreat from "It is red" to "It seems red to me," I cannot retreat from "The heat caused the wine to sour" to "The heat seemed to cause the wine to sour"—in such a context "seemed to cause" makes no literal sense. In talking about how something causes something I am making a claim about how things are really tied together out there. This kind of objective knowledge claim Kant calls a "judgment of experience."

Talk about how the world really is requires judgments of experience. And judgments of experience cannot be made without recourse to such notions as those of enduring things—substances—that are more than sets of regularly associated traits, and real relations between them, such especially as causes. Now if the notion of cause, for instance, were reducible to that of a habit of expectation, as Hume had maintained, judgments of experience would turn out to be really no different from mere judgments of perception. In that case there would be no objective knowledge of a real world at all.

But there is such knowledge. Therefore, just as in sensing it is the mind's faculty of intuition and not the object sensed that contributes the forms of space and time, so in judging it is the understanding of the knower rather than any characteristic of the object known that contributes the formal aspects, the scheme of organization, to the judgment. The mind is passive only at the level of mere receipt of sensations. Every judgment of experience, on the other hand, involves the mind's activity of synthesis. The forms by which experience is organized Kant calls "pure concepts of the understanding," or *categories*. There are twelve of them, of which the most important are substance and cause.

In calling cause a category and maintaining that we have transcendental knowledge of causation, Kant was not claiming that our knowledge of any particular causal relation, such as that boiling water hardens eggs, can be *a priori*. He meant only that the notion of causation is indispensable for organizing our intuitions into experiences, and that cause is one of these organizing notions that we bring to experience rather than derive from it.

> When I say that experience teaches me something, I mean only the perception that lies in experience,—for example, that heat always follows the shining of the sun on a stone; consequently the proposition of experience is always so far accidental. That this heat necessarily follows the shining of the sun is contained indeed in the judgment of experience (by means of the concept of cause), yet is a fact not learned by experience; for conversely, experience is first of all generated by this addition of the concept of the understanding (of cause) to perception.[2]

Kant's point can perhaps be put this way: According to Hume our belief in causation is a habit. Well, suppose we did not have the habit or suppose we rid ourselves of it. The world then would revert to being the blooming buzzing confusion that William James says is the baby's world. If the mind in perception were entirely passive, if we merely sat back and let the perceptions flow in upon us, if in Kant's terminology our consciousness consisted of awareness of the "sensuous manifold" and nothing else, this confused awareness would not constitute experience. Before we can say anything about the sensuous manifold, the mind's faculty of understanding must contribute organization to that manifold. From what is given simply as a varying field of color, shapes, sound, smells, and the like, the understanding picks out elements (which in themselves are only the fleeting individual "impressions" of Hume) and unifies them into "a pan of boiling water." Other collections of bits of white and hard and oval are molded into traits of an object we call an egg; this process exhibits the category of substance at work. Those complex configurations that we call dropping an egg into a pan of boiling water, leaving it there for 15 minutes, taking it out, cracking it, and finding it a gelatinous mass, are summed up by the understanding under the category of cause as boiling-hardening-an-egg. Thus what was said of "The wine is sour" being a judgment of perception was not strictly accurate. For even to call something wine is already to have subsumed a perception under one or more categories—in this case that of substance at least.

Thus the metaphor of space-colored glasses used in discussing the forms of sensibility needs to be made more complicated. Now we need to think of the mind as a camera which records a picture of the world through a space-colored lens onto a film that then can be developed only by the use of substantial and causal and ten other kinds of chemicals.

The metaphor can be carried further. If we are never allowed to look directly at the world but are restricted to knowing it only through pictures we take with a certain camera, then we can know in advance that our knowledge of the world must conform to what the camera is capable of photographing. If we have only black and white film, we shall never find out that there are colors in the world, nor shall we even form a notion of what a color is. In short, the object of our knowledge will be the photograph, not the thing photographed. Just so, in Kant's philosophy the object of knowledge is the experience, not the thing in itself that contributes the content to experience or the self that has the experience. The camera does not photograph itself. Nevertheless, the knowledge we get from the photographs is real knowledge; it is not an imposture produced internally by the camera. So also our knowledge of the world is knowledge of the world, not a subjective reverie.

> We cannot think an object save through categories; we cannot *know* an object so thought save through intuitions corresponding to these concepts. Now all our intuitions are sensible; and this knowledge, in so far as its object is given, is empirical. But empirical knowledge is experienced. *Consequently, there can be no a priori knowledge, except of objects of possible experience.*[3]

> *The understanding does not derive its laws (a priori) from, but prescribes them to, nature.*[4]

Kant called this doctrine his "Copernican revolution" in philosophy. Previous philosophies had run into skeptical difficulties, he thought, because they had supposed that in the knowledge situation the knower must conform to the object known. Kant claimed to have avoided these difficulties by making the known object conform instead to the knower.

The Illusions of Reason

If we were prisoners with only a photograph album to look at, we would be tempted to suppose that the world outside was, like the photographs, black and white, two dimensional, and cut up into rectangles. We would be wrong, but we would have no way of finding out that we were wrong.

As things are, we are tempted to suppose that things in themselves are spatial, temporal, substantial, and causally related. This is a mistake, as we have seen, because if it were so synthetic *a priori* judgments would be impossible. But according to Kant we have another way of knowing that the forms of sensibility and of the understanding cannot apply to things in themselves. The attempt to reason in accordance with the forms of intuition and the categories outside any reference to possible experiences generates what Kant calls Transcendental Dialectic, the production of valid arguments leading to incompatible conclusions: *antinomies*. This happens, for example, when we try to think of the universe as a completed whole—which is not a possible, must less actual, object of experience. We may think we can show that this whole must have had a beginning in time.

> For if we assumed that the world had no beginning in time, then an eternity must have elapsed up to every given point of time, and therefore an infinite series of successive states of things must have passed in the world. The infinity of a series, however, consists in this, that it never can be completed by means of a successive synthesis. Hence an infinite past series of worlds is impossible, and the beginning of the world a necessary condition of its existence.[5]

This argument was urged by St. Bonaventura, among others.

On the other hand, to this thesis our reason protests with the antithesis that the world could not have had a beginning in time.

> For let us assume that it has a beginning. Then, as beginning is an existence preceded by a time in which a thing is not, it would follow that antecedently there was a time in which the world was not, that is, an empty time. In an empty time, however, it is impossible that anything should take its beginning, because of such a time no part possesses any condition as to existence rather than nonexistence, which condition could distinguish that part from any other (whether produced by itself or through another cause). Hence, though many a series of things may take its beginning in the world, the world itself can have no beginning, and in reference to time past is infinite.[6]

Parmenides and Hobbes advanced this reasoning.

Kant held that the solution to this conflict of Reason with itself consists in recognizing that time, as the form of inner sense, has no application to the world as a whole but only to possible experience, which must be distinguished from things in themselves. Thus both thesis and antithesis are false. Similarly with respect to arguments purporting to show that the world is spatially infinite or finite.

With respect to the category of cause, reason is driven to admit that determinism is universally true, while at the same time we have to admit that in our own case there is another kind of causality, that of freedom. Kant here maintains that both thesis and antithesis are true. Of the appearances that are the objects of our experience, determinism is absolutely true; yet the demands of morality show that the causality of freedom must be operative in moral agents considered as things in themselves. We shall try to see how (according to Kant) this can be, when we discuss Kant's ethics.

Hume had confessed that his own philosophy foundered on the shoals of personal identity. The self is nothing but a bundle or heap of perceptions. But what distinguishes one heap from another? There is no perception that can serve as the distinguishing mark; yet the reality of the difference cannot be denied.

Kant pointed out that there is given in experience a difference between succession of perceptions and perception of successions. Suppose I had a rare disease called one-second recurring amnesia: I remember things for just one second and then I forget them. In this condition if the clock in the steeple strikes twelve, I shall hear twelve separate strokes, but I shall not hear them *as* twelve. In order to hear them as twelve, there has to be in my consciousness a synthesis of present perception with memory of the past. To this faculty Kant gives the name "transcendental unity of apperception." That is the self of my experience. It is not another perception over and above the twelve perceptions of strokes of the bell; it is the context in which those perceptions find themselves. In this sense we are aware of a self that has experiences.

Reason, however, is drawn to the illusion of supposing that the Self is a perfectly simple substance, not given in experience but responsible for experience, and assimilated to the Soul of religion. This illusion, a typical metaphysical doctrine, is mainly the result of the illegitimate extension of the category of substance outside possible experience.

Ethics

"Nothing in the world—indeed nothing even beyond the world—can possibly be conceived which could be called good without qualification except a *good will*." This famous opening sentence of Kant's *Foundations of the Metaphysics of Morals* puts Kant squarely in the camp of those who, like the Stoics, center their theory on the motives for action. The ethics of duty (deontology) is commonly contrasted with goal ethics (consequentialism), which seeks first to determine what it is that we ought to aim at, whether happiness or pleasure or the glory of God, and then defines duty as a secondary term referring to action with the proper aim. There is something to this contrast, but it can be overstressed, as we shall see.

Kant means his opening sentence to be taken literally and seriously. To be good without qualification is to be good no matter in what context. Thus, as Kant goes on to point out, the talents of the mind and the gifts of fortune are usually rightly considered good, but not without qualification. If scoundrel *A* is intelligent and scoundrel *B* is stupid, then to that extent *A* is more scoundrelly than *B*; hence intelligence in that context is not a good thing. Nor is even happiness a good if it is the happiness of scoundrels.

The good will, however, is subject to no such qualifications. It is always a good thing for an individual to have a good will, whatever else he or she has or has not, and in whatever circumstances.

The good will is not defined in terms of "what it effects or accomplishes or . . . its adequacy to achieve some proposed end." If all of Jones' projects end happily, it does not follow that Jones is a good person. Nor if everything Robinson does ends in disaster, do we necessarily conclude that Robinson is bad. She may be unlucky, or a blundering idiot, but these are not moral failings. Undoubtedly Kant was right in claiming that common usage agrees; moreover, the law does. Attempted murder is still a crime even if in fact the intended victim, being insane, recovers sanity from the shock of the wound.

The good will is the will to do your duty because it is your duty. Kant makes a sharp distinction between acting according to duty and acting from duty, that is, for duty's sake. A shopkeeper may deal honestly with customers because of the knowledge that dishonesty will lead to a bad reputation and loss of business. To behave honestly because honesty is the best policy is to act in accordance with duty; but if that is the only motive, the action is not *from* duty and has no moral worth. Nor is the shopkeeper's action moral if the reason is love toward the customers and caring for their welfare.

> To be kind where one can is duty, and there are, moreover, many persons so sympathetically constituted that without any motive of vanity or selfishness they find an inner satisfaction in spreading joy, and rejoice in the contentment of others which

they have made possible. But I say that, however dutiful and amiable it may be, that kind of action has no true moral worth. It is on a level with actions arising from other inclinations, such as the inclination to honor, which, if fortunately directed to what in fact accords with duty and is generally useful and thus honorable, deserves praise and encouragement but no esteem. For the maxim lacks the moral import of an action done not from inclination but from duty. But assume that the mind of that friend to mankind was clouded by a sorrow of his own which extinguished all sympathy with the lot of others and that he still had the power to benefit others in distress, but that their need left him untouched because he was preoccupied with his own need. And now suppose him to tear himself, unsolicited by inclination, out of this dead insensibility and to perform this action only from duty and without any inclination—then for the first time his action has genuine moral worth.[7]

In this and similar passages Kant has put his point in such a way as to lead to the misconception that only what we dislike doing can have moral worth. Perhaps some persons have held this unattractive and indeed absurd doctrine, but not Kant. He is only making the point, with which common sense would not disagree, that my inclinations have nothing to do with my obligations. They may, of course, coincide. But if I do something that is right—that is, in accordance with duty— and if I can honestly say either (a) "I wasn't at all inclined to do it, but I did it anyway because it was my duty" or (b) "I did it, and in doing it I followed my inclination; but even had I not been inclined to do it, I know I would have done it just the same, because I realized it was my duty," then and only then does my action have moral worth. But to Kant, and to us too if we are aware of our powers of rationalization, it is an open question whether anyone ever could say either of these things honestly. Therefore, it is also an open question whether any action having moral worth has ever been done by anybody.

Kant makes the point in his own terminology this way.

> For the will stands, as it were, at the crossroads halfway between its *a priori* principle which is formal and its *a posteriori* incentive which is material. Since it must be determined by something, if it is done from duty it must be determined by the formal principle of volition as such since every material principle has been withdrawn from it.[8]

An "*a posteriori* incentive" to the will is an inclination based on experience, in the sense that only through experience can I know or guess what the usual consequences of action will be. For instance, you have an incentive to punt on the fourth down because experience of football games has shown that other courses of action are usually riskier. If you deal fairly with your customers because honesty is the best policy, it is only experience that can teach you that honesty is rewarded financially. These incentives are material: they point to some particular gain to you, some material advantage, that you hope to reap. But if you avoid unnecessary roughness even though you could get away with it or deal honestly with your customers simply because that is right, you do so regardless of material advantage; you adhere strictly to the form of rightness, the "rules of the game." Thus the principle of your action is formal, and also *a priori* because rules of games and of morals are not generalizations from experience. Nobody *discovered* that touchdowns count six points or that cheating is dishonest.

The Nature of Duty

Kant defines duty as "the necessity of an action executed from respect for law."[9] This difficult saying is the key to Kant's ethical theory. We shall approach it through an example he discusses concerning the wrongness of telling lies.

You are in a tight spot, and you think you might get out of it by making a promise that you have no intention of keeping. How shall you decide whether to do this? There are two lines of thought that both lead to a decision not to make the false promise.

In the first you picture to yourself the probable consequences of making a false promise. You convince yourself that when you are found out (as is likely), your credit will sink so low that in the end you will be in more trouble than you are already. So out of prudence you decide not to lie. What then is the maxim of your action, that is, the rule you are following? It is "When the probable consequences to yourself of lying are more disastrous than those of telling the truth, don't lie." In other words, "Lie only if you are pretty sure to get away with it."

In the second you simply decide that lying is not the thing to do, not even pondering the probable consequences. The maxim of your action in this case is the simple command, "Don't lie."

In the second case you act from duty, in the first only in accordance with duty. Wherein lies the difference?

Kant's answer is this. Let us try to imagine each of these maxims turned into a universal law. To imagine the maxim "Don't lie" turned into a universal law is just to imagine that everybody acts in accordance with it; in short, to picture a world in which "Nobody lies" is a true description of behavior. It is clear (Kant holds) that we can imagine such a condition.

But now let us try to imagine a state of things in which "Everybody lies when he or she is pretty sure to get away with it" is a true description. We find (again Kant holds) that we cannot imagine this. The reason is that if making false promises in difficulties were the universal practice, no false promise would get anyone out of any difficulty, because none would be believed. "Thus my maxim would necessarily destroy itself as soon as it was made a universal law." Universal lying would not just be unpleasant or inconvenient, it would be self-defeating. Thus there could not be universal lying. More strictly speaking, if lying were universal no lie could ever achieve its purpose of deceiving, so lying would be pointless. A lie would no longer *be* a (what we now understand by the word) lie if it were inevitably and routinely recognized as such.

Now to return to your situation where you are trying to decide whether to lie or not, in the world as it is, where lying is common but not universal practice. If you did not believe the lie might succeed, you would have no temptation to tell it. But you now see that in willing a false promise, you are incapable of willing that everybody else in similar circumstances should act the same way; for if you did, and got your wish, there would be nothing for you to gain by lying. "You could will the lie but not a universal law to lie."

This is not merely a curious fact about lying. It explains, Kant holds, why lying is contrary to duty. What is a duty for you must be a duty for anybody else in the same situation. But as we have seen it is impossible for you to will that everybody in your situation should lie; hence your duty is in the opposite direction.

Now we can return to the definition of duty. We have seen that "An action performed from duty does not have its moral worth in the purpose which is to be achieved through it but in the maxim by which it is determined."[10] Now we know why the moral worth lies in the maxim. Only those maxims that are fit to be universal laws are moral maxims. No action can be moral unless it is all right for everybody to act that way. To have your will determined by a maxim that can be universalized is, in ordinary speech, to act in a principled way—or, as Kant puts it, to act "from respect for law." To say that duty is the *necessity* of an action executed from respect for law is to emphasize that as a rational being acting from respect for law you acknowledge that the law lays a demand on you, that the law is not just a piece of advice you are free to follow or reject.

Kant points out that "the conception of the law in itself . . . can be present only in a rational being."[11] It does not make sense to speak of the beasts of the field as moral or as immoral either; Kant finds the connection between morality and reason precisely in this fact—that only a rational being can form a universal conception. Not only that, but only a rational being can act from *respect* for law.

Kant claims that his doctrine of the nature of morality is only what common human reason has always recognized, that "the knowledge of what everyone is obliged to do and thus also to know is within the reach of everyone, even the most ordinary man."[12] And indeed his doctrine is to a large extent a development of what is implicit in the ordinary question "What if everybody behaved that way?" Kant praises the simple unspoiled natural man at the expense of the philosopher who, he thinks, is too inclined to quibble.

The Categorical Imperative

Even though there is no mystery about what morality requires and why it does, in order "to escape from the perplexity of opposing claims and to avoid the danger of losing all genuine moral principles through the equivocation in which reason is easily involved,"[13] Kant deemed it necessary to place the principles of morality on the foundation of proof. He begins his rational reconstruction of ethics with a series of arguments to show that duty is not an empirical concept. The first depends on an interesting principle that there must be really existing examples of empirical concepts, though not of *a priori* notions. Red is an empirical concept—we could not know the meaning of the word apart from experience of instances of what it applies to. So too for happiness. We cannot sensibly ask whether no one has ever been happy, for someone must have been happy sometime in order for the concept to have arisen at all.

If duty were an empirical concept, the word would be a name that we give to a certain aspect of experienced acts, and we would know that since we have the concept there must be instances to which it applies. But as we have seen, Kant denied that we *know* whether in fact there has ever been a single action performed from duty. In taking this position Kant was not being absurdly misanthropic, as at first blush he might seem. The doctrine called psychological hedonism, according to which every deliberate action is motivated by anticipation of pleasure, has had its adherents throughout history and still has. Jeremy Bentham (1748–1832) wrote

> The man who affects to have withdrawn himself from the despotic sway [of pleasure and pain] does not know what he is talking about. To seek pleasure and to shun pain is his sole aim, even at the moment when he is denying himself the greatest enjoyment or courting penalties the most severe.[14]

Bentham thus denies that duty in Kant's sense is as a matter of fact the motive of any human action. Kant treats it as an open question.

Furthermore, Kant held, moral laws are like mathematical statements and principles of science such as the law of causality in holding universally and necessarily. If it is wrong for me to cheat on a fair examination, it must be equally wrong for you or any other rational being—whether here, in Madagascar, or in another galaxy. But as we have seen already, experience cannot give rise to universal and necessary principles. Finally Kant points out that in order to classify what we come upon in experience as moral or the opposite, we must already be in possession of some standard of morality. The standard cannot itself be simply given in experience; for if it were it would have to be some quality of objects, or relation between them, obvious to the perception. Clearly there is no such thing. This is the same point that Hume made in remarking that experience can reveal only how things are, not how they ought to be.

Hume used this argument to support the conclusion that "moral distinctions are not based on reason." Kant, precisely to the contrary, concludes that "all moral concepts have their seat and origin entirely *a priori* in reason . . . Since moral laws should hold for every rational being as such, the principles must be derived from the universal concept of a rational being generally."[15]

Rational Beings and Imperatives

What does it mean to be rational in behavior? We can begin finding the answer to this difficult question by forming the conception of a perfectly good will. Such a will would in every case will "that which reason, independently of inclination, recognizes as practically necessary, i.e., as good."[16] Thus it would always act according to principles. It would recognize the principles but it would not experience them as exercising constraint: the perfect will, by definition, would never have to struggle against temptation, for mere inclinations would have no power over it.

Beasts presumably act only according to their inclinations. They know nothing of principles of morality; thus (like the perfect will) they experience no constraint from them. Only we human beings, because of our unique position between angels and beasts, can experience constraint by a moral law. We often have to fight out the internal battle between what we want, impulsively, to do and what as rational beings we know we ought to do. In this situation reason commands or constrains the rebellious will to act in a principled manner. "The formula of this command is called an *imperative*."

Not every imperative, however, is an imperative of morality. We come to recognize, as a result of deliberation, rules of the form "If you want to achieve the end *E*, adopt the means *M*." These Kant calls *hypothetical* imperatives. They exert constraint on us only to the extent that we do, in fact, desire the end *E*. *E* may be anything—healing a sick person or poisoning a healthy one.

But is there not one end that everyone desires, namely, happiness? Kant admits that there is. Therefore imperatives of *prudence*, of the form "If you want to secure your happiness, do such and such," are not arbitrary or transitory. Many moralists have based their systems on them. Nevertheless, Kant insists, they are "still only hypothetical; the action is not absolutely commanded but commanded only as a means to another end."

Then is every imperative conditional on some presupposed end, and in consequence hypothetical? No, says Kant.

> There is one imperative which directly commands a certain conduct without making its condition some purpose to be reached by it. This imperative is categorical. It concerns not the material of the action and its intended result but the form and the principle from which it results. What is essentially good in it consists in the intention, the result being what it may. This imperative may be called the imperative of morality.[17]

Consider:

A. If you want to confuse Jones, who expects you to lie, tell him the truth. (Rule of Skill)
B. If you want to be happy, always tell the truth. (It works out to your advantage in the long run.) (Rule of Prudence)
C. Tell the truth. (Categorical Imperative)

A is sound advice in case you are interested in bamboozling Jones; otherwise it is irrelevant. *B* is perhaps never irrelevant, yet its relevance is dependent on the existence and nature of the end. Only *C* is unconditional. We do not preface it with an 'if' clause, not even "If you want to be a moral man." For the obligation to tell the truth holds irrespective of anyone's desires. You are not released from the obligations of morality by declaring that you have no interest in morality.

But why should you acknowledge any obligation other than the pursuit of your own interests? Kant's answer is, "Because you are a rational being." The connection between being rational and being under unconditional moral obligation is derived as follows.

(1) Any categorical (nonhypothetical) imperative must be of the form "You must do such and such"; it cannot have an 'if' clause. It is also a law obliging all rational beings. Therefore we can rewrite it, at this point, as "All rational beings must do such and such."

(2) But we cannot replace "such and such" with the name of any particular action, such as brushing the teeth, since particular acts presuppose particular circumstances that make them appropriate. We would be back at the hypothetical imperative, "All rational beings, who are both interested in retaining their teeth and in danger of incurring dental decay, must brush their teeth."

(3) Hence "such and such" must refer to a principle of action rather than a particular act. We can rewrite it, "All rational beings must act according to such and such a principle (or principles)."

(4) "Acting according to such and such a principle" means "acting so that the maxim of your action conforms to the principle." Then the categorical imperative becomes "All rational beings must act so that their maxims conform to such and such a principle (or principles)."

(5) But for the same reason that no particular act can be prescribed to all rational beings, neither can any particular principle be prescribed. There is then nothing left for the maxim to conform to except the idea of principle (or of law) as such. "All rational beings must act so that their maxims conform to the idea of law as such."

(6) The idea of law as such is just the conception of universality, exceptionlessness. Therefore when a maxim of action conforms to the idea of law as such, what this amounts to is that the maxim must not admit of exceptions. And this means that it must be capable of being universalized; there must be nothing about it that would lead to absurdity if we tried to conceive of the maxim as describing universal behavior.

So at last we come to Kant's first formulation of the categorical imperative: "Act only according to that maxim by which you can at the same time will that it should become a universal law."[18]

Kant formulated the categorical imperative in two other ways as well. The second statement involves the notion of a *rational end*, "something the existence of which in itself has absolute worth." The goals of our pursuits are in general relative to our interests. However, Kant declares, "man and, in general, every rational being exists as an end in himself and not merely as a means to be arbitrarily used by this or that will."[19] Things have worth relative to persons who desire them; the worth of persons, however, is not relative but absolute. At any rate, *you* think of yourself in this way. And if you have any right so to think, you are bound, as a rational being, to admit that every other human being has the same right—that is, has absolute worth.

If rational nature is an absolute end, then the determination of the will by a motive referring to that end will be an unconditional ground of morality. Hence the second form of the categorical imperative: "Act so that you treat humanity, whether in your own person or in that of another, always as an end and never as a means only."[20]

The word "only" in this formula should be emphasized. Kant does not mean that it is always or even ever wrong to treat humanity as a means; if it were, hiring a plumber would be immoral. What is wrong is treating a plumber or any other rational being as a *mere* means, as a "living tool" (Aristotle's definition of a slave)—or as we say, using people.

The two forms are combined in a third: "Act as if you were a legislator in the realm of ends." The conception of a realm of ends is that of a "systematic union of different rational beings through common laws." Ideally, rational beings would make for themselves just those laws prescribed by objective reason, not laws serving the interest of any particular individual or clique. Obedience to those laws would never be a matter of bowing to force, nor indeed of deferring to the will of another, for every rational will would prescribe the same laws. Hence in this realm everyone would be at once the legislator and the subject. This would be government by consent in a strict and absolute sense.

It is fairly easy to see that the three versions of the categorical imperative are, as Kant claimed, equivalent. At any rate, all of them forbid sharp practices. Whether one can deduce from them the immorality of suicide, as Kant maintained, is not so clear perhaps.

Freedom of the Will

> When Duty whispers low, *Thou must,*
> The youth replies, *I can.*

Emerson's verses are (not coincidentally) thoroughly Kantian. The categorical imperative tells us what moral action is like, but not that it is even possible. One thing more is needed: assurance that nothing prevents us from following the dictates of duty.

Kant, as we have seen, held that nature forms a determined system; the law of causation holds without exception throughout. We—our bodies at any rate—are parts of nature, therefore determined in our motions. Thus there seems no difference, save in complication, between the motion of the earth, sun, and moon that constitutes an eclipse and the motion of my larynx and tongue that constitutes telling a lie. If there was an eclipse, there could not have *not* been one. Likewise it seems that if I told a lie I could not have told the truth. But I could not have been under an obligation that I could not have fulfilled. Morality evaporates.

Kant's maneuver to get out of this difficulty is similar to Descartes' (the pineal gland), but more subtle. He refuses to hold that human behavior—the motions of the human body including larynx and tongue—are exceptional. They are determined, caused. If, then, the world of nature were the only world, freedom and hence morality would be illusory. Let us not forget, however, that nature is only the world of possible experience, of phenomena or appearances, and that behind nature lies the intelligible world (as Kant paradoxically calls it) of things in themselves. Man is a citizen of both worlds; the contradiction between freedom and determinism is an illusion that is resolved if we "think of man in a different sense and relationship when we call him free from that in which we consider him as part of nature and subject to its laws." Kant did not claim to have demonstrated that man, considered as thing in itself, must enjoy the advantage of a kind of causality called freedom; nor did Kant claim even to have rendered the notion of freedom intelligible. What he did maintain was that since causality is a category applying only within the world of phenomena, we are not entitled to conclude that it applies to things in themselves. They (including the "intelligible" self) may act in some quite different manner satisfying the requisites of morality. Demonstration of the possibility is sufficient for moral purposes, since we are in any case obliged at every moment to *assume* that we can act morally.

The human will stands between the two worlds. On the side of the sensible world it is buffeted like everything else by sticks and stones and temptations. But on the side of the intelligible world it is, in the end, master of its fate, a giver of universal laws in the realm of ends—or at least it may be. That is how a categorical imperative is possible.

God

Experience is open-ended, but it is the nature of the mind always to postulate completion. We have seen how this inevitable tendency leads us to the attempt to prove that the world had (or had not) a beginning. This Cosmological Idea (the word 'Idea' is here used disparagingly) is, however, only one of the transcendental illusions. More notoriously still, Reason in chafing at the bonds of experience tries to prove the existence of God.

Ultimately, Kant held, there are only three arguments for the existence of God. The most popular, the argument from design or "physico-theological proof," as he calls it, is the weakest. As Hume had noted, even if we grant all its premises this argument by itself can prove neither the immateriality nor oneness nor even continued existence of the designer of the world—for the architects and craftsmen we meet with, and who furnish the analogy, are fleshly, mortal, and many. Hence this proof cannot yield the desired conclusion unless supplemented by the Cosmological Argument, or argument to an ultimate cause or reason of everything there is—the argument that the contingency of everything in the world must be grounded in a necessary being. But that argument, in turn, cannot work unless its conclusion is true, that is, unless there really does exist a necessary being. Now a necessary being is by definition a being whose essence includes existence—a being such that from a clear conception of what sort of thing it is, we can infer with certainty that it exists in reality. But if there is such a being, then the Ontological Argument of Anselm and Descartes must be valid—for that argument simply amounts to asserting that in the case of God, the inference from notion to reality is warranted and necessitated. Therefore the Ontological Argument turns out to be basic. If it works, the others are redundant; if it fails, they fail with it.

Kant's demolition of the Ontological Argument is famous. The gist of the argument is that when we think of God we must assign to Him suitable predicates: we must acknowledge that God is most powerful, most wise, most just, and so on. For no being that was not perfectly just, wise, and so on could be God, by definition, however interesting, comforting, or frightening he might otherwise be. This train of thought led Anselm and Descartes to infer that among the predicates that must apply to God, existence must be included—a being lacking that supremely important property would surely not be God.

This thought takes for granted that existence is a predicate, and that is what Kant denied. To form the concept 'tiger' is to add together all the predicates applicable to tigers—striped, carnivorous, growling, having-retractile-claws, whiskered, ferocious, and so on. But the "and so on" cannot include 'existent' (or any synonym or near-synonym such as 'real'), for existence, unlike ferocity, is no part of the concept. To say that tigers are striped, ferocious, and existent tells us that the concept of striped and ferocious animals applies to some things—has instances.

> A hundred real dollars do not contain a penny more than a hundred possible dollars. For as the latter signify the concept, and the former the object and the positing of the object, should the former contain more than the latter, my concept would not, in that case, express the whole object, and would not therefore be an adequate concept of it.[21]

The point is the same as Hume's, "To reflect on anything simply, and to reflect on it as existent, are nothing different from each other."[22] This may not seem evident to us; we protest that to think of the philosopher king is one thing, to think that the philosopher king exists is another. Yes, but the *notion* we have of the philosopher king in the two cases is not different—as it would be if existence were an added predicate.

> By whatever and by however many predicates I may think a thing (even in completely determining it), nothing is really added to it, if I add that the thing exists. Otherwise, it would not be the same that exists, but something more than was contained in the concept, and I could not say that the exact object of my concept existed.[23]

Kant has a second and equally devastating criticism of the argument. Even waiving the point about existence not being a predicate and allowing that God possesses by definition the property of existence, it still does not follow that God exists. For letting 'divine' mean the sum of properties that God has by definition, including existence, then it is indeed a necessary truth that whatever is divine must exist. But this does not tell us that anything divine exists. All it says is that *if* anything is divine, then that thing must be, among other things, real.

> The attempt to establish the existence of a supreme being by means of the famous ontological argument of Descartes is therefore merely so much labor and effort lost; we can no more extend our stock of knowledge by mere ideas, than a merchant can better his position by adding a few zeroes to his cash account.[24]

The Regulative Use of the Ideas of Pure Reason

You might think that one who so ruthlessly demolished the rational props of religion would have done so with the intention of discouraging religious practices and institutions. And indeed, when in 1786 the bigoted Frederick William II succeeded the enlightened Frederick the Great on the Prussian throne, Kant was forbidden to publish anything further on religion. (He complied without a murmur.) Yet in the Preface to his first *Critique*, Kant wrote that he had "found it necessary to deny knowledge, in order to make room for faith." In fact Kant's attitude was a complex one.

Although we cannot establish on rational grounds the reality of God, freedom, and immortality, or show that the world as a whole has limits in time and space, Kant declared these ideas indispensable as guides for thought. We cannot understand the world unless we can look on it as a totality, the unified production of a unified intelligence. In our activities as moral agents we must suppose that we are free; we can make no sense of our practices on the opposite supposition. The Ideas of Reason thus are to some extent analogous to the categories. The difference is that the categories are constitutive of experience—the phenomenal world, the world of experience, really is, and really is known to be, substantial and causally related, for instance—but the Ideas are merely regulative. We do know that there is a reality outside experience, but we cannot *know* whether it contains anything to which the notion of God would be applicable, nor can we know in what sense it constitutes a unity.

It may be cold comfort to the pious to tell them that no one can know whether God exists, but at any rate it is all right to behave as if He did. However, the religious should perhaps not complain. We have seen how the theistic worldview was threatened with intellectual annihilation by the new science. Kant in "denying knowledge," that is, denying the unrestricted applicability of scientific concepts, was doing all that could be done to make room for faith.

Kant sometimes went farther than the mere demonstration that we do not know for certain that religion is false. He produced what has come to be called, somewhat inaccurately, the moral argument for the existence of God and the immortality of the soul. Kant held it to be a demand of reason that moral progress, the improvement of the moral nature, should reach its goal, and that ultimately happiness and moral worth should be correlated. The former demand requires the existence of the soul, if not forever, at least immensely longer than the mortal span; while the latter requires not only an afterlife but a supernatural dispenser of reward. Therefore, God and immortality are postulates of practical reason.

Kant here undoubtedly touched upon an important source of religious sentiment, one so powerful indeed that it made Kant himself seemingly oblivious to his own noble insistence that acts done with an eye toward reward are not moral acts.

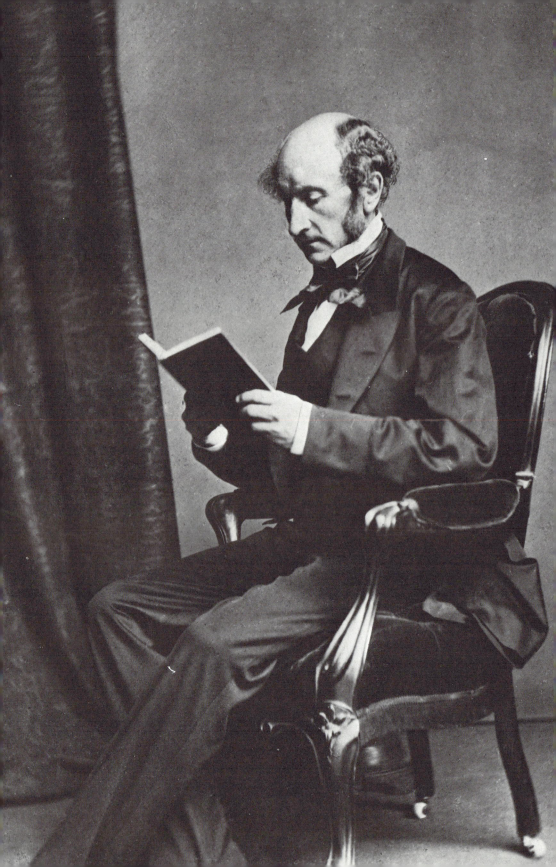

VII

The Nineteenth Century

42

Hegel

HERACLITUS, PARMENIDES, PLOTINUS, SPINOZA, and Hegel hold that "It is wise to agree that all things are one." They are the holistic, integrative philosophers. Analytic philosophers such as Democritus and Hume try to understand complexes by reducing them to their simple parts and to the relations in which these parts stand—so as to rebuild the complex, at least in imagination. You comprehend a motorcycle when you can take it apart and put it back together. Integrative philosophers, on the other hand, believe that the things we deal with and whose significance we try to grasp are parts of larger unities; they become intelligible only when fit, actually or imaginatively, into that unity. You cannot understand the carburetor in isolation; it makes no sense just sitting there; its reality consists in the role it plays in the whole functioning of the motorcycle. But the cycle itself cannot be understood except in relation to the interests and values of the motorcycle club, the police, and the Japanese economy. You cannot fully understand anything until you understand everything.

Integrative philosophies are perennially fascinating. The notion that the universe must make sense and that to do so it must constitute an organic whole in which nothing partial is fully intelligible has inherent appeal, as does the complementary dispraise of analysis as falsification or worse: cutting up kills. Uncompromisingly analytic philosophies such as Hume's, in which "objects have no discoverable connexion together," are apt to seem gloomy and frightening even to their authors. Analysis breeds loneliness; companionship is integration. Religions—at least monotheisms—are integrative.

The philosophy of Hegel is, so to speak, the negative of Hume's. It is the most thorough attempt at an integrative philosophy that the world has yet seen.

Life

Georg Wilhelm Friedrich Hegel was born in Stuttgart in 1770. His life had more variety than Kant's, and almost some excitement: he finished his first big book in Jena the night before the battle in which Napoleon crushed the Prussians. Clutching the last pages of the manuscript, he fled to his publisher in Bamberg. But on the whole he lived in academic tranquillity.

Hegel was educated as a theologian, but decided not to follow that profession when he found he could not accept the orthodoxy of the time. He was attracted to a pantheistic and naturalistic conception of God's relation to the world; he even wrote (but did not publish) a book about Jesus in which the virgin birth was not mentioned. He was a private tutor in aristocratic households until the age of thirty, when he went to the University of Jena as a *Privatdozent* in philosophy. From 1808 until 1816 he was principal of a high school in Nuremberg. The book completed in Jena was *The Phenomenology of Mind*, an enormous work though intended merely as an introduction to his philosophy. In Nuremberg he wrote and published the two volumes of his *Logic*; in 1816–1818, while Professor at Heidelberg, the *Encyclopedia of the Philosophical Sciences in Outline*. He then accepted a call to the University of Berlin, where in connection with lectures on philosophy of law he wrote the *Philosophy of Right* (1821). After his death in the cholera epidemic of 1831, his students pooled their notes to publish his lectures on aesthetics, philosophy of religion, history of philosophy, and philosophy of history, in the *Collected Works* (18 volumes) 1832–1840.

Leading Principles

Philosophy is the attempt to understand what is ultimate: the whole of things, the Absolute, God. The Absolute is the antithesis of abstraction; it is the ultimate concrete thing. However, it must be grasped in its manifold aspects. Hence the title Hegel gave to his principal work, *Encyclopedia*. This is not a book of alphabetized entries in which you can look things up. It mirrors the Absolute in being not a collection but a Whole.

The simplest kind of integrative philosophy, mysticism, attains its goal quickly by asserting that reality is a unity—multiplicity and differentiation are only appearance or illusion. Hegel ridiculed the Absolute set up in this manner as "the night in which all cows are black." His integration was to be one in which differences were explained and ultimately reconciled, not airily abolished.

Thus unlike mystics he did not deny the distinction of subject and object in all experience. He insisted upon it. However, there are degrees of interpenetration of subject and object, corresponding to different kinds of experience. In mere sense experience this interpenetration is least, subject and object barely touching, so to speak. In perceptual knowledge, where the reality of the object is inferred and affirmed, there is the beginning of a fusion. It becomes more intimate in scientific, moral, and religious experience, reaching its culmination in the self-knowledge of the Absolute, where the object is itself the mind that knows.

Reality is a living, evolving process, not a mere succession but a rational development, as shown by the order both of the heavens and of living creatures. The process is teleological: later stages of development are the reasons for the earlier. Man—more specifically, man in the State—is, up to now at least, the goal of the process.

Understanding, Reason, Dialectic

The method of philosophy, the process whereby comprehension of the Absolute is to be attained, consists in development of Concepts ("Notions" in some translations). To grasp what Hegel means by a Concept, let us begin with his account of the kind of thinking that develops it.

Hegel makes a distinction between Reason and Understanding that is somewhat different from Kant's. Understanding is exhibited in the common sense of the people, in the natural sciences and mathematics, and in analytical philosophy. To the understanding, things are fixed and separate. Laying down definitions, demonstrating conclusions, analyzing—these are the works of the Understanding. Reason, on the other hand, is what thinks dialectically. Kant offered a similar characterization, but for him dialectical thinking oscillated between contradictory conclusions. To Hegel, on the contrary, dialectical thinking proceeds deliberately by means of contradictions to attain direct insight into ultimate reality. Every abstract idea, when thought about strenuously enough, leads to its own negation; but idea and negation both are then taken up into a further idea richer and more concrete than either, until we come at last to the "concrete universal," the Concept.

For example, let us consider the most abstract of all ideas, that of Being. Everything there is has Being. It follows that if we are told about something only that it has Being, we have not particularized that thing, we know nothing of it. There is no difference between saying of a thing that it has Being and saying nothing about it. The concept Being has led us to its own negation, Nothing. Having got this far, analytical thinking—Understanding—halts. Hume pointed out that "To reflect on any thing simply, and to reflect on it as existent, are nothing different from each other," and adjourned to the backgammon table. Dialectical thinking, however, notes that from the contradiction—the union of Being with its negation Nothing or Nonbeing—there emerges the idea of Becoming, the transition from the one to the other; the Becoming, moreover, of something definite. To be definite is to have some Quality or other—as neither Being nor Nothing, as such, has. Quality, admitting as it does of the opposition of more and less, implies a unit, hence Quantity.

This example has illustrated a nontemporal development from abstract to (relatively) concrete. Dialectical development of a Concept may also be a process in time; there is no ultimate distinction between the processes of thought and of history, for "the real is the rational, the rational is the real." The history of philosophy exhibits this dialectical enrichment of concepts. Plato was thinking dialectically when he took up the motionless Being of Parmenides and the restless Becoming of Heraclitus into the reconciling notion of Participation. In more recent times the opposition between Continental Rationalism and British Empiricism led to the Critical philosophy of Kant and ultimately to Hegel, in whose all-encompassing philosophy every insight of the past was to have its place, according to its author.

The dialectical development of the "Concept in itself" is what Hegel calls Logic, a use of the term with more affinity to the Heraclitean and Stoic notion of *logos* than with theory of argument. Philosophy of Nature, in opposition to this, is the development of the Concept not "in itself" but "for itself": the Concept as externalized. (Again we must remember the essential unity of thought and nature.) Nature is what exists in space, "the non-sensible sensible" as Hegel in a brilliant paradox summed up the Kantian doctrine—which he accepted—of space as the form of outer intuition. All the parts of Nature are external to each other—yet Nature is a whole.

In Logic, thinking takes place in terms of pure universality; that is, the notions dealt with are all universals, no names of particulars occur. In Philosophy of Nature, on the other hand, the subject is pure particularity or difference: every element in Nature is an individual. The synthesis of Logic and Philosophy of Nature is Philosophy of Mind. Mind, as we saw when discussing Leibniz, is the only thing that is an absolute unity, an individual thing, while yet containing difference within itself. It contains representations of space without itself being spatial, and temporal sequences without itself being a temporal sequence—at any rate not in the same sense; the memory of a play that went on for three hours is not itself a three-hour-long memory.

The Absolute Mind and the Absolute Idea

Thus the requirement that the Absolute be an integral unity of all that is real in experience entails that it is a mind, or mind-like being. Hegel argued also for the mental nature of the Absolute in this way. The Absolute must be free. For from the very conception we see that nothing can limit it; it must be infinite. Therefore the Absolute cannot be matter, for the nature of matter is to be unfree, pushed and pulled from outside. Freedom is characteristic of mind and only of mind. And indeed only in self-consciousness does freedom reach its completion. Therefore, the Absolute is self-conscious mind.

Our own finite minds are capable of integrating the universal and the particular to a certain extent; the process is carried to completion in the Absolute Mind. All the Concepts, the various aspects of the Absolute, are therein apprehended as a unity, the Absolute Idea. This integrative apprehension is the activity of God. We are reminded of Aristotle's God, thought thinking of thought. Though the comparison is just, the difference is considerable. Aristotle's God eternally apprehended the timeless relations of abstract entities, as in geometry. For Hegel, however, geometry and all mathematics belong to the Understanding. The Hegelian Absolute in its self-consciousness is conscious of everything there is, everything concrete and temporal as well as everything abstract and eternal—or rather, even more so; the merely abstract and eternal drop out of the Concrete Universal that is the content of the Absolute Mind.

Perhaps an example can help to make this clear. There are various ways in which we can apprehend falling bodies. We can look at them, we can time their descent with stopwatches. In sense knowledge, or perception, the object is from our point of view entirely external to us. Or we can study falling bodies scientifically; we can work out the formula $s = \frac{1}{2} gt^2$, and use it to predict time of impact given time of release. Here, however, we are only at the level of Understanding. Another mode of apprehension is achieved if we take up skydiving so that we *are* a falling body. Our knowledge in this case will be concrete—but only of one particular falling body. Perhaps, though, we can attain to some glimmering of what it would be like to know all falling bodies in the same intimate way that we as finite beings can know only one. Our knowledge would then be immediate and noninferential; we could dispense with formulas and calculations, since direct awareness of all facts would preclude the need for inferences. The unity of thought and its object would then be achieved. This may suggest the kind of consciousness that, multiplied to infinity, is the Absolute Idea.

However, it would be a mistake to suppose that in Hegel's view God, the Absolute Mind, is a being over and above the consciousnesses of you and me and all the other minds there are and have been and will be, or that God thinks thoughts over and above your thoughts and mine. To the contrary, Hegel like Spinoza holds God to be immanent in the world, not separate from it. God is the integral unity of you and me and the rest; you and I have no reality or meaning apart from God but neither does God, even in His thought, have any aspects not to be found in the finite beings integrated in Him—you and I and the others. The progress of philosophy is, literally, the process whereby the Absolute attains self-consciousness.

According to Hegel this philosophical result is symbolized in religion, which also develops dialectically. The divine, first conceived as absolute Being, undergoes dialectical transformation into its negation in the Greek gods—who were so concrete and particularized that they were nothing but human beings writ large. The third stage is Christianity, whose central doctrine is the Incarnation of the divine in man, infinite Being manifested in the finite. For this reason Christianity is the absolute religion.

Philosophy of History and Politics

History (Hegel claimed) makes sense. Its theme is the development of the Concept of freedom. The passions of men are the means by which this development is furthered; its fulfillment is the State.

Freedom is not to be found in the realm of mere matter; it is a quality of mind, specifically of will, which is even more essential to mind than is the faculty of cognition. By freedom Hegel did not mean the liberty to do as you please. That is only the liberty of indifference, or "abstract or negative" freedom, which is destructive and irrational—as the French Revolution made horrifyingly plain. Concrete freedom, the good kind, is not opposed to constraint, but even requires it, for it is the rational organization of feelings and impulses.

Rationality in action is a conception that has no application outside a society. The rational man conforms himself to the needs of society, obeys the social imperatives, and thereby achieves his rational ends. Therefore the rational man, and only he, is free. The criminal, insofar as he is rational, wills the punishment of crime; therefore, he wills his own punishment.

The State, the total culture, is the concrete union of objective freedom and subjective passion. The individual has freedom and significance only in a State. The Absolute Mind historically manifests itself in particular States and even individual human beings. After witnessing Napoleon's ride through Jena, Hegel is reported to have said that he had seen the World Spirit on horseback.

At every stage of world history one people preeminently manifests the progress of the Spirit. Once upon a time China was in the vanguard. But in an Oriental despotism only one man is free, the despot; and not even he, really, for his freedom is of the negative, capricious, irrational kind. Greece and Rome successively though imperfectly manifested the advance to rational freedom under law. After many backings and turnings—Hegel did not suppose the course of history to be straightforward—freedom in the nineteenth century reached its highest expression in the Prussian State.

World history, the development of the Concept of Freedom, like other dialectical developments proceeds by means of conflicts—mostly wars—in which, however, the vanquished is never utterly destroyed; what there was of value in the defeated culture is taken up into the next stage, we are assured.

Whether or not the world develops dialectically, Hegel's philosophy did after the author's death, as we shall soon see.

43

Positivism

THE VIEW IS VERY old that there can be no human knowledge beyond what is given in experience and systematized from that experience in science. Perhaps Anaximenes in rejecting Anaximander's Boundless assumed some such principle. In more modern times this antimetaphysical outlook has been especially associated with the British. William of Ockham and Francis Bacon were among the founders of a movement that culminated in Hume's advice to commit to the flames the books of metaphysics because they contained neither mathematical nor experimental reasoning. Most French philosophers of the eighteenth century subscribed to this tenet. Kant's philosophy issued in the same conclusion, though expressed less harshly than Hume's.

It remained, however, to confer unity on this shared viewpoint by giving it a label. To Claude Henri de Rouvroy, Comte de Saint-Simon (1760–1825) came the happy inspiration to call this essentially negative philosophy Positivism.

Comte

Definitive form was given to Positivism by Saint-Simon's pupil and secretary, Auguste Comte (1798–1857), in lectures published as *Course in Positive Philosophy*, six volumes 1830–1842.

Comte differed from most of his antimetaphysical predecessors through his interest in and respect for the history of ideas. A concept can be understood, he declared, only through knowledge of its development. In this emphasis, Comte almost shares a point of contact with the arch-metaphysician Hegel.

At the outset of the *Positive Philosophy*, Comte announced the Law of Three Stages according to which all departments of knowledge pass successively through theological and metaphysical forms to the positive. In the theological or fictitious stage, events are explained as due to the will of the gods. It is no accident or aberration that early thought is mythical; in order for facts to be explained there must be a theory, and in primitive conditions no framework for explanation can exist except that provided by the model of human activity. Theological explanation culminates in monotheism, the unified world picture that ascribes everything to the intentions of one great spirit.

In the metaphysical or abstract stage, explanation in personal terms is discarded as too crude. Instead, there is accounting for events in terms of impersonal and hidden causes: forces, essences, faculties. The ideal of metaphysical explanation is reached when everything is referred to one Nature, or Absolute, as in the philosophies of Spinoza and Hegel. This stage is transitional between theology and the final stage, the scientific or Positive, in which explanation becomes "simply the establishment of a connection between single phenomena and some general facts, the number of which continually diminishes with the progress of science." Particular phenomena are explained when shown to be instances of a law of nature, a regularity of experience. The laws themselves are explained by being shown to be consequences of more general laws. Falling bodies on the surface of the earth conform to Galileo's law. The orbits of the planets are predictable through deduction from Kepler's three laws of planetary motion. But Galileo's and Kepler's laws are themselves all deducible from Newton's one law of universal gravitation, which explains all these phenomena by showing their interconnections as manifestations of the same set of regularities, however diverse they may appear to be. However, it is senseless to ask "What is gravity?"; positive science does not deal in essences.

The ideal of positive science would be a unification of explanation under a single all-embracing law or "general fact." If, for example, electricity and magnetism could be shown to be gravitational phenomena at the micro level, the ultimate unity might be achieved. Comte, however, was skeptical of the possibility of completing science in this way even theoretically, and he was sure that in practice we will never be able to predict the complicated motions of living creatures from the fundamental laws of physics.

Every thinking man, Comte assures us, will remember personally having passed through the three stages: as a child he was a theologian, as a youth a metaphysician, and finally in maturity a natural scientist.

Classification of the Sciences

The sciences, according to Comte, are

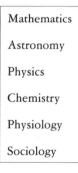

Mathematics

Astronomy

Physics

Chemistry

Physiology

Sociology

This order is both logical and historical: logical, in that each science presupposes all the others higher on the list; historical, for the order is that in which these disciplines have passed (or are passing) through the three stages. Physiology or biology in Comte's day was still metaphysical insofar as many biologists considered the phenomena of life to have a different essence from the rest of nature and to be explainable only in terms of a mysterious vital force.

Comte invented the name 'sociology', and claimed to be the man who pushed the study of society across the line from metaphysics into science. In the theological stage the interactions of men were explained by the interventions of the gods, as in Homer. In the metaphysical stage the political philosophers had recourse to abstract notions such as sovereignty, the general will, or the state of nature. In the positive era it will be realized that the conditions of social existence can be studied like any other collection of phenomena, its laws ascertained and used for prediction and control. We shall then have a "social physics," divisible into two parts: social statics, the theory of order; social dynamics, the theory of progress.

The practical application, the social engineering so to speak, is to be based on a utilitarian conception of the good. But utopia cannot be produced by simply appealing to people's reasoned estimate of even their own good. If altruism (another word invented by Comte) is to triumph over egoism, there must be a moral regeneration—nothing less than a new religion—to take the emotional place of Christianity, which is no longer an effective force in guiding human behavior. In his *System of Positive Politics* (1851–1854), Comte proceeded to invent the Religion of Humanity. Religion, he held, is the submission to a Power outside ourselves; the Positive stage of religion will find that power not in myths or occult forces but in experience. There really does exist a Great Being to which we owe submission: Humanity. Earth the Great Fetish and Space the Great Way make up the remainder of the Positivist Trinity. The calendar is to be reformed, with days commemorating not saints but men who have benefitted humanity; major figures such as Gutenberg and Shakespeare give their names to the thirteen months. There is to be a ritual and a priesthood. (Unsympathetic persons derided this scheme as "Catholicism minus Christianity.")

Positive society, or "sociocracy," will revive the advantages of cohesion, vitality, the respect for authority that characterized society in the theological stage—but without the drawback of belief in fictions. In the scientific world, what it is necessary to believe will be true. Since this will be so, there can be no valid objection, Comte thought, to the absolutism of the sociocracy, which is to be ruled like Plato's ideal state by philosophers.

Comte, like Rousseau, died in poverty and obscurity, leaving his ideas to simmer and later come to a boil in the events of the world. But as his poverty was less extreme than Rousseau's, so his influence was less world-shaking. Only in Latin America was Comtean Positivism adopted by men of action. The Brazilian revolution of 1889 that overthrew the monarchy was largely the work of Positivists. In consequence the flag of Brazil bears the motto ORDEM E PROGRESO. A Positivist church exists in Rio de Janeiro.

Mach

Comte did not concern himself overmuch with fundamental problems of theory of knowledge, such as what the immediate object of awareness is and what might be its relation to an external world. Comte was an outside-in philosopher who took for granted the existence of facts and the ability of the human mind to know them, if only not distracted by metaphysics.

On the other hand, the Austrian physicist and philosopher of science Ernst Mach (1838–1916) deemed it necessary to analyze the nature of a fact if science was to be scraped clean of metaphysical accretions. The problem to Mach was not one of ensuring the intellectual supremacy of science by beating down its rivals; the elimination of metaphysics was rather a necessary task within science. Thus

Mach, so far from styling himself a positivist, demurred at being called a philosopher at all. His principal book of interest to philosophers, the *Analysis of Sensation* (1886), is in form a report of certain experiments bearing on the physiology of the sensory apparatus.

Mach's scientific interests were very wide. He complained that the state of scientific thought in his time was such that when he passed from one realm of scientific discourse to another it was as if he were literally traveling between different worlds. The world of electricity was composed of rubbery fields; the chemists made theirs of hard atoms; the psychologists talked of egos. Which was the real world? None of them, Mach concluded, remembering Kant, whose *Prolegomena to Any Future Metaphysics* had so impressed him when he was a boy of fifteen. The scientist no more than anyone else is able to penetrate behind experience to the thing-in-itself. If words like 'atom' and 'field' have any reference to reality, they must be fully explicable in terms of what we are, immediately and indubitably, in contact with: our sensations. Indeed, even Kant went astray when he postulated an unknowable thing-in-itself; here Mach followed Berkeley and Hume.

All the sciences deal with one world, the only one there is. Science is description of facts and their connections. Facts are what are immediately given in experience: sense impressions. The world, therefore, consists of sensations, or as Mach sometimes less mentalistically called them, elements. These elements are colors, sounds, pressures, tastes, and the like—Berkeley's ideas, Hume's perceptions, Kant's phenomena. They make up consciousness and the "external world" as well as the body, which is the linkage between them. The difference between the redness and juiciness in the tomato, and in your consciousness, is not of kind but only of relation. "What we call matter is a combination of the elements or sensations according to certain laws."

Scientific conceptions such as field and molecule are fictions, but useful ones. All names, indeed, are conveniences. A word such as 'tomato' designates a certain relatively permanent compound of color, shape, and taste. 'Volcano' and 'war' refer to vastly complicated collections of unlike elements. It is useful to have such words, but they are dangerous insofar as they suggest that wars and volcanoes are unities, things, in the way tomatoes or particular murders are, and can enter into causal and other relations in the same way. Terms in scientific theories are of a special sort, likewise useful but dangerous. Description of heat as a fluid, flowing from hot bodies to cold as water goes from high to low, facilitated understanding of many phenomena. However, the supposition made by literal-minded physicists, that heat was really a subtle fluid, obscured the investigation of frictional production of heat. Just so, Mach advised, the wise chemist will talk *as if* things consisted of tiny molecules strung together from even tinier atoms. He will talk this way because that is how multitudinous facts can be referred to with brevity. But he will not fall into the superstition of believing that there actually are such things in nature. "The concept is to the physicist what a musical note is to a piano player."

44

Marx and Engels

IN THE GENERATION AFTER Hegel's death, his doctrines underwent dialectical development. His followers split into two more or less well-defined groups, Left-Wing and Right-Wing, originally over theological issues but increasingly over the political implications of the dialectic. The right wing tended to view politics in terms of a gradual liberalization; the left conceived it as proceeding by revolutions. Moreover, the left wing substituted a materialist conception of Being for Hegel's idealism.

Ludwig Feuerbach (1804–1872), philosophically the most important of these "young Hegelians," was an atheist and a materialist, in consequence of which he was deprived of his teaching post at the age of 32 and lived thereafter in poverty. Nevertheless he stayed out of politics, a stance that provoked his most famous follower to remark

> Philosophers have only *interpreted* the world in various ways; the point is to *change* it.[1]

Life of Marx

The author, Karl Marx, was born in 1818 in the ancient Rhineland town of Trier, son of a prominent and prosperous Jewish lawyer. When Karl was six, the entire family were baptized Lutherans in order to circumvent disabilities imposed on Jews by the Prussian government, which had annexed the region. The elder Marx was a Voltairean, uninterested in religion. Karl was also in his youthful period something of a protégé of another Voltairean, the Marxes' neighbor Baron von Westphalen, with whose daughter Jenny he fell in love and eventually married.

Karl attended the Universities of Bonn and Berlin, first as a law student but then changing to philosophy. He was not a diligent scholar and provoked parental displeasure by roistering and extravagant expenditures. Eventually he submitted a Hegelian dissertation on Democritus and Epicurus to the University of Jena, for which he was awarded a doctorate in philosophy.

Barred from an academic career because of atheism, which he did not conceal, after a year of drifting he took a position as editor of the Cologne *Rheinische Zeitung*, a liberal paper whose policies he moved even farther left. He resigned the editorship in 1842 in a futile effort to forestall the banning of the paper. In the following year he and Jenny were married, despite opposition from the families of both, and moved to Paris, where Marx soon made the acquaintance of leading radical intellectuals including the poet Heinrich Heine, the anarchist Mikhail Bakunin, the socialist Pierre-Joseph Proudhon—and another unemployed German, Friedrich Engels.

Engels, a Rhinelander like Marx and two years younger, came from a family of considerable wealth, part owners of textile mills in Bremen and Manchester. Although he never attended a university, being put to on-the-job training in factory management from the age of 18, through his own studies he had made himself a man of broad culture, a student of Hegel, and an accomplished linguist. During a two-year stint at the mill in Manchester, he had found time to write *The Condition of the Working Class in England in 1844*, his first book.

Marx and Engels, finding themselves in agreement in their outlooks, collaborated on a book of social criticism, *The Holy Family*, in 1845. In the same year the French government ordered Marx to leave France. He went to Brussels, where he became associated with a working men's association, the League of the Just, which was in process of reorganizing itself as the Communist Party. He secured for himself and Engels the job of writing a statement of their purpose and principles: *The Communist Manifesto*. It was published in London in 1848, a few weeks before the first of the revolutions that swept Europe in that year. However, it played no part in causing them, despite its prophetic opening line "A specter is haunting Europe—the specter of communism" and its concluding exhortation "WORKINGMEN OF ALL COUNTRIES, UNITE!", and it attracted little notice at the time.

In the turmoil of 1848, the authorities expelled Marx from Brussels. A democratic government having been set up in Cologne, he returned to that city and undertook to edit a revived *Rheinische Zeitung*. In a short time, however, both democracy and paper were suppressed, and Marx, among others, was put on trial for treason. He was acquitted—the jury thanked him for a most instructive discourse—but forced to leave Germany. He proceeded to London where, except for a few brief trips, he was to remain for the rest of his life.

At about the same time, Engels returned to Manchester to work as manager of the family factory. He detested the job but undertook it with the conscious purpose of obtaining funds to support the Marxes, who had nothing but what they could get from family donations (despite Marx's bad relationship with his widowed mother), occasional inheritances, loans, gifts, and (1851–1862) earnings from articles written for the New York *Tribune*. (However, the extreme penury of their circumstances from 1850 to 1870 was due more to mismanagement and occasional splurges than to destitution; their average income was lower middle class, about three times that of a laborer.) Engels helped in other ways also; for instance, when (1851) the Marx's maid—Helene Demuth, with the family from 1845 on—bore Karl's bastard son, Friedrich falsely confessed paternity to avoid upsetting Jenny.

Only after settling in London did Marx, antecedently convinced of the supreme importance of economics in the historical process, take up the serious study of the science. For years he read every day in the British Museum, then after supper worked on his magnum opus, *Capital*. The first volume was published at Hamburg in 1867. He made an enormous collection of notes for the projected second and third volumes, which however he never put into publishable form; Engels, with the help of Karl Kautsky, devoted many years of labor to the task after Marx's death.

Besides poverty, Marx suffered from chronic illness, the early deaths of three children (three daughters survived), and from obscurity and intellectual isolation. In the 1860s he and Engels got control of the International Working Men's Association (First International)—intended to be a grand alliance of the European Left—but in 1872 they torpedoed it (by having its official headquarters moved to New York!) rather than let it fall under the domination of the anarchist Bakunin. Outside such limited circles, Marx was unknown. Four years following publication, *Capital* had sold only a thousand copies. For twenty years John Stuart Mill lived in the same city and dealt with the same topics as Marx but never heard of him.

In 1870 Engels, by then a wealthy man, retired and settled an annuity on the Marxes that put an end to their financial woes. But although Marx had twelve more years to live and continued to write voluminously, the product was diffuse. Jenny died early in 1882, and Karl followed her fifteen months later.

At the burial in Highgate Cemetery Engels delivered the eulogy, beginning "On the 14th day of March, at a quarter to three in the afternoon, the greatest living thinker ceased to think." He attributed to Marx the discovery of the laws of historical development, which he compared in importance to Darwin's achievement in biology.

Engels was Marx's single lifelong friend. All the others, from Heinrich Heine and before, sooner or later were driven away by his arrogance and sarcasm. The German-American statesman Carl Schurz summarized the general opinion of Marx's personality in these words:

> I have never seen a man whose bearing was so provoking and intolerable. To no opinion, which differed from his, he accorded the honor of even a condescending consideration. Everyone who contradicted him he treated with abject contempt; every argument that he did not like he answered either with biting scorn at the unfathomable ignorance that had prompted it, or with opprobrious aspersions upon the motives of him who had advanced it.[2]

He was, however, a kind and loving husband and father.

The Genesis of Marxism

The mature Marx considered himself a scientist, and was contemptuous of philosophy, an enterprise that he looked upon as destined to have no place in the rational society of the future. He held, in agreement with Comte, that it would be superseded by the empirical study of nature, which, he declared, is related to philosophy as sexual love is related to masturbation.

Be that as it may, the most accurate capsule description of Marx's worldview is—in his own words—"Hegel turned upside down." Marx never doubted that reality is a dynamic process; that it has a single internal driving force; that it advances by discrete steps; that it is intelligible—the pattern of development can be perceived by the intellect and its future stages predicted; that it is progressive—the later stages are in some sense 'better' than the earlier; and that the process is destined to come to completion in a stable condition of perfection wherein there will be no possibility of further change. This entire schema is Hegelian. But whereas for the sage of Berlin the process was the coming to full self-consciousness of the Absolute Idea, the exile in London saw it as the succession of class-structured societies issuing at last in the classless society—the restoration of the primeval human community but at a high level of technology and culture. The force keeping the process in motion was not a cosmic logic but that which is necessarily at the basis of any society whatsoever: the production of the material goods essential for the continuance of life.

Alienation

A particular Hegelian concept that Marx turned upside down was that of *Ent-fremdung*. The plain English equivalent of this word is "estrangement," making-into-something-strange, but it is usually translated as "alienation." This notion had a complex role in Hegel's metaphysics; primarily it signified the Absolute Spirit's producing Nature out of itself and appearing to separate from it as if it were a distinct entity—somewhat like Emanation in Neoplatonism. Marx, however, meant the estrangement of the individual worker from the product of labor in the societies that superseded the primitive community and the consequent (alleged) feeling of being cut off from the core of one's own being.

Marx's conception of human good was basically the same as Aristotle's: it is the happiness of self-fulfillment, actualizing one's innate potentialities. And again like Aristotle, Marx thought that the human good could be achieved only in a community: man is a "political animal." A small group or tribe in which no one specialized but everyone took part on equal terms in hunting, growing food, building shelters, and the like, would allow for such fulfillment—at the primitive level of technology and culture.

But with progress—growth in numbers, and refinements of techniques so that the making of (say) baskets and pots required special training and competence— division of labor would be introduced. This would have many effects, the one chiefly emphasized by Marx being the *Entfremdung* of basket-weaver from basket. There is a profound and basic difference—so Marx thought—between the out-looks of people who labor to make things solely for their own use and workers who produce articles in order to exchange them for other things made by other people. Goods made for the market seem to take on an active role of their own that can be oppressive, as if they were whispering "Hurry up and get me made, or you will starve!" And they stereotype their makers, who are no longer identified simply as men and women but as butchers, bakers, and so forth.

> The division of labor offers us the first example of how, as long as . . . a cleavage exists between the particular and the common interest, as long therefore as activity is not voluntarily, but naturally, divided, man's own deed becomes an alien power opposed to him, which enslaves him instead of being controlled by him. For as soon as labor is distributed, each man has a particular, exclusive sphere of activity, which is forced upon him and from which he cannot escape. He is a hunter, a fisherman, a shepherd, or a critic, and must remain so if he does not want to lose his means of livelihood . . .[3]

This separation of producer from product issues in what Marx calls the "fetishism of commodities," the virtual endowment of lifeless material things with power over the living human beings who should be their masters.

Division of labor also brings into being the institution of private property, since the need to be scrupulous about what is mine and what is thine arises in the process of exchange. Further complexity in the organization of production leads to further trauma: the *dehumanization* of the worker who is separated from his own essence, his labor power, once it becomes possible for one person—the Capitalist—to hire others to work at his bidding. In that situation the worker's labor power itself becomes a commodity, one with (according to Marx) the unique potential for making a *profit*—not for the worker but for the purchaser, the employer, who in appropriating the profit *exploits* the worker. The sum of all these developments—fetishism of commodities, dehumanization, and exploitation—is the alienation experienced by the worker in capitalist society, estrangement not merely from product but from the human essence itself. "Man is a debased, enslaved, abandoned, contemptible being."[4]

Classes

A further consequence of division of labor, of immense significance, was the creation of classes. The *Manifesto* declares

> The history of all hitherto existing society [excepting primitive communism, as Engels later explained] is the history of class struggles.
> Free man and slave, patrician and plebeian, lord and serf, guild master and journeyman, in a word, oppressor and oppressed, stood in constant opposition to one another, carried on an uninterrupted, now hidden, now open fight, a fight that each time ended either in a revolutionary reconstitution of society at large or in the common ruin of the contending classes.[5]

History is a dialectic, as Hegel had maintained—but of classes, not of ideas.

The French Revolution, the most spectacular "reconstitution of society" in European history, was only a limited success in the view of Marx and others who looked toward the reestablishment of community. The revolutionary slogan "Liberty, Equality, Fraternity" had seemed to promise it; but it was never delivered. Only *formal* liberty and equality had been promoted. In theory every citizen was free and the equal of every other citizen; in reality this meant only liberty to practice a policy of unbridled egoism. Fraternity, the essence of community, was forgotten altogether, or interpreted merely as the sentiment of nationalism.

> The political emancipators reduce citizenship, the *political community*, to a mere means for preserving these so-called rights of man, so that the *citoyen* [citizen] is proclaimed to be the servant of the egoistic *homme* [man]. The sphere in which man conducts himself as a communal being is degraded, put below the sphere in which he conducts himself as a sectional being.[6]

Marx had an explanation for this disappointing outcome. Every revolution is made by a class, which purports to speak for the whole of the society (except the class to be overthrown), but which in fact serves its own limited interests. In the France of the eighteenth century, the oppressing class was the aristocracy and the rising power was the bourgeoisie (defined by Engels as "the class of modern capitalists, owners of the means of social production and employers of wage labor").

> This class emancipates all of society, but only on the condition that all of society is in the same position as this class, e.g., that it has money and education or can easily acquire them.[7]

The bourgeoisie really emancipated themselves; they emancipated the proletariat ("the class of modern wage laborers who, having no means of production of their own, are reduced to selling their labor power in order to live") only formally. Community remained a mere ideal, indeed farther off than ever in the new capitalist society which has

> put an end to all feudal, patriarchal, idyllic relations . . . left remaining no other nexus between man and man than naked self-interest, than callous "cash payment" . . . resolved personal worth into exchange value and, in place of the numberless indefeasible chartered freedoms, set up that single, unconscionable freedom—free trade . . . stripped of its halo every occupation hitherto honored . . . torn away from the family its sentimental veil, and reduced the family relation to a mere money relation.[8]

Historical Materialism

Disappointment with the outcome of the French Revolution and revulsion at the degraded conditions of working-class life incident to the industrial revolution were nothing new in the middle of the nineteenth century. Robert Owen (1771–1858) in England and Claude Henri de Rouvroy, Comte de Saint-Simon (1760–1825) and Charles Fourier (1772–1837) in France were prominent among the socialists—the word came into use about 1825—who developed proposals for restructuring society on an economic basis of cooperation rather than profit seeking. Communities based on their principles were founded, notably New Harmony and Brook Farm in the United States.

Marx and Engels disparaged all such schemes as "Utopian Socialism": consciously devised plans, advocated on the general ground of being morally better than the unplanned state of things, and intended to be put into practice—whether peaceably or forcibly—by convincing people of their desirability and thus spurring them to take action. The "Utopian Socialists" took for granted that ideas are the causes of which historically significant changes in the social order are (or at any rate can be) the effects. Philosophy—in the broad sense of the dominant system of ideas—then determines the nature of society.

On the contrary, Marx contended, "it is not the consciousness of men that determines their being but . . . their social being that determines their consciousness."[9] By the mid-1840s Marx claimed to have worked out the fundamentals of the *science*—not the philosophy—of historical development. He called it "materialist" both to distinguish it from religious or speculative "idealist" theories and to emphasize that forms of society are rooted in the material conditions of people's existence.

Previous thinkers (Marx held) had not sufficiently appreciated the truism that the absolutely indispensable condition for the existence of any social group is the provision of the essentials of livelihood: food, clothing, shelter. The "relations of production"—who produces what, how production is organized, what technology is available, how the products are distributed—determine the basic structure of the society. For example, where agriculture depends on irrigation works there must be a centralized bureaucratic government. The "ideology"—philosophy, religion, law, art, social stratification—will be dictated by this basic fact: philosophy will prove the rightness of bureaucracy, religion will declare the ruler sacred, social status will be correlated with water rights, and so on.

In some places, such as Egypt and the Orient, the relations of production, hence the ideological superstructure, remain the same for ages. Elsewhere, especially in Europe, these relations change, mainly because of technological developments. The institutions that were appropriate for the former system of production then become obstacles in the way of getting the most out of the methods that are newly available. But as the welfare of the dominant class depends on preserving those institutions, a tension develops leading to class conflict.

This happened when the bourgeoisie overthrew the feudal aristocracy. Feudalism was the form that fit subsistence agriculture. Its very success created relatively peaceable conditions in which commerce could be carried on, coupled with a demand for kinds of goods beyond the productive resources of local workers—leading to the rise of towns with their craftsmen, merchants, and bankers: the beginnings of the bourgeoisie. The rise of this class, accelerated first by the opening of trade routes to the New World and Orient and then by the development of power machinery for centralized mass production, led after three centuries of struggle to the victory of the bourgeoisie in the French Revolution.

In the *Manifesto*, Marx and Engels credit the bourgeoisie with many good things: urbanization, spread of civilization, unleashing of productive forces on an unheard-of scale. But this class, we are assured, carries within itself the seeds of its own destruction. As feudal aristocracy gave birth to bourgeoisie, so bourgeoisie brings forth "its own gravediggers," the industrial proletariat.

Struggle between these classes is inevitable inasmuch as their interests are diametrically opposed. Marx's major work, *Capital*, was intended to show by a scientific analysis of the capitalist process of production why the victory of the proletariat is assured. But the essentials of the argument were present already in the *Manifesto*. Besides the alienation of the workers, which creates a resentment eager to seize every opportunity to smash the oppressor, capitalism is subject to four fatal flaws. (1) By the inner dynamic of capitalism, its enterprises tend to consolidation and the creation of monopolies, which in turn assure that the rich get richer—and fewer; while the poor get poorer (relatively, at any rate)—and multiply. The petty bourgeoisie—professional people, landlords, shopkeepers, pawnbrokers, and the like—cannot keep up, and sink into the proletariat, augmenting that class not just quantitatively but more importantly with educated people conscious of their class interests and capable of leadership. (2) By the "iron law of wages," capitalist competition keeps wages at the subsistence level—the minimum needed to keep the workers alive and reproductive. These two factors constitute the "law of increasing misery" under capitalism. (3) The centralization of production in large factories brings workers into physical proximity with one another, so that they are capable of concerted action in their own interest. (The dispersion of the peasantry, Marx held, was a principal reason for the inability of agricultural laborers throughout history to better their lot as a class.) (4) Finally, capitalist competition by its nature leads to periodic episodes of overproduction with consequent industrial dislocation and unemployment. These *business cycles* will grow more severe until they become intolerable.

The Revolution

Thus the occurrence of the proletarian revolution against capitalism, the "expropriation of the expropriators," is as inevitable as the next appearance of Halley's comet—though of course its date and circumstances are not amenable to precise prediction. However, as a natural event it both must come, and can only come, when the time is ripe, when the necessary steps of social development have been gone through—without skipping. So at any rate Marx thought in the 1860s.

> And even when a society has got upon the right track for the discovery of the natural laws of its movement—and it is the ultimate aim of this work to lay bare the economic law of motion of modern society—it can neither clear by bold leaps, nor remove by legal enactments, the obstacles offered by successive phases of its normal development. But it can shorten and lessen the birth-pangs.

The last sentence of this quotation (from the Preface to *Capital* Volume I) expresses why political activity in furtherance of revolution is useful, and also what the limit of its usefulness is.

It is taken for granted in the *Manifesto* that the overthrow of the bourgeoisie will be violent. Later in life Marx entertained the possibility that in liberal democracies it might be peaceably brought about by legal means. But Marx did not deplore the use of force.

> The workers must, above all during the conflict and immediately after the struggle, as far as possible work against bourgeois appeasement and force the democrats to carry out their present terrorist slogans. They must work to ensure that direct revolutionary agitation is not suppressed again immediately after victory. They must, on the contrary, keep it alive as long as possible. Far from opposing the so-called excesses, examples of popular revenge against hated individuals or against public buildings with hateful associations, they must not only allow them but themselves undertake their direction.[10]

Marx attributed the failure of the Paris Commune of 1870 mainly to the reluctance of its leaders to implement a vigorous terror.

In order to prevent counterrevolution and to make the transition to the classless society, seizure of power must be followed by the *dictatorship of the proletariat*. This is of course not a government in which decisions are made actually by the whole proletariat, but by a cadre of Communists, class conscious representatives schooled in the theory of historical materialism. The cadre does not merely take over the positions of power—the ministry of this or that—established by the constitution of the overthrown State ("a committee for managing the common affairs of the whole bourgeoisie"[11]); it abolishes that organization and sets up appropriate organs of its own whereby to rebuild society from scratch.

> For us it cannot be a question of changing private property but only of destroying it, not of smothering class antagonisms but only of wiping out classes, not of improving existing society but of founding a new one.[12]

The Classless Society

It might be supposed that according to historical materialism the victory of the proletariat would be followed by the rise of another class in dialectical opposition, which would eventually triumph over the proletariat, generate still another class, and so *ad infinitum*. Not at all, said Marx. After the victory of the proletariat, there will be no other class for it to oppose. Class struggle will have come to an end, forever. The reason is that there will be no more separation of workers from the means of production and consequently no further clash of interests. (Classes are *defined* by their interests.)

True community, never actual in all of *recorded* history, will be restored. The division of labor will be abolished.[13]

> In communist society, where nobody has one exclusive sphere of activity but each can become accomplished in any branch he wishes, society regulates the general production and thus makes it possible for me to do one thing today and another tomorrow, to hunt in the morning, fish in the afternoon, rear cattle in the evening, criticize after dinner, just as I have a mind, without ever becoming hunter, fisherman, shepherd or critic.[14]

With the end of alienation, coercion will no longer be needed to insure production, which will be so abundant that money and wages can be abolished, everyone simply taking what he or she requires from the common store. Nor will there be further use for the apparatus of the State, which will "wither away."

Dialectical Materialism

Historical materialism purports to be a science. Underlying it, however, despite Marx's rejection of speculative philosophy, is a distinctive worldview including a theory of knowledge, a theory of being, and even a logic. The principal text in which these are set out is Engels' book *Herr Eugen Dühring's Revolution in Science* (1877–78), usually referred to as *Anti-Dühring*, which was read and officially approved by Marx. The label "Dialectical Materialism" was applied to this philosophy in 1891 by Georgi Valentinovich Plekhanov (1856–1918), the founder of Russian Marxism.

Marx and Engels were of course materialists in the sense of anti-idealists. They thought that Idealism—denial of the full reality of the material world—was a dishonest philosophy, in effect a mask for religion. They rejected mind-body dualisms. However, they were at some pains to distinguish their position from what they referred to as the "vulgar materialism" popular in Germany, especially among scientists, which took Force and Matter as the only realities and tried to reduce all so-called mental phenomena to them.

Marx held all knowledge to be based on sense perception, the process in which stimulation of the sense organs by the external world produces representations of the stimulus objects. But if we can never get directly in touch with the objects represented, how can we know that the so-called representations really represent them? This stock objection to representationalism is answered by pointing out that man is more than a mere spectator of the world (or of his own mind), he *interacts* with it.

> The question whether human thought can attain to objective truth is not a theoretical but a *practical* question. Man must prove the truth, i.e. the reality and power, the thissidedness of his thinking in practice. The dispute over the reality or nonreality of thinking which is isolated from practice is a purely *scholastic* question.[15]

This is reminiscent of Locke's recipe for determining the meaning of solidity by taking a football in one's hands and trying to bring the hands together, and of his answer to the skeptic that "this certainty [of the reality of the external world] is as great as our happiness or misery, beyond which we have no concernment to know, or to be." It is also, as we shall see, a forerunner of Pragmatism.

There are three Laws of Dialectics.

1. *Law of Conflict and Interpenetration of Opposites* Aristotle's Law of Noncontradiction holds that nothing can both have, and not have, any property at the same time and in the same respect. Engels criticized this law as static; the world is *dynamic*, constantly changing in all respects, and change requires the presence of real contradictions in nature. Any instance of motion, for example, is an objective contradiction: the moving thing must both be and not be in the same place. Everything is what it is, but also everything is what it is *not*.

2. *Law of Quantity and Quality* As quantitative changes accumulate, at some point they give rise to a sudden qualitative change. For example, when water is being cooled (quantitative change) it retains the qualities of water until zero degrees centigrade is reached, whereupon it changes—all at once—from liquid to solid (qualitative change). And the power of the proletariat increases steadily to the point where suddenly society changes from capitalist to socialist.

3. *Law of Negation of Negation* Qualitative changes ("negations") are in their turn succeeded by further qualitative changes. The negation of ice is water; the negation of water is steam. An individual organism is negated by death, which is itself negated by the development of a new organism from the seed of the old. The negation of feudalism is capitalism; the negation of capitalism is socialism. (The never-to-be-negated classless society seems to constitute an exception to this law.)

Marxism-Leninism

During the nineteenth century, mainstream socialism in western Europe was what Marx and Engels called "Utopian," aiming usually at the capture of political power by peaceful means. Marxists did not hesitate to ally themselves (for temporary advantage) with these movements, which developed into the British Labour Party and the various Social Democratic parties of the Continent. The "Utopians" on their part adopted much from Marx; *Capital*, for instance, achieved recognition as the chief theoretical work of the socialist movement as a whole. Around the turn of the century it might have been reasonably predicted that the place in history of Marx and Engels would be on a par with Owen, Fourier, and Lassalle. But because the *Russian* socialist movement was dominated by revolutionary Marxists, events turned out differently.

Lenin (Vladimir Ilyich Ulyanov, 1870–1924) devoted much attention and energy to philosophy, producing a book, *Materialism and Empirio-Criticism* (1909) vigorously defending the representationalist-realist philosophy of Engels against other Marxists who, emphasizing the Positivist strain in Marx's thought, were flirting with the phenomenalism of Ernst Mach. Lenin followed Marx and especially Engels in his philosophy, but greatly emphasized certain aspects such as activism (union of theory and practice)—which to him implied the supreme importance of upholding philosophical correctness among party members—and dialectic in all its ramifications. He also declared it possible to institute socialism in a single country, and that Russia could advance from feudalism to socialism skipping the capitalist stage—a position difficult to reconcile with Marx's Law of Historical Development. The official philosophy of the "socialist" countries is now usually referred to as Marxism-Leninism. We cannot here delve into later developments, except to note that shortly before his death (1953) Stalin saw fit to lift the ban on formal (nondialectical) logic, which is fundamental to the theory of computers.

Marxism as a Religion

The two philosophers who have had the most widespread *direct* impact on world history are Augustine and Marx. Neither thought of himself as a philosopher, neither had much respect for the recognized and established philosophers and philosophies of his day, and in turn neither has been judged by the consensus of philosophers to be of the first rank—considered *as* philosophers. The parallels can be drawn further.

Christianity before Augustine was primarily a way to salvation, implying a worldview, which however was unsystematic and without ready rejoinders to objections raised by intellectual sophisticates. Augustine, drawing on Platonism, made up this deficiency, creating a grand view of the universe that lasted (with a major overhaul by St. Thomas Aquinas) essentially unchallenged for a thousand years. This system satisfied many human needs.

(1) *For Understanding* It authoritatively explained what reality consists of (heaven, earth, hell), what beings it contains (God, angels, men, women, animals, vegetables, minerals, devils), how they came to be (by God's creative fiat), when (a few thousand years ago), why (to glorify God and to serve man), and how it will end (with the second coming and the last judgment).

(2) *For Meaning* It explained what a human being is (a supernatural immortal soul temporarily united to a natural mortal body) and proclaimed a purpose for human life (service and glorification of God) beyond the mere routine of getting and spending.

(3) *For Hope* This life, with its disappointments, injustices, and miseries of all kinds, is not the only one. Good people may expect an eternal, and blissful, life beyond the grave.

(4) *For Revenge* Furthermore, wicked people who oppress the virtuous in this life will find their triumph short-lived and hollow. They will be punished excruciatingly and eternally.

(5) *For Comfort* All suffering somehow furthers God's purpose, which is good, and will in some way benefit the sufferer (if he or she is good).

(6) *For Community* Membership in the Church, the mystical body of Christ, unites one in brotherhood with all other believers.

(7) *For a Moral Order* What God commands is absolutely and objectively right, and what He forbids is wrong, regardless of personal interest, likes and dislikes.

(8) *For Social Order* God has ordained the State, its rulers, and its laws for our good. That is why we have an obligation to obey the powers that be, even when to do so seems against our interest.

Probably the need for understanding is not, for most people, the most important of these needs. Nevertheless, the ability of Christianity to satisfy all the other needs depended crucially on its satisfaction of this need. To doubt whether in fact the world was as described—created and ruled by an omnipotent and benevolent God—was to jeopardize the basis for meaning, comfort, and all the rest. No wonder that astronomy, geology, biology, history, and even classical scholarship were regarded as dangerous, and that opposition to their results was so intense and emotional.

But despite all attempts at suppression—or accommodation by allegorical interpretation of Scripture and other stratagems—and despite intellectual inertia, the cumulative effect of science (which in the words of Albert Einstein is "nothing more than a refinement of everyday thinking"[16]) from Copernicus to Darwin was to render the Christian story increasingly incredible to more and more people. And while the view of the world to be derived from science might satisfy the need for understanding, it could not of itself assuage any other of the enumerated cravings. Nothing in physiology suggests an afterlife, astronomy and geology reveal neither heaven nor hell.

Like Spinoza some people were content to accept, even with awe, the scientific worldview, to regard morals as based on human nature and the needs appropriate to it, to find sufficient meaning for life in this-worldly activities and satisfactions, and to do without hope or fear of postmortem rewards and punishments. But for most, philosophy was not enough. They sought a new *faith*—a system of beliefs, compatible with science, that would satisfy the needs formerly satisfied by the Church.

The beginning of such a faith can be discerned in the rise of "Utopian Socialism." On the whole the Church counseled a resigned acceptance of the social and political order as it was, but the American and French revolutions had demonstrated the possibility of planned changes of great magnitude. The idea was abroad that society might be reshaped in accordance with Reason, by deliberate human choice and effort. Arbitrary inequalities could be done away with, worldly goods—rapidly becoming more abundant as production was industrialized— could be distributed in accordance with desert, justice might at last triumph on earth. Superstition could be abolished by universal and secular education. Enlightened and well-fed humanity could live in harmonious cooperation.

But utopian socialism lacked unity, as evidenced by the bewildering variety of schemes actually proposed. It was not such as to engage the emotions at a deep level, being concerned mainly with external goods; and it lacked grounding in a comprehensive view of being and human destiny. That is to say, it lacked a philosophy.

Karl Marx's achievement was to provide that philosophy. Building on Hegel much as Augustine had built on Plato, he invented a worldview that could satisfy all the human needs that the Church had satisfied, while not coming into conflict with the ascertained results of science—indeed, while proclaiming itself to *be* "social science." Dialectical and historical materialism presented socialism not merely as a good idea that might be put into effect if people would work hard enough for it; the triumph of socialism was *inevitable* because the awesome forces that direct history had been working to that end from the beginning of the race.

Let us review the human needs to which the Church responded and see how they fare with Marxism.

(1) *For Understanding* Marx and Engels wisely left the description of the world at large to the sciences, with allowance for revision. The view taken of human nature, however, is more rigid: thought and behavior are determined by social environment, so that all undesirable traits can be removed by suitable restructuring of society, that is, by political means. Humanity under socialism will be free of superstition, competitiveness, greed, laziness, and so forth.

(2)   *For Meaning* Life devoted to "lessening the birth-pangs" of the new society involves the same satisfaction as the Christian derives from serving God.

(3)   *For Hope* Suffering in the cause is not in vain. Compensation is bound to come in the lifetime of one's grandchildren, and—so swift is progress—quite possibly in one's own.

(4)   *For Revenge* The capitalist enemy's liquidation is assured, and probably in short order.

(5) and (6)   *For Comfort and Community* The Party offers them here and now. The classless society to come will be the reestablishment of the original human community, torn asunder by the division of labor and its sinister (but fortunately reversible) effects.

(7)   *For Moral Order* There is an absolute standard of right and wrong. Whatever furthers the revolution is right, whatever seeks to oppose it is wrong. The Party authoritatively decides what specific acts fit these descriptions.

(8)   *For Social Order* In the classless society the social order will coincide with human nature, so that the apparatus of laws and compulsion will be dispensed with. At last the free development of human potential will be assured for everyone.

This belief system certainly constitutes a faith, according to the classic definition of St. Paul: "The substance of things hoped for, the evidence of things not seen."[17] As is well known, Marxism-Leninism has its scriptures, its orthodoxy, its heresies, its pope, its college of cardinals, its inquisition, its confessionals, its penances, and its excommunications. And from time to time this apparatus has been deployed against straightforward scientific research—Einsteinian physics and Mendelian genetics for instance. Whether it is to be counted a religion hinges on the definitional point of whether a religion must involve belief in a personal God. (If it must, then original Buddhism is not a religion.)

Marx was conscious of the need for religion in the world as it is. The context of his famous characterization of religion as a drug follows.

> Religion is the general theory of this world, its encyclopedia, its logic in popular form, its spiritualistic *point d'honneur*, its enthusiasm, its moral sanction, its solemn complement, and the general ground for the consummation and justification of this world. It is the *ghostly realization* of the human essence, ghostly because the *human essence* possesses no true reality. The struggle against religion is therefore indirectly the struggle against *that world* whose spiritual aroma is religion.
>
> Religious suffering is at once the *expression* of real suffering and the *protest* against real suffering. Religion is the sigh of the oppressed creature, the heart of a heartless world, just as it is the spirit of spiritless conditions. It is the *opium* of the people.
>
> The overcoming of religion as the *illusory* happiness of the people is the demand for their real happiness . . .[18]

However, in evaluating the contrast between Marxist 'reality' and religious 'illusion', it should be borne in mind that the Marxist eschatology is every bit as speculative as the Christian.

Engels explicitly noted many of the parallels between Marxism and Christianity to which we have called attention.

> The history of early Christianity has notable points of resemblance with the modern working-class movement. Like the latter, Christianity was originally a movement of oppressed people: it first appeared as the religion of slaves and emancipated slaves,

of poor people deprived of all rights, of peoples subjugated or dispersed by Rome. Both Christianity and the workers' socialism preach forthcoming salvation from bondage and misery; Christianity places this salvation in a life beyond, after death, in heaven; socialism places it in this world, in a transformation of society. Both are persecuted and baited, their adherents are despised and made the objects of exclusive laws, the former as enemies of the human race, the latter as enemies of the state, enemies of religion, the family, social order. And in spite of all persecution, nay, even spurred on by it, they forge victoriously, irresistibly ahead. Three hundred years after its appearance Christianity was the recognized state religion in the Roman world empire, and in barely sixty years socialism has won itself a position which makes its victory absolutely certain.[19]

45

The Utilitarians

HUME AND OTHER EIGHTEENTH-CENTURY moralists found the source of the moral sentiments to lie in our feeling of approval for what is socially useful. Social usefulness consists in the tendency to further the general well-being. Hume seems to have regarded his task as a moralist to be primarily descriptive: to analyze the moral concepts and trace them to their sources.

There were others who felt that attainment of clarity on these issues should be but the preliminary to reform. Although utility is the criterion of right and wrong, many people who actually employ it are not aware that they do. They may suppose that they judge in accordance with some other standard, for instance the command of God or the prompting of conscience. In particular cases these people may reach mistaken conclusions—for instance, that certain forms of sexual behavior are wrong which in fact promote happiness or at least do not decrease it. There is need then to bring the principle of utility to public consciousness, to explain it, answer objections to it, and reform social practices to conform to it. Because social interest is the standard but individual interest is the motive, ways must be devised to ensure that one pursuing one's own profit will be acting in conformity to public interest.

In late eighteenth- and early nineteenth-century Britain, a group of men dedicated themselves to this program. They were not a party nor otherwise formally organized, and did not have an official label. For some time they were referred to as the Philosophical Radicals, later as the Utilitarians. They were extraordinarily successful: although they were not men of political power or influence in the usual sense, and moreover relied on reasoned argument with minimal emotional appeal, nearly all the specific legislative reforms they advocated were adopted at one time or another in the nineteenth century.

Their leader was Jeremy Bentham (1748–1832), a Londoner all his long life. He was a wealthy man who studied law but never practiced; instead he devoted himself to the reform of the law in the broadest sense. In his works, collected in eleven large volumes, he is never sketchy or content to enunciate principles and leave the filling in of details to others. The *Introduction to the Principles of Morals and Legislation* (printed 1780 but, in accordance with Bentham's curious reticence about publishing, not issued until 1789), his chief work, contains both the grand principles of human nature and a list of the 21 offenses "to which the condition of a husband stands exposed."

J. Watts, Jeremy Bentham, *detail, late eighteenth century. Oil.*

The Principle of Utility

The book begins

> Nature has placed mankind under the governance of two sovereign masters, *pain* and *pleasure*. It is for them alone to point out what we ought to do, as well as to determine what we shall do. On the one hand the standard of right and wrong, on the other the chain of causes and effects, are fastened to their throne. They govern us in all we do, in all we say, in all we think: every effort we can make to throw off our subjection, will serve but to demonstrate and confirm it. In words a man may pretend to abjure their empire: but in reality he will remain subject to it all the while. The *principle of utility* recognises this subjection, and assumes it for the foundation of that system, the object of which is to rear the fabric of felicity by the hands of reason and law. Systems which attempt to question it, deal in sounds instead of sense, in caprice instead of reason, in darkness instead of light.

Bentham thus subscribes in a single sentence to two kinds of hedonism. Psychological Hedonism is the doctrine that, as a matter of fact, all motives of action come down to desire for pleasure or avoidance of pain. Ethical Hedonism declares that pleasure is the only good and action is right only as it tends to produce pleasure.

Is either of them true? Psychological Hedonism has been attacked on the ground that anything at all can be desired, even severe pain, as masochists and mountain climbers show. It seems unsatisfactory to reply that the masochist's pain *is* his pleasure, for to do so would trivialize the doctrine. But for Bentham the notion of pleasure had definite content. Indeed he distinguished 14 species of simple pleasures: the senses (further distinguished into nine kinds), wealth, skill, amity, good name, power, piety, benevolence, malevolence, memory, imagination, expectation, association, and relief; and 11 of pain. Cases such as those of monks who whip themselves bloody he explained away as proceeding from the monks' belief that such action would be rewarded by great pleasure in the hereafter. Benevolence is on the list: you can get pleasure from making someone else happy, even at expense of pain to yourself. On the whole it may be best to say that Psychological Hedonism, in some cautious version such as that people do not deliberately aim at *ends* that they (consciously or unconsciously) dislike, is true or near the truth; at any rate no practical policy would be likely to succeed that did not assume it.

If Psychological Hedonism is true, then it must be pointless to recommend the pursuit of anything other than pleasure. So then Ethical Hedonism must be true but redundant. However, this point should not be dwelt upon, for there is still plenty of advice for the sage to give concerning strategies for maximizing pleasure. The hedonist will admit that the prescriptions consist of factual statements, but this will be no embarrassment. On the contrary, the hedonist will say, ethics has at last become scientific.

Bentham found that pleasures and pains vary in seven ways: according to intensity, duration, certainty or uncertainty of occurrence, propinquity or remoteness (*i.e.* whether near—the cigarette now; or remote—the cancer thirty years away), fecundity (the chance it has of being followed by others of the same kind; the pleasures of benevolence and the pains of malevolence are both fecund), purity (chance of not being followed by the opposite; the pleasure of healthiness is pure, that of drunkenness impure), and extent (number of persons affected).

> *Intense, long, certain, speedy, fruitful, pure—*
> Such marks in *pleasures* and in *pains* endure.
> Such pleasures seek, if *private* be thy end:
> If it be *public*, wide let them *extend*.
> Such *pains* avoid, whichever be thy view:
> If pains *must* come, let them *extend* to few.[1]

The notion of a "hedonic calculus," with so many points for a steak dinner and so many negative points for a broken leg, does not occur in Bentham's writings. He advocates only the methodical pursuance of the process we all go through when we somehow sum up pros and cons where a decision is important enough for us to take much time in weighing it. Actually we do manage somehow or other to reason quantitatively about pleasures and pains, at least when expenditure of money is involved.

The primary area of application for the scheme, in Bentham's intention, is legislation, the aim of which ought to be nothing other than the greatest happiness.

Whether abortion and marijuana are to be forbidden, permitted, or mandatory should be decided in accordance with these considerations and not, as Bentham complains they often are, superstitiously or by the "principle of sympathy and antipathy"—the raw sentiments of the legislator or of his or her constituency. But moral rules themselves, such as the prohibition of lying, must stand up to scrutiny in light of these factors. Presumably they can; if not, they are mere taboos. It is, moreover, moral *rules* that are to be judged by this procedure; if they pass, then, being rules, we are not to consider anew in every particular situation whether it would further the greatest happiness to abide by them. If we did, they would not be rules; they would be pieces of advice holding by and large. It is to the advantage of society that there should be rules imposing real obligations. The utility principle can, moreover, make allowance for the violation of rules in extreme cases—where the social interest in telling a lie, say in a case where it will save an innocent life, is great enough to offset the peril to the general interest presumed to attach to failure to abide by an established precept.

Sanctions

"For a man not to pursue what he deems likely to produce to him the greatest sum of enjoyment, is in the very nature of things impossible."[2] Yet morality consists in furthering the greatest happiness for all concerned, which in a particular case may not coincide with the agent's greatest satisfaction. If moral conduct is to be possible, conflict situations of this sort must be prevented. This is the task of the legislator.

Bentham found that the *sanctions*, the pressures that can be brought to bear to influence conduct, are of four kinds. 1. The physical: for example, the pains of hangover may persuade the drunkard to temperance, the fear of venereal disease may discourage lewdness. 2. The political or legal. 3. The moral or popular or social: hope of admiration or fear of disapproval. 4. The religious: fear of divine punishment or hope of heavenly reward.

Since Bentham regarded the religious sanction as superstition and the physical as hardly changeable, the practical problem was narrowed to operations concerning the moral and above all the political sanctions: reform of the law. Three tasks were needful. First, introduce rationality into the lawmaking process by making Parliament a really representative body. This required the equalization of electoral districts, extension of the right to vote to all adult literate males, secret ballot, and abolition of the House of Lords. Second, the laws themselves should be codified and made reasonable so that only really harmful deeds were criminal, and punishments should be proportioned to offenses. Third, the judicial system should be overhauled to make the administration of justice a reality. The bulk of the *Principles* is occupied with questions of what offenses are really offensive and how they should be punished. Bentham is rigorously and unsentimentally faithful to his principle. Capital punishment for offenses other than murder, for example, is condemned not on the ground that it is cruel but that it does not deter—the reason being that juries are reluctant to convict where the death penalty is mandatory. Harshness of punishment is no substitute for certainty of it. Whipping he deems suitable for certain offenses such as theft, but finds a drawback in that the flogger

> may make the punishment as trifling or as severe as he pleases. He may derive from this power a source of revenue, so that the offender will be punished, not in proportion to his offence, but to his poverty. . . . The following contrivance would, in a measure, obviate this inconvenience:—A machine might be made, which should put in motion certain elastic rods of cane or whalebone, the number and size of which might be determined by the law: the body of the delinquent might be subjected to the strokes of these rods, and the force and rapidity with which they should be applied, might be prescribed by the judge: thus everything which is arbitrary might be removed. A public officer, of more responsible character than the common executioner, might preside over the infliction of the punishment; and when there were many delinquents to be punished, his time might be saved, and the terror of the scene heightened, without increasing the actual suffering, by increasing the number of the machines, and subjecting all the offenders to punishment at the same time.[3]

Despite such evidences of mechanical ingenuity and attention to detail, Bentham was no rigid doctrinaire. Again and again he emphasized points often overlooked in his day: that a policy right for England might yet be disastrously wrong for India; that punishments should fit not only the crime but the criminal—a fine of ten pounds would be nothing to the Duke of Bedford, but the ruin of his tenant (conversely, ten lashes might be nothing to the yeoman but a disgrace that could drive the Duke to suicide). He was aware too that the abolition of abuses might incidentally work underserved hardship. Slavery ought to be abolished, but Bentham did not think it right thereby to reduce to poverty those persons whose wealth was invested, legally, in slaves. They should be compensated from public funds. This was an application of what he called the "Non-Disappointment Principle": the suffering of individuals ought not to be disregarded on the ground that it would bring about an increase in general happiness. In later years Bentham dropped the words "of the Greatest Number" from the Utilitarian slogan, leaving it simply "The Greatest Happiness." He did this not because he was unconcerned with the numbers of people to share happiness but exactly to the contrary, because he was convinced that happiness not shared as equally as feasible among the whole number affected could never be the greatest.[4]

The program for legal and electoral reform, which got off to an auspicious beginning, was stopped dead by the outbreak of the French Revolution. The British would not even adopt the metric system, for grams and centimeters "smelled of the guillotine." For a whole generation Bentham—who in 1792 had been made an honorary citizen of the French Republic—could accomplish nothing, even though he was opposed to the highflown principles of the revolutionaries and denounced their Declaration of the Rights of Man as "nonsense on stilts." Not until the 1820s was it possible again to make some headway. Bentham lived just long enough to witness the passage of the Reform Bill of 1832 which, though limited in the extent of its provisions, was the breakthrough that made further innovations possible.

Bentham was one of the founders of University College, the nucleus from which the University of London developed. In accordance with his will, his mummified body, seated and dressed in the style of 1832, is kept there in a cabinet that must be present at each meeting of the Board.

John Stuart Mill

One of Bentham's principal co-workers was James Mill (1773–1836), by birth a Scot of a poor rural family. The local laird, John Stuart, perceived his intelligence and saw to his education, which was intended to make him a parson. However, he went to London in 1802 where for sixteen years he made a meager living as a journalist. Bentham helped support him while he worked on a *History of British India*. When this was published in 1818, the East India Company appointed him to a responsible position.

His firstborn (1806) he named John Stuart after his Scottish benefactor, and proceeded without delay to apply his theories of education to him. When the son was three years old his father began teaching him Greek; four years later, Latin. At six and one-half, John Stuart Mill wrote a *History of Rome*, with footnotes. Besides languages and history, he studied logic and experimental science. Whenever he learned a subject, he was required to teach it to his younger brothers and sisters, who eventually numbered five. He disliked the task. He rounded out his student days with a thorough study of political economy, his notes later serving as the basis for his father's textbook on the subject. He was then thirteen years old and better educated than any university graduate of the time. All this was accomplished, he declared, without forcing, and proved that ordinary methods are appallingly wasteful of young people's time.

> If I had been by nature extremely quick of apprehension, or had possessed a very accurate and retentive memory, or were of a remarkably active and energetic character, the trial would not be conclusive; but in all these natural gifts I am rather below than above par; what I could do, could assuredly be done by any boy or girl of average capacity and healthy physical constitution: and if I have accomplished anything, I owe it, among other fortunate circumstances, to the fact that through the early training bestowed on me by my father, I started, I may fairly say, with an advantage of a quarter of a century over my contemporaries.[5]

Mill when fourteen spent a year in France, in the household of Jeremy Bentham's brother. On returning to England he began his career as a writer with some enthusiastic Benthamite articles. He and the young men with whom he associated had "an almost unbounded confidence in the efficacy of . . . representative government, and complete freedom of discussion." They shared the opinion of the French philosophers of the Enlightenment that human beings are naturally reasonable; so if the people were given access to reason by universal education, and to power by universal suffrage, the world would be improved rapidly.

Suddenly, when he was twenty, Mill's enthusiasm for reform collapsed in a mental crisis. One day, while in a listless mood,

> it occurred to me to put the question directly to myself: "Suppose that all your objects in life were realized; that all the changes in institutions and opinions which you are looking forward to, could be completely effected at this very instant: would this be a great joy and happiness to you?" And an irrepressible self-consciousness distinctly answered, "No!" At this my heart sank within me: the whole foundation on which my life was constructed fell down. All my happiness was to have been found in the continual pursuit of this end. The end had ceased to charm, and how could there ever again be any interest in the means? I seemed to have nothing left to live for.[6]

When several months later Mill emerged from this despondency, his outlook was altered in two respects: he realized that happiness must not be the direct aim of life but can only ensue as by-product from successful endeavor toward some definite goal, and that intellectual development could not dispense with the cultivation of feeling and appreciation for the arts.

In 1830 Mill met a young lady of beauty and intellect who, though two years younger than he, was married and already mother of three. Mill and Harriet Taylor were closely associated through the rest of her life. In 1849 Mr. Taylor died, and in 1851 the two were married. Mill gave his wife credit for some of his best ideas. On account of his admiration for her talents, Mill became the leader of the movement for women's suffrage. In 1867, when for one term he was a member of Parliament, he tried to amend the Reform Bill of that year to give the vote to women.

Mill earned his living, as his father had done, by working in the office of the East India Company. He began as a junior clerk at the age of 17; in 1856 he succeeded to the office his father had held, Chief Examiner of the India Correspondence. When two years later the Company was nationalized, Mill retired with a pension after 35 years' service. Some of his most important writings, including the two for which he is best known today, belong to the fifteen years of his retirement, a great part of which he spent in southern France. In 1873 he died in Avignon and was buried there.

Utilitarianism

Mill's brief *Utilitarianism* (1861) is the classic statement of the ethical position known as Consequentialism, from its central tenet that the rightness of acts is to be judged in terms of their (actual or probable) consequences. In doctrine Mill agreed with Bentham except on one point, connected with Mill's changed outlook after his mental crisis. Bentham gave minute directions for estimating the relative quantities of pleasure to be got from different experiences, but he refused to make further distinctions apart from considerations of intensity and the like: "Quantity of pleasure being the same, pushpin [a trivial pastime] is as good as poetry." Mill argued to the contrary.

> It is quite compatible with the principle of utility to recognise the fact, that some *kinds* of pleasure are more desirable and more valuable than others. It would be absurd that while, in estimating all other things, quality is considered as well as quantity, the estimation of pleasures should be supposed to depend on quantity alone. . . . It is better to be a human being dissatisfied than a pig satisfied; better to be Socrates dissatisfied than a fool satisfied. And if the fool, or the pig, are of a different opinion, it is because they only know their own side of the question. The other party to the comparison knows both sides.[7]

The decision between pushpin and poetry must be made by an impartial jury familiar with all the delights of both. If "irrespective of any feeling of moral obligation to prefer it" they award the preference to poetry, then that is the more desirable pleasure.

On Liberty

In 1859 Mill published a defense of the liberty of the individual against what was at the time a relatively new danger: the tyranny not of a king or small ruling class but of the majority, manifested not so much in oppressive legislation as in the coercive pressure of public opinion. The principle he enunciated is

> That the sole end for which mankind are warranted, individually or collectively, in interfering with the liberty of action of any of their number, is self-protection. That the only purpose for which power can be rightfully exercised over any member of a civilized community, against his will, is to prevent harm to others.[8]

Mill based his defense on utility "in the largest sense, grounded on the permanent interests of man as a progressive being."[9] Progress is really the key notion, as we see from his advocacy of free thought and discussion—not merely insofar as they further the greatest happiness, but absolutely. For free thought is indispensable to the advance of thought in the direction of truth.

An opinion threatened with suppression may be true or false, or partly true and partly false. If it is true, its suppression deprives society of truth—and to Mill it was self-evident that hushing up the truth is a bad thing. Even if it is false and pernicious, its advocacy has value in keeping the defenders of truth on their toes; doctrines not discussed become dead dogmas. If the opinion is partly true and partly false—the most usual case—there is loss of both kinds. Since Mill's opponents were mainly defenders of Protestant Christian orthodoxy, he was able to make effective use of historical examples taken from the persecution of Christians by pagans and of Protestants by Catholics. Mill allows one restriction on freedom of speech:

> An opinion that corn-dealers are starvers of the poor . . . ought to be unmolested when simply circulated through the press, but may justly incur punishment when delivered orally to an excited mob assembled before the house of a corn-dealer.[10]

This is an example of the "clear and present danger" criterion subsequently recognized by the United States Supreme Court.

Mill deplored the drab conformity in action and mode of life, already widespread in his day. By definition, conformists do not instigate progress. Where complete conformity has been achieved, as in China, culture is fossilized. Individuality, originality, even eccentricity should be recognized as socially valuable.

Society has a right to regulate only those of a person's actions that affect others. But can we make such a distinction in practice? Getting drunk may seem a personal affair, but the drunkard may leave his or her family to starve. Thus drunkenness is socially harmful, therefore justly punishable. Mill replied that in such a case punishment should be for nonsupport—the actual damage done. There could be no objection to exhorting the drunkard to mend his or her ways, but he or she must not be coerced.

It would be wrong to suppose that Mill's viewpoint has been generally adopted, even in liberal democracies, in the years since the publication of *On Liberty*. He gave specific examples of unjustifiable (according to his principle) encroachments on personal freedom: the suppression of polygamy among the Mormons of Utah; prohibition of the drug traffic, gambling, and prostitution; and restrictions (other than registration) on the sale of poisons.

The Methods of Science

Utilitarianism is the moral philosophy that makes the most consistent and thorough effort to base ethics on ascertainable facts, eliminating from consideration all "intuitions." The appeal to alleged self-evidence was in Mill's opinion not only mistaken but immoral and the support of immorality.

> By the aid of this theory, every inveterate belief and every intense feeling, of which the origin is not remembered, is enabled to dispense with the obligation of justifying itself by reason, and is erected into its own all-sufficient voucher and justification. There never was such an instrument devised for consecrating all deep-seated prejudices.[11]

This dislike of intuitionism pervades Mill's metaphysics and philosophy of science as well as his ethics.

The only truths knowable independently of experience, Mill held, are propositions which do nothing but explicate the meanings of words, such as "Bachelors are unmarried." These "identical" propositions tell us nothing about the world—not even what our ideas are; in this respect Mill is stricter than Hume. On the status of mathematics, Mill held, as Kant did, that the axioms are informative and not disguised definitions; this is true not only of "a straight line is the shortest distance between two points" but even of the common notions at the base of arithmetic, such as that if equals are added to equals the sums are equal. Disagreeing with Kant, Mill concluded that mathematical axioms must be generalizations from experience, the best established of all because of their pervasiveness and simplicity.

Mill accordingly held that deductive inference cannot be a method for discovering new truth. If I assert that all men are mortal and that Socrates is a man, then from the principles of the syllogism I am committed to asserting also that Socrates is mortal. However, the premises do not constitute a reason for accepting the conclusion; if they did, I would be reasoning in a circle. In order to know that all men are mortal, I must *already* know that Socrates is mortal.

Genuine inference is the process whereby from what we know we discover something that we do not already know. Looking at the question of the mortality of Socrates from this standpoint, we see that what we already know is that Smith, a man, has died; Jones, a man, has died; Robinson, a man, has died; and so on—but only for a finite number of particular men. From these particulars we can and do make two inferences. First, we infer the truth of another particular statement, the assertion that Socrates is mortal. Here is inference directly from particulars to another particular, without any intervening general proposition. Second, from the same evidence we make the inductive generalization that all men are mortal. The fact that we can now arrange the evidence and the two conclusions of inference into a syllogism—in which the generalization and the evidence logically entail the conclusion of the particular inference—ought not to be allowed to obscure the actual evidence relation, which is induction from the minor premise to both major premise and conclusion.

When we reason from particulars to particulars we assume the validity of the principle of induction, or law of cause and effect; otherwise there would be no ground for supposing that the deaths of men in the past constitute evidence for the mortality of the present President. But how do we know that the law of cause and effect holds? By induction, Mill said. "We may even regard the certainty of that great induction as not merely comparative, but, for all practical purposes, complete."[12] To the Humean objection that to prove the principle of induction inductively is to reason in a circle, Mill replied that the appearance of circularity vanishes once we grasp the true role of the minor premise in the syllogism. The success of particular inductions is at once the warrant for predicting the success of other particular inductions and the evidence for the general law of cause and effect.

Mill, like Francis Bacon, tried to formulate the procedures whereby causes can be discovered. According to Mill there are four methods, which he called agreement, difference, concomitant variation, and residues. We take as example the method of difference.

> If an instance in which the phenomenon under investigation occurs, and an instance in which it does not occur, have every circumstance in common save one, that one occurring only in the former; the circumstance in which alone the two instances differ is the effect, or the cause, or an indispensable part of the cause, of the phenomenon.[13]

For instance, if we take a litter of rats with identical heredities, divide them into two groups, raise each group in identical environments—save only that Group *A* is fed polished rice and Group *B* unpolished—if then all the rats in Group *A* but none in Group *B* develop scurvy, we can infer that scurvy is causally connected to deficiency of some ingredient found in rice polishings. This method is at the base of all use of control groups in experimentation. In practice, inference will not be certain because of the difficulty of being sure that the groups are really identical with the sole exception of the element under investigation.

The method of difference, however, is limited as a procedure for scientific discovery, if indeed it is a method of discovery at all. For it cannot work unless we have identified properly all the possibly relevant circumstances in the cases under comparison. To do this we must already possess all the concepts in terms of which the conclusions will be stated. Recall Anaximenes' experiment of blowing on his hand; this was an application of the method of difference. The two breaths, according to Anaximenes, differed only in that one consisted of thick air, the other of thin. Since in one instance, that of the thin air, heat occurred, and in the other, the thick air, heat was absent, Anaximenes inferred that heat and thinness are causally connected. He was wrong because the really relevant difference was not between presence and absence of thick air but presence and absence of expanding air. But Anaximenes was not to blame for not thinking of the situation in terms of expansion. It is doubtful whether he had the notion, and even if he did it could not have been obvious that air blown hard expands.

The method of difference, and the other three, can lead to discovery of the cause when the situation has been properly conceptualized and the investigator is familiar with all the possibly relevant factors. They have established the connection between smoking and lung cancer. But the great discoveries in science typically are, or require, conceptual breakthroughs—in the making of which Mill's methods play no part. Furthermore, these discoveries are not always nor even often answers to questions of the form "What causes it?" The great triumph of physics in Mill's era was the theory of electricity and magnetism. Here the problems were not about causation but about how to conceive these "strange twisty forces." The key to the mysteries was Faraday's conception of the field of force: a model for understanding.

Permanent Possibilities of Sensation

Dislike of intuitions led Mill also to affirm a Berkeleyan conception of matter. He took for granted the Cartesian principle that our immediate awareness is directed to our own sensations, so that the external world must be not perceived but inferred. His psychological account of the inference was like Hume's: the laws of association lead us to fill in the gaps and smooth out the irregularities of our actual sensations.

> I see a piece of white paper on a table. I go into another room, and though I have ceased to see it, I am persuaded that the paper is still there. I no longer have the sensations which it gave me; but I believe that when I again place myself in the circumstances in which I had those sensations, that is, when I go again into the room, I shall again have them; and further, that there has been no intervening moment at which this would not have been the case. . . . The conception I form of the world existing at any moment, comprises, along with the sensations I am feeling, a countless variety of possibilities of sensation. . . . These various possibilities are the important thing to me in the world. . . . Matter, then, may be defined, a Permanent Possibility of Sensation. . . . I affirm with confidence, that this conception of Matter includes the whole meaning attached to it by the common world, apart from philosophical, and sometimes from theological, theories.[14]

The Self, complementarily, is Permanent Possibility of Feeling.

This is a puzzling theory. We might ask first what the force of the word "permanent" is? Presumably there are temporary possibilities of sensation to contrast, but what these are we are not told; nor why, supposing they are such things as lightning and rainbows, they must be less material than mayflies and tidal waves; or indeed where the line is to be drawn. Perhaps the function of the word is to reassure us by retaining in the new definition of matter a relic of the solid permanence that formerly consoled us. The chief difficulty, however, lies in the paradoxicality of grounding the actual in the possible rather than vice versa. We might describe a stick of dynamite as a permanent possibility of explosion, or a restaurant as a permanent possibility of dinner. But on unpacking these rather poetical phrases, what we mean appears to be that dynamite—on account of chemical properties it actually has here and now—is such that in certain circumstances it will explode; and that because there exists, whether I see it or not, an actual kitchen containing actual foodstuffs, saucepans, and cooks, dinner will be forthcoming when I please to order it. By analogy, if matter is to be called a Permanent Possibility of Sensation, the phrase ought to mean that it is because of something actually existing on Mill's actual desk that there is the possibility for Mill, if he reenters the room, to have a certain sensation. But Mill seems to be using the definition as a means of dispensing with what he regards as a metaphysical entity, the actually existing (but unsensed) piece of paper. This theory, whatever its merits, can hardly claim to be unmetaphysical. An unsupported possibility, even if Permanent, seems to be the ultimate in metaphysical entities.

46

The Will in Germany

HEGEL AND HIS FOLLOWERS dominated German philosophy through the first half of the nineteenth century. Their slogan "The real is the rational, the rational is the real" being the extreme claim for the cosmic supremacy of Reason, anti-Hegelians were stigmatized as irrationalists; unfairly, for to dispute the exalted status assigned by Hegel to what he presumed to call Reason—a faculty of extracting profundity from contradictions—was in itself hardly a sign of disloyalty to evidence and logic. Moreover, much so-called irrationalism consisted in pointing out that human behavior is often lacking in rational justification or motivation; it is hardly irrational to call attention to these lamentable facts.

Two Germans, one a younger contemporary of Hegel, the other half a century later, emphasized the dominance of will over intellect. One was a comfortable and sensual man whose philosophy was ascetic and pessimistic; the other was an ascetic invalid who sang the joys of strength and sensuality.

Schopenhauer

Arthur Schopenhauer was born in 1788 in the (then) free city of Danzig. His father was a rich merchant who admired Voltaire; his mother was a feminist and avant-garde novelist. When Arthur was five, Danzig was annexed to Prussia. The father, who could not abide the clergy-dominated government of Frederick William II, moved the family to Hamburg, still a free city. The boy, an only child, was given an international education—in France and England, Austria, and Switzerland, as well as Hamburg—in preparation for the business career that, his father assumed, he would follow despite his dislike of commerce and desire for a studious life. The conflict did not come to a crisis, for when Arthur was seventeen his father underwent a mental collapse and killed himself.

Thereupon Frau Schopenhauer removed herself and her son to Weimar, the literary capital of Germany. There young Schopenhauer enjoyed the patronage and friendship of Goethe (1749–1832). However, he stayed no longer than he had to. He and his mother quarreled incessantly. As soon as he turned 21 and came into money of his own, he left. For two years he studied medicine, and then in 1811 went to Berlin to take up philosophy.

Unaffected by the nationalism that at the time was whipping so many young Germans to a martial frenzy, Schopenhauer spent the years from 1813 to 1818 in rural solitude writing first his doctoral dissertation and then *The World as Will and*

Idea, his principal work in philosophy, which in 1818 fell deadborn from the press. Schopenhauer did not react to disappointment so calmly and sensibly as Hume had done in similar circumstances. When next year he was favored with an appointment as *Privatdozent* in the University of Berlin, he deliberately scheduled his lectures for the same hours as those of Hegel, who had just arrived in triumph, acclaimed as the leading philosopher of all Germany. After one year, during which he failed to attract even a few auditors away from the "great windbag," Schopenhauer abandoned the academic life forever.

His inheritance, which he managed prudently, assured him the means to live comfortably if not grandly. When not traveling, he lived principally in a boarding-house in Frankfurt-am-Main. From time to time he published books, which like his masterpiece attracted little attention until a collection of *Essays*, 1851—including his notorious denunciation of women and defense of suicide—caught on and aroused interest in his previous works. Schopenhauer was delighted by the fame that came to him so late, and in 1860 the great pessimist died happy.

The World as Idea

Schopenhauer regarded himself as the first genuine philosopher since Kant and as Kant's true heir. His metaphysics consists approximately of Kant's, tidied up. The twelve Categories are reduced to one, the Principle of Sufficient Reason, which has four forms: in logic, the relation of ground to consequent; in physics, the spatiotemporal and causal relations; and in psychology, the relation of motive to action. And Schopenhauer claimed to have discovered what the Thing in Itself is.

> "The world is my idea [*Vorstellung*, in some translations 'representation']": this is a truth which holds good for everything that lives and knows, though man alone can bring it into reflective and abstract consciousness. If he really does this, he has attained to philosophical wisdom.[1]

What is known and experienced is not out there but in here. We cannot see the sun but only the sun-in-relation-to-consciousness, the phenomenon that is the interaction of two unseens and unseeables.

That "all that exists, exists only for the subject"[2] is as true of a man's body as of any other so-called material object. Your arms, as you perceive them, are your ideas, and so are their movements, and all the actions in which you engage.

The World as Will

But of course you are not a mere spectator of your own actions. They are known to you also as manifestations of your will. What is the relation between the will to throw the stone and the throwing of the stone? Hume and most philosophers have thought of it as cause and effect. This is a mistake, Schopenhauer insisted. You do not observe the willing, then the throwing, and proceed to infer a connection. You *are* the being that wills and throws; the willing and the throwing are not two events but one and the same, though known under two aspects. The body is "nothing but objectified will, i.e., will become idea."[3]

In ourselves we are conscious of will, but will is not the same as consciousness; it is what underlies consciousness. That is why Schopenhauer equates it to the Kantian thing-in-itself. Indeed (Schopenhauer averred) Kant was on the point of saying so, when in his writings on "practical reason" he made the will the locus of the character as virtuous or wicked, and at the same time asserted that the possibility of being virtuous or wicked must be referred not to the self of experience (that is, the body) but to the "noumenal self," the self as a thing-in-itself. Kant was right to deny that the noumenal self is knowable in experience, where by experience is meant ideas; but there is, so Schopenhauer claimed, an "underground passage" to it.

Through this passage you have access not to something personal to you, but to the fundamental reality. Just as the *whole* world is your idea, and also mine, so you are the *whole* will, in which the real nature of the world consists. Will is the same in you as in me; not only in us, but in everything. Individuation—separation— applies only to ideas, and is, in the end, illusory. Our bodies are objectified will; so is a lion, a tree striving to overtop its neighbors, a boulder pressing against a sapling and at last breaking it and rolling to the bottom of the canyon. Gravity, indeed, is the lowest grade of objectification of the will. Every phenomenon is a manifestation of this blind desire, striving, impulse.

In giving a specially eminent metaphysical status to will, Schopenhauer's philosophy had many precedents. Spinoza, Leibniz, even Berkeley found will at the core of things. The latter two supposed, however, that there are as many distinct wills as there are persons—and that these are either subordinate to the associated intellects in some way, or at least they cooperate with them to bring about a world that is ultimately an intelligible harmony. Schopenhauer emphatically rejected these assumptions. It is not the nature of will to aim at anything other than its own continuation. It is blind and knows nothing of harmony. So far from being subordinate to intellect, will creates intellect; consciousness is nothing but an instrument the will makes in order to have its way. Conscious thought is hardly more than a froth on the wave; Schopenhauer saw how few of our real motives are apparent to us. He therefore denied the principle taken as fundamental by Descartes and all his successors, that mind is essentially conscious and immediately and infallibly known.

Having proclaimed will to be the core of reality, Schopenhauer proceeded to take a position hitherto unheard of in European philosophy: he declared reality to be fundamentally evil.

> All *willing* arises from want, therefore from deficiency, and therefore from suffering. The satisfaction of a wish ends it; yet for one wish that is satisfied there remain at least ten which are denied. Further, the desire lasts long, the demands are infinite; the satisfaction is short and scantily measured out. But even the final satisfaction is itself only apparent; every satisfied wish at once makes room for a new one; both are illusions; the one is known to be so, the other not yet. No attained object of desire can give lasting satisfaction, but merely a fleeting gratification; it is like the alms thrown to the beggar, that keeps him alive to-day that his misery may be prolonged till the morrow.[4]
>
> The basis of all willing is need, deficiency, and thus pain. Consequently, the nature of brutes and man is subject to pain originally and through its very being. If, on the other hand, it lacks objects of desire, because it is at once deprived of them by a too easy satisfaction, a terrible void and boredom comes over it, *i.e.*, its being and existence itself becomes an unbearable burden to it. Thus its life swings like a pendulum backwards and forwards between pain and boredom.[5]

Art and Asceticism

Is there then no hope, no alleviation?—Cheer up, there are three.

The contemplation of art is "will-less perception." Here at least temporarily is rest from the oscillation between frustration and boredom. To enjoy a painting, a play, or a symphony is to put yourself outside the arena and regard with detachment the goings-on inside. Music, Schopenhauer held, is the most direct representation of the will. It is the highest art form just because in listening we are in intimate touch with the world as will, yet without willing. For the moment we have made the will into idea.

While the will to live necessitates suffering, some pains are worse than others. Sympathy for suffering, then, and effort to comfort, are not useless. Sympathy is the basis of Schopenhauer's ethics. Only the pessimist is properly sympathetic; optimism, denying the ultimate reality of pain, is heartless. Schopenhauer, though not religious, admired Christianity and Buddhism for their pessimism and exaltation of compassion.

The most radical stratagem is the turning of the will to destroy itself. Schopenhauer did not mean suicide which, though in a way a good thing, is still a sign of passionate involvement. He intended rather the intellectual denial of the will to live, manifested in an ascetic cessation of all desire. Since the will is not free, not everyone can attain this complete indifference, this *Nirvana* of the Hindus. Schopenhauer himself did not.

Nietzsche

Friedrich Nietzsche's father and both his grandfathers were Lutheran ministers; he almost became one himself. Born in Roecken, Prussia, in 1844, when he was only five he lost his father and so was brought up as the only male in a household of five females. His life gruesomely illustrated Schopenhauer's declamations on human misery. Having been, understandably enough, a rather sissified boy, when he went to the University of Bonn to study theology he tried hard to be a regular fellow. He joined a fraternity and visited a brothel once or twice. These may have been his last as well as his first sexual experiences. From them he contracted syphilis, which made him an invalid all his life and resulted in paresis and extinction of his intellect when he was in his forty-fifth year.

Nietzsche abandoned theology and went to Leipzig to study Greek. His professor considered him the most brilliant student he had ever taught. When only twenty-four he was awarded a doctorate without a dissertation, so that he could be appointed Associate Professor of Greek at the University of Basel. He was promoted to the professorship two years later, just before the outbreak of the Franco-Prussian War. Though by then a Swiss citizen, he volunteered as a hospital corpsman in the Prussian army but was given a medical discharge after a short period of service.

At the time he was writing his first book, *The Birth of Tragedy from the Spirit of Music*, a lively and insightful essay but not a work of exact scholarship (or pedantry). Its publication in 1872 aroused the hostility of conventional classical scholars, including his Leipzig benefactor Ritschl; he found himself more or less boycotted and without students. In any case Nietzsche had no fondness for academic routine as the aggravations of his ill health made it more and more difficult to keep up. In

Friedrich Nietzsche, *1873*.

1879 he retired from the faculty with a pension, supplemented by income from a bequest from an uncle who had prospered in America. He had ten more years of sanity ahead. However, he was nearly blind, and suffering from migraine headaches and insomnia, to combat which he took chloral hydrate ("Mickey Finn"). He moved about from boardinghouse to boardinghouse in Italy, Switzerland, and southern France. During this period he wrote a book a year, which were published mostly at his own expense and almost completely ignored. This indifference infuriated the author against the Germans (Nietzsche believed, wrongly, that he was of Polish descent). In January 1889 in Turin, excited by the effort of trying to protect a horse from being beaten, he suffered complete mental breakdown. Nursed by his mother and sister, he vegetated for eleven years, expiring in 1900. By that time his books had made him a celebrity, but he never knew it.

Truth and Philosophy

Most of Nietzsche's books consist of aphorisms and short essays, loosely (if subtly) connected. He was opposed to philosophical argumentation, "dialectic," on principle: it was in his view an innovation by Socrates, the decadent corrupter of the sound instinctive Greek attitude to life. "What must first be proved is worth little."[6] He admired Heraclitus and imitated his epigrammatic, paradoxical, and enigmatic style. Thus

> Truth is that kind of error without which a certain species of living being cannot exist. The value for *life* is ultimately decisive.[7]

Elsewhere, however, Nietzsche numbers himself among those holding to the conviction that

> *nothing* is needed *more* than truth, and in relation to it everything else has only second-rate value.[8]

It might seem, then, that not only does Nietzsche not argue, he does not even maintain the same views but says whatever occurs to him. This would be a mistake, or at least an exaggeration. Nietzsche is probably as consistent as most philosophers who wrote as much as he did. The statements about truth just quoted are not incompatible. In the first one Nietzsche is emphasizing the doctrine, which he took from Schopenhauer, of the intellect as instrument of the will to live. What we in fact call truth at a given time and place is that set of beliefs that helps us to get on with living. This set includes many dubious items, and many that are patently false. Nietzsche believed that most religious and metaphysical beliefs are of this sort: they have survival value (though for the wrong kind of people, usually) but no correspondence to fact. The kind of truth, on the other hand, that has supreme value is found in the natural sciences. This is a different matter entirely. It is strange that Nietzsche should so often be called an antirationalist. He was indeed opposed to so-called rationalist metaphysics, but only in the way that Hume was.

Nietzsche admitted, however, that to exalt truth as the supreme value requires faith. Experience does not show that truth is always valuable; on the contrary, it is often useless, repulsive, even dangerous. Faith in science is consequently a moral matter, not justified by utilitarian calculation. Nietzsche went so far as to say that

> even we devotees of knowledge today, we godless ones and anti-metaphysicians, still take *our* fire too from the flame which a faith thousands of years old has kindled: that Christian faith, which was also Plato's faith, that God is truth, that truth is divine.[9]

A New Morality

But *God is dead*, Nietzsche announced.[10] When He was 'alive', belief in Him had provided the focus for morality and the reason for all other existence; He had made life worthwhile. However, European thought had passed beyond the stage where it was any longer possible to regard the universe as the effect of a superhuman personal cause.

The death of God presaged the collapse of the whole moral system and the onset of "nihilism," that is, rejection of moral distinctions and a policy of utter permissiveness. Nietzsche often used the expression "we immoralists" and made disparaging remarks about "moralic acid" and the like, giving rise to the misconception that he was himself a nihilist ("nothing-ist"). He did indeed hold that the traditional value system needed a thorough overhauling—a "re-evaluation of all values" (*Umwertung aller Werte*)—but in order that a new code more in keeping with the best in human nature might consciously be created. This, he thought, was the great opportunity made possible by the death of God.

What Nietzsche wanted was the fullest possible scope for the Will to Power. In the lurid light of the twentieth century, this has seemed ominous; but in fact Nietzsche was merely Aristotelian, desiring the maximum realization of human potential. He was like Aristotle too in deeming the most important potentialities to be intellectual.

It is obviously false, Nietzsche held, that every human being has the same potential for development. Besides such natural inferiorities as those of women to men and Germans to Frenchmen, there are everywhere individual differences. Most people, the "many-all-too-many," are "botched and bungled." They can be useful but only as servitors, means to the ends of the few natural aristocrats. The noble values—in primitive societies those of the warrior caste—are truthfulness, spontaneity, pride, loyalty, friendship, boldness, and lack of rancor. The moral code of a society is good insofar as it encourages the development and predominance of men of this type—or as Nietzsche more vividly put it in the poetic-prophetic language of *Thus Spoke Zarathustra*, prepares for the advent of the Superman (*Uebermensch*, "Overman" in some translations). This figure, despite his notoriety, is somewhat vaguely delineated. Man, we are told, is a creature to be surpassed; Superman is he who shall surpass him. Although this suggests a projection of evolutionary ideas, Nietzsche did not have in mind gross biological alterations of the human frame. Superman was his ideal human being: Goethe, approximately.

Superman is a warrior, at any rate the human type who in rude warlike societies assumes leadership. Nietzsche sometimes seemed to glorify bloody combat: "You say it is the good cause that hallows even war? I say unto you: it is the good war that hallows any cause."[11] However, the vigor and zest that manifest themselves in combat are found sublimated in the intellectual hero. Nietzsche was as far removed as possible from glorifying the aggressions of Prussia or any other state. In predicting the great wars of the twentieth century, he foresaw the future more clearly than anyone else of his time; but the prospect did not enrapture him. The State, he said, "is the name of the coldest of all cold monsters. Coldly it tells lies too; and this lie crawls out of its mouth: 'I, the state, am the people.'"[12] Georg Brandes, the Danish critic who first publicized Nietzsche, described his philosophy as "aristocratic anarchism." Nietzsche approved.

There are, alas, other kinds of leaders besides warriors, and they are the reason why progress toward the Superman is not a fact. There are priests. The priest is devious, mock-humble, clever, untrustworthy, dissimulating, envious, and resentful. Where the warrior says Yea to life the priest says Nay. The moral sickness of Europe is due to its having fallen under the domination of priests, beginning with St. Paul.

The morality of Greece and Rome in their great days was the code of the warrior. The will to power and its honest direct satisfaction were recognized as good. What was associated with the rabble—humility, weakness, envy, pity, resentment—were bad, worthless, the traits of plebeians and slaves. Then Christianity in St. Paul's version reversed the value system. The botched and the bungled triumphed; what had been bad became good; what had been good became, not bad, but evil. This is the slave morality, the exaltation of impotence: "The meek shall inherit the earth." The will to power is condemned—a piece of hypocrisy, for the priests exercised power undreamed of by the deposed aristocrats.

The extreme of slave morality is reached in the equalitarianism of socialist democracy. (Marx and Engels, however, are nowhere mentioned in Nietzsche's writings.) Nietzsche discerned behind the passion for equality mere spitefulness, the craving for revenge on those who have outdone us.

> *That man be delivered from revenge*, that is for me the bridge to the highest hope, and a rainbow after long storms.
> The tarantulas, of course, would have it otherwise. "What justice means to us is precisely that the world be filled with the storms of our revenge"—thus they speak to each other. "We shall wreak vengeance and abuse on all whose equals we are not"—thus do the tarantula-hearts vow. "And 'will to equality' shall henceforth be the name for virtue; and against all that has power we want to raise our clamor!" . . .
> But thus I counsel you, my friends: mistrust all in whom the impulse to punish is powerful. They are people of a low sort and stock; the hangman and the bloodhound look out of their faces. Mistrust all who talk much of their justice! Verily, their souls lack more than honey. And when they call themselves the good and the just, do not forget that they would be pharisees, if only they had—power.[13]

When the demand for equality is linked to the belief in general happiness and universal education, only disaster can result. The culture that values book learning

> requires a slave class for its continued existence, but in its optimism it denies the necessity for such a class; therefore, it courts disaster once the effect of its nice slogans concerning the dignity of man and the dignity of labor have worn thin. Nothing can be more terrible than a barbaric slave class that has learned to view its existence as an injustice and prepares to avenge not only its own wrongs but those of all past generations.[14]

The supremacy (officially at least) of the slave morality has caused two thousand years of European degeneration. But now, because God is dead, the possibility lies open for the restoration of the master morality: the *Re-evaluation of All Values*. Nietzsche planned to write a book with this title, but his breakdown occurred just after completion of the first part: *The Antichrist*, perhaps the most stinging attack on Christianity ever written.

Eternal Recurrence

In his last years Nietzsche was fascinated by the notion of eternal recurrence, the belief that time is cyclical; every series of events must be—indeed, already has been—repeated exactly, down to the tiniest detail, an infinite number of times. The Stoics endorsed this speculation, which is itself recurrent. Nietzsche supposed that the doctrine was implied by physics, which teaches that matter and energy are finite, time is infinite. Therefore there are only a finite number of possible arrangements of things; when these have been gone through, as in time they must, the series must begin again.

The thought awed and bemused Nietzsche, who drew from it, inconsistently, the moral conclusion that you should be especially careful about what you do, since you are destined to do it over and over ad infinitum. To him the courage to face the concept of eternal recurrence became the criterion by which the noble could be distinguished from the slave. It seems to have played the emotional role in his thinking of "Where will you spend eternity?" in the Lutheranism of his forefathers that he supposed he had rejected altogether.

VIII

Up to Now

47

Pragmatism

PRAGMATISM, THE FIRST DISTINCTIVELY American philosophical movement to achieve international recognition, was invented by Charles Sanders Peirce (1839–1914) and popularized by William James (1842–1910), two Harvard graduates and lifelong friends who were, however, of very different philosophical and personal temperaments.

Peirce

Peirce, the son of a distinguished mathematician and astronomer, was in many respects the American Leibniz: in his extraordinarily penetrating intelligence, the breadth of his scientific and philosophical interests, his bent for logic (to which he made contributions of fundamental importance), his preferred method of production (papers, not books), his respect for the medieval schoolmen, his Realist position on universals, and his passion for system (he produced no fewer than four more-or-less complete versions of his worldview, each one after the first a response to technical and for the most part self-discovered inadequacies in the previous formulation). He studied chemistry, worked as an astronomer and (for thirty years) as a physicist with the U.S. Coast and Geodetic Survey, and was for eight years Professor of Philosophy in the then new Johns Hopkins University. Yet he achieved little fame in his lifetime, and no permanent remunerative employment. His latter years were spent in solitary poverty, alleviated by the generosity of his wealthy friend William James, in gratitude to whom he took the additional middle name Santiago (*i.e.* St. James).

The Origin of Pragmatism

Despite the many similarities of Leibniz and Peirce, in one crucial respect they were polar opposites. Leibniz pressed the claims of *a priori* knowledge further than any other philosopher. Peirce, on the other hand, regarded metaphysical theorizing (unchecked by experience) about how things *must* be as only more or less sophisticated indulgence in wishful thinking and of no cognitive value. This difference was not merely temperamental but was related to their views about logic.

A tenet of Aristotelian logic, which Leibniz did not question, is that every proposition is really of subject-predicate form—that is, it ascribes some quality to

Charles Sanders Peirce

some substance, for instance mortality to Socrates. If so, then relations must really be qualities: "Socrates is shorter than Theodorus" must ascribe the quality, being-shorter-than-Theodorus, to Socrates. But this kind of quality cannot pertain to the essence of a substance; Socrates would not cease to be Socrates if Theodorus were shortened. A devastating consequence for the theory of knowledge is that nothing learned by perception can pertain to the essence of anything. For perception can reveal only the *relations* in which things stand to perceivers. (This inference was made explicitly by Spinoza, for example.)

Peirce's discovery of the logic of relations, about 1870, made possible the philosophical rehabilitation of perception. He showed that relations are logically just as fundamental as properties. 'Socrates is snub-nosed' ascribes the property of being snub-nosed to a single substance. 'Socrates is shorter than Theodorus' ascribes the relation 'shorter than' to the *ordered pair* Socrates/Theodorus. Hence 'snub-nosed' can be thought of as a *one-place predicate*—meaning that a complete proposition results when it is complemented by the name of a single individual. 'Shorter than' is a *two-place predicate* that forms a proposition by association with an ordered couple of substances. (There can of course be three-, four-, . . . *n*-place predicates.)

It thus turns out that there is no metaphysical distinction between qualities and relations. If the essence of a thing is the set of predicates that necessarily apply to it, then the essence can include the relations in which the thing necessarily stands. Indeed there will be things whose essences are entirely relational—for example the South Pole, which is just that point on the earth's surface that uniquely stands in the relation 'south of' to every other point.

The consequence for theory of knowledge is that perception is no longer debarred from access to the essences of things by the argument that observation involves relation. The traditional logic upheld a sharp distinction between what a thing *is*—its qualities—and what it *does*, for acting (including affecting the sense organs of a perceiver) can be described only relationally. Explanation then had to be thought of as showing how the accidental, relational properties—what the thing does—stem from the essential nonrelational predicates, which were strictly unobservable. (Put in these terms, it is easy to see why Hume was right when he declared an objective "necessary connexion between cause and effect" to be undiscoverable in experience.) But the logic of relations abolished the distinction between being and doing, so that a thing could be thought of as identical with its actions—with what it does to other things, including human perceivers.

Thus, for example, when we discover that if we look at sugar we have a sensation of white color; if we put it on our tongue we experience a sweet taste; if we put it into hot coffee it dissolves; if we burn it it leaves a black residue which, when subjected to laboratory analysis, proves to be carbon;—and so on; we are learning what sugar *is*, not merely what is done by an inner nature 'behind' these processes. "This is sugar" *means* the whole infinite set of if-then statements describing experience of its behavior in all possible circumstances, a sample of which is given above. To make these statements is to state the essence of sugar.

> Consider what effects, that might conceivably have practical bearings, we conceive the object of our conception to have. Then, our conception of these effects is the whole of our conception of the object.

These two sentences from Peirce's paper "How to Make our Ideas Clear" (1878) comprise the Pragmatist theory of *meaning*.

A companion essay, "The Fixation of Belief" (1877), develops the Pragmatist conception of *inquiry*. A genuine inquiry is the struggle to get rid of doubt, an irritating condition of not knowing what to do, and to replace it with the "calm and satisfactory" state of belief. Peirce distinguishes four methods of bringing about this transition: *tenacity*, consisting in the adoption of whatever belief we may fancy and holding on to it come what may by closing our minds to criticism and contrary evidence; *authority*, the equivalent method adopted by the State rather than the individual; the *a priori* method of selecting the answer that is most "agreeable to reason," *i.e.* to antecedent prejudice; and finally *science*. Peirce pays his sardonic respects to the popularity and convenience of the first three methods, but notes that as they lack connection to "external permanency" they cannot prevent the eventual reawakening of doubt. Only the method of science is "such that the ultimate conclusion of every man shall be the same."

> Its fundamental hypothesis . . . is this: There are Real things, whose characters are entirely independent of our opinions about them; those Reals affect our senses according to regular laws, and, though our sensations are as different as are our relations to the objects, yet, by taking advantage of the laws of perception, we can

ascertain by reasoning how things really and truly are; and any man, if he have sufficient experience and he reason enough about it, will be led to the one True conclusion.

Peirce held that different inquirers, if only they proceed scientifically and conscientiously about the same question, are "fated" to converge on an agreed conclusion: the truth.

But how could he be sure that there are "Reals" in the sense required? Peirce's answer was fourfold.

> 1. If investigation cannot be regarded as proving that there are Real things, it at least does not lead to a contrary conclusion; but the method and the conception on which it is based remain ever in harmony. No doubts of the method, therefore, necessarily arise from its practice, as is the case with all the others. 2. The feeling which gives rise to any method of fixing belief is a dissatisfaction at two repugnant propositions. But here already is a vague concession that there is some *one* thing which a proposition should represent. Nobody, therefore, can really doubt that there are Reals, for, if he did, doubt would not be a source of dissatisfaction. The hypothesis, therefore, is one which every mind admits. So that the social impulse does not cause men to doubt it. 3. Everybody uses the scientific method about a great many things, and only ceases to use it when he does not know how to apply it. 4. Experience of the method has not led us to doubt it, but, on the contrary, scientific investigation has had the most wonderful triumphs in the way of settling opinion.

James

William James studied science, medicine, and painting in France, Switzerland, Germany, and the United States, earning the M.D. degree from Harvard in 1869 where he was appointed Instructor in Anatomy. His interests turned to psychology, then in its infancy as an experimental science. In 1880 he joined the Department of Philosophy, where he taught philosophy and psychology until 1907. His book *Principles of Psychology* (1890) is a classic both of psychology and of philosophy. By all accounts he was one of the sweetest men who ever lived.

James shared Peirce's distaste for *a priori* speculation and called himself a "radical empiricist." Nevertheless a major motive in his philosophizing was a desire to vindicate freedom, which he saw as threatened by determinism and rationalistic philosophies stemming from Hegel that set up what he called a "block universe" in which nothing could be otherwise than as it is. Peirce's logic of relations restored experience to the role of arbiter of reality—and nothing in experience reveals any such constraining necessity, James insisted.

Peirce's foundational essays on Pragmatism, though published in the *Popular Science Monthly*, went unnoticed for twenty years until James expounded the ideas in "Philosophical Conceptions and Practical Results," a lecture delivered at the University of California in 1898. James accepted Peirce's theories unmodified. However, in his version there is a difference in emphasis concerning the nature of the experience that gives meaning to our concepts. This appears in the definition of Pragmatism that James wrote for Baldwin's *Dictionary of Philosophy and Psychology* (1902).

> The whole meaning of a conception expresses itself in practical consequences, either in the shape of conduct to be recommended or in that of experience to be expected

if the conception is true, which consequences would be different if it were untrue, and must be different from the consequences by which the meaning of other conceptions is in turn expressed.

No doubt "conduct to be recommended" might be included among the "effects, that might conceivably have practical bearing" in which Peirce had located the meaning of our concepts; but Peirce was astonished by some of James' examples, such as "'God' means that 'you can dismiss certain kinds of fear.'"[1]

James' concern for the effects of belief on the quality of life of the believer was most famously expressed in "The Will to Believe" (1896). Against agnosticism, James upheld the thesis that

> *Our passional nature not only lawfully may, but must, decide an option between propositions, whenever it is a genuine option that cannot by its nature be decided on intellectual grounds; for to say, under such circumstances, "Do not decide, but leave the question open," is itself a passional decision,—just like deciding yes or no,—and is attended with the same risk of losing the truth.*

A "genuine option" is defined as one that is living, forced (*i.e.* unavoidable practical consequences attend both acceptance and rejection), and momentous (the consequences are serious). James held that the religious hypothesis—which he stated exceedingly nondoctrinally as

> the best things are the more eternal things, the overlapping things, the things in the universe that throw the last stone, so to speak, and say the final word. 'Perfection is eternal' . . . [and] we are better off even now if we believe [the foregoing]—

is a genuine option for most people. Believing it increases confidence and adds zest to life. So there can be no objection to belief. Moreover, the majority of religions teach that the universe is a 'thou' not an 'it', an even more advantageous opinion.

Such sentiments were unpalatable to Peirce, who had written

> Logicality in regard to practical matters . . . is the most useful quality an animal can possess, and might, therefore, result from the action of natural selection; but outside of these it is probably of more advantage to the animal to have his mind filled with pleasing and encouraging visions, independently of their truth; and thus, upon unpractical subjects, natural selection might occasion a fallacious tendency of thought.[2]

While Peirce had advanced only a Pragmatic theory of meaning—taking for granted the traditional conception of truth as correspondence of assertion with fact—James seemed to be propounding a new notion of what it means to say of a proposition that it is true.

> *True ideas are those that we can assimilate, validate, corroborate, and verify. False ideas are those that we cannot.* That is the practical difference it makes to us to have true ideas, that therefore is the meaning of truth . . .
> *The true . . . is only the expedient in the way of our thinking, just as the right is only the expedient in the way of our behaving.* Expedient in almost any fashion, and expedient in the long run and on the whole, of course . . .[3]

Peirce was impelled to rechristen his own philosophy "Pragmaticism," saying he hoped the new name was so ugly that no one would be tempted to kidnap it.

James' "Pragmatic Theory of Truth" provoked numerous hostile criticisms, notably from Bertrand Russell. However, James reiterated that he never intended to redefine truth or to deny that a true proposition must correspond with an objective reality; he was offering, he insisted, only an insight into the means of discovering truth.

Dewey

John Dewey (1859–1952) was the son of a grocer in Burlington, Vermont, and was educated there in the tiny (faculty of eight) University of Vermont. After graduation he taught school for two years and then, with the combined encouragement of his teacher of philosophy and of W. T. Harris, the Hegelian editor of the only American philosophical journal, he borrowed $500 from an aunt and entered the Johns Hopkins University for graduate study in philosophy. Peirce was one of his teachers. In 1884 he took the Ph.D. and joined the faculty of the University of Michigan where he taught for ten years, and then went to the University of Chicago as head of the Department of Philosophy, Psychology, and Pedagogy— Dewey's three principal interests. By this time he had been much influenced by James' *Principles of Psychology*, and in cooperation with the Michigan Department of Education had written books for teachers in training.

The "Dewey School" at Chicago, which he founded as a laboratory for his students, became the fountainhead of the progressive education movement: learning by doing (instead of rote memorization and recitation), the student-centered approach. *School and Society* (1900), probably the most influential of Dewey's books, began as fund-raising lectures for the school. When in 1904 the President of the University of Chicago sabotaged the school, Dewey resigned, soon thereafter accepting an offer to go to Columbia University where he remained until his retirement in 1929.

Dewey lectured on education to great effect in Japan, China, Turkey, Mexico, and the Soviet Union—which last he visited in 1928, a time when experimental approaches were being discouraged in favor of Stalinist indoctrination. Dewey, who like many liberal thinkers had had high hopes for the new regime, was disillusioned by what he saw and was confirmed in his distrust of all dogmatisms. A decade afterward and as an indirect consequence of his visit, he became chairman of the international (but unofficial) tribunal investigating the charges brought against Leon Trotsky *in absentia* by Stalin after the latter had won the power struggle of the twenties. The findings were published in a volume entitled *Not Guilty*—which, however, did not prevent Stalinist agents from seeking out Trotsky in Mexico, whither he had fled, and assassinating him.

Dewey continued to lecture and write for nearly a quarter of a century after his official retirement. The bibliography of his works runs to 150 pages. After James' death in 1910 he was the acknowledged dean of American philosophy, indeed of the academic community, having been a founder of the American Association of University Professors.

Instrumentalism

The earliest philosophical influence on Dewey was Hegelian and, as he acknowledged, something of it remained permanently: the organic antianalytic viewpoint and the notion of process as fundamental. These were reinforced by studies in physiology and in evolutionary biology that began when he was an undergraduate in Vermont.

Processes are classified by Dewey into three groups of "transactions": first, those that are merely physicochemical; next, those involving psychophysical relations; finally, human *experiences*, the processes of primary interest to the philosopher. But the distinctions are not sharp, all three types forming a continuum in which the later developed from the earlier in the course of evolution. Dewey said that the main purpose of his philosophical writings was "to reintegrate human knowledge and activity in the general framework of reality and natural processes."[4]

Though all knowing is experiencing, experience is a wider concept than knowledge, including all (human) *action* as well. Indeed, knowing is a kind of doing.

> Every experience in its direct occurrence is an interaction of environing conditions and an organism. As such it contains in a fused union somewhat experienc*ed* and some processes of experienc*ing*. In its identity with a life-function, it is temporally and spatially more extensive and more internally complex than is a single thing like a stone, or a single quality like red.[5]

The extensiveness and complexity mentioned in the last sentence are the *only* types of difference that Dewey admitted between experiences—conscious processes—and simpler things like stones and qualities. Although reluctant to be called a Materialist, preferring "Naturalist," he repudiated all doctrines that imply a discontinuity between minds on the one hand and the subject matter of physics and of chemistry on the other.

The kind of experience from which knowledge emerges Dewey called *inquiry*, following Peirce, and conceived it in much the same way. Genuine inquiry begins in a problem situation, a felt difficulty. The first step in inquiry is the articulation of the problem—the coming to consciousness of what the difficulty is. Then hypotheses are proposed that, if satisfactory, will clear up the difficulty. These hypotheses are refined and made more precise, to the point at which they can be subjected to experimental testing. If successful, the inquirer finds that the initial problem situation has been transformed into a "unified whole." Some of the steps, of course, may need to be repeated.

Articulating the problem and proposing hypotheses require the introduction of *concepts*, which in this scheme have the status of tools of inquiry. For this reason Dewey called his theory of knowledge "Instrumentalism": concepts are instruments useful in inquiry.

The aim of inquiry is to obtain knowledge, which is expressed in a proposition that is "warrantedly assertible." Dewey, like James, was suspicious of the notion of *truth* because of its association with metaphysical absolutes outside experience. To say that a proposition is warrantedly assertible, however, claims no more than that it describes a situation that in the experience of the community of inquirers is felt not as problematic but as a "unified whole." In further agreement with Peirce, Dewey held that inquiry is self-correcting—the results of (serious) inquiries will "converge." Dewey intended this pattern sketch of inquiry to fit both commonsense problem-solving and the most sophisticated scientific procedures, though of course different subject matters require different detailed methods for their investigation.

The philosophical importance of the conception of inquiry as the process from which alone knowledge emerges is primarily that it affords a strictly 'empirical' theory of knowledge that need not seek 'foundations'—Hume's 'impressions', the 'sense-data' of more recent philosophers—for which dubious claims of infallibility must be made. Deweyan inquiry can begin anywhere, with anything, and no element enjoys any preferred status. The growth of knowledge may be compared, on this model, to the increasing clarity and detail of a landscape perceived as the fog lifts.

Although Dewey made the successful termination of inquiry, "warranted assertibility," to consist in the *experience* of a unified whole—that is to say, in a *feeling* of satisfaction on the part of investigators—he drew back from the precipice over which James was in danger of falling when he allowed "our passional nature" to decide what to believe. Dewey insisted that the satisfaction warranting assertibility must not be just any satisfaction—including that which comes to true believers when they close their eyes—but must be the special kind of cognitive satisfaction appropriate to serious and unbiased inquirers. However, his repeated attempts to formulate a criterion by which to judge whether the satisfaction is of the right type did not allay the fears of all his critics.

Dewey claimed that the theory of inquiry dissolved many of the most venerable philosophical conundrums.

> Some of the gratuitous dualisms done away with . . . are those of the objective and subjective, the real and apparent, the mental and physical, scientific physical objects and objects of perception, things of experience and things-in-themselves concealed behind experience, the latter being an impenetrable veil which prevents cognitive access to the things of nature.
> The source of these dualisms . . . is isolation of cognitive experience and its subject-matter from other modes of experience and *their* subject-matters, this isolation leading inevitably to disparagement of the things of ordinary qualitative experiences . . .[6]

In other words, many traditional problems of philosophy do not arise in genuine experience but merely reflect the confusions of philosophers about the nature of experience. This, as we shall see, is one—but only one—of the attempts made in the twentieth century to demote problems to the status of 'pseudoproblems', calling not for solution but for *dis*solution. For example, Dewey suggested that the "problem of the existence of an 'external world'"

> is artificially generated by the kind of premises I call epistemological. When we *act* and find environing things in stubborn opposition to our desires and efforts, the externality of the environment to the *self* is a direct constituent of direct experience.[7]

It may be interesting to compare this treatment of the problem with Dr. Johnson's tactic of kicking the stone to refute Berkeley.

Ethics

> The problem of restoring integration and cooperation between man's beliefs about the world in which he lives and his beliefs about values and purposes that should direct his conduct is the deepest problem of any philosophy that is not isolated from that life.[8]

The problem is particularly acute in twentieth-century philosophy because of the prevalence of theories of language holding that there is an unbridgeable gap between descriptive utterances ("The cat is on the mat") and prescriptions ("The cat ought not to be on the mat"). The former, if true, correspond to verifiable facts; but what is there for the latter expressions to correspond to? The desires of the utterers? Then sentences containing "ought," "right," "wrong," and the like express merely subjective preferences—which have little connection, logical or factual, with the way the world is—and one is 'as good as another'?

Philosophers have sought to rescue ethical objectivity in various ways. Dewey characteristically found the fact-value dichotomy to be just another gratuitous dualism. He saw no reason why valuations might not be objects of inquiry just as facts are, and in much the same way. There is no need (he held) to have one method in natural science, another in morals.

Genuine inquiry into values begins in an unintegrated situation, one in which a difficulty—What is to be done?—is felt. The application of intelligence consists in analysis of the situation (the facts, determination of which may require a separate inquiry), formulation of alternative lines of possible conduct, imaginative projection of their probable consequences, and deliberation of their relative desirabilities. Prejudice and ignorance must be eliminated in this process, just as in any scientific investigation. Valuation, furthermore, if serious is done in a social context—there is a community of valuers—so there is nothing 'subjective' about it.

Democracy, because it allows for social experimentation and selection of the most successfully progressive ideas, is the best political organization of society.

The Fate of Pragmatism

Today few philosophers call themselves Pragmatists. The reason is not, however, that Pragmatism has been refuted or discredited. Rather—being more an attitude than a school—its major insights have been largely absorbed into the fiber of most twentieth-century philosophy, at least in North America and Britain.

48

Russell

BERTRAND ARTHUR WILLIAM RUSSELL was born in Wales, May 18, 1872; he died in Wales, February 2, 1970. His position in British philosophy for most of his life was similar to that enjoyed by Locke and Mill in their days. In addition, his enlightened and witty humanity made him the first citizen of the world, fit to stand comparison to Voltaire.

His parents, who were advanced thinkers and close friends of John Stuart Mill, died young—the father when Bertrand was only two, the mother in the following year. Their will provided that Bertrand and his elder brother were to be brought up by a guardian who was a freethinker; it was set aside by court order. The boys were entrusted to their paternal grandparents.

The Russell family, of which the Duke of Bedford is head, for centuries has produced statesmen of liberal policies. One of the most eminent was John, first Earl Russell, who was eighty-five when his grandsons came to live with him. It was he who introduced in Parliament the Reform Bill of 1832. He served in various offices, including that of Foreign Secretary, and was twice Prime Minister. He died, aged eighty-six, when Bertrand was six. The boy's education was directed by his grandmother, the dowager Countess, a Scottish lady with a Puritan outlook on life. Russell is kind to her memory in his autobiographical writings, but from her letters she appears never to have let pass an opportunity to nag, scold, and whine. She disapproved of boarding schools and had the boys taught at home by governesses and tutors, so that Bertrand, unlike most English upper-class boys, had no respite from home life. In adolescence he often contemplated killing himself, but was "restrained by the desire to know more mathematics."

His education was thorough. His recreation, in lonely surroundings, was mainly the reading of history and poetry and the study of mathematics, which fascinated him as it had Hobbes, but happily at a younger age. At eighteen he was awarded an entrance scholarship to Cambridge University.

Russell's undergraduate career was scholastically brilliant and the happiest period of his life. For the first time he had many friends—young men who were bright and energetic.

> The world seemed hopeful and solid; we all felt convinced that nineteenth-century progress would continue, and that we ourselves should be able to contribute something of value. For those who have been young since 1914 it must be difficult to imagine the happiness of those days.[1]

At Cambridge he studied mostly mathematics and philosophy, and in 1895 was elected to a fellowship of Trinity College, where he lived for six years. Again, 1910 to 1916, he was lecturer in philosophy until dismissed on account of his opposition to the continuation of World War I. The fellowship was reinstated in 1919, but he resigned it. Not until 1944–1949 did he again lecture in Cambridge.

The twenty years beginning about 1900 were those of Russell's greatest productivity in logic and the more technical branches of philosophy. During this time he wrote *Principles of Mathematics* (1903), *Principia Mathematica* (with Alfred North Whitehead, 1910–1913), *Our Knowledge of the External World* (1914), *Introduction to Mathematical Philosophy* (written in prison and published in 1919), and *The Analysis of Mind* (1921), besides numerous papers. These works are the foundation of Russell's reputation as a philosopher. At the same time he was a socialist and active in politics on behalf of unpopular causes, mainly women's suffrage. His lack of religious belief debarred him from Parliament. He believed in God (so he tells us) until he was eighteen, because the first cause argument convinced him; but then he read, in Mill's *Autobiography*, that it is futile to argue that God must exist to be Cause of the universe, for this only raises the further question "Who made God?" While an undergraduate and under the influence of British Hegelians, for some time he thought the ontological argument to be valid; that faith too disappeared when he abandoned Hegelianism.

During World War I, Russell was already in his forties and overage for military service. He made himself unpopular by advocating a negotiated peace—not from doctrinaire pacifism but because he thought that even victory for the Germans, who were in the wrong, would be preferable to continuation of the hideous slaughter. In 1918 he was imprisoned for six months, having been convicted of libeling American troops by alleging that at home they were used for strikebreaking.

In 1920 Russell visited the newly constituted Soviet Union. He was not favorably impressed. Russia, he wrote, "seemed to me one vast prison in which the jailors were cruel bigots." His little book *The Theory and Practice of Bolshevism* accurately predicted the course that Communist dictatorship was to take in the next twenty years. This outraged his socialist friends, as his opposition to the war had alienated the others.

Russell when in his early twenties decided to write two series of books: one, the scientific, beginning with the most abstract departments of logic and mathematics and proceeding to the relative concreteness of biology; the other, social and political, taking departure from the immediate problems of the times and becoming more abstract. The two series were to meet in the middle. He did not carry out this plan in detail, but the long shelf of his writings consists of these two kinds of books. The twenty years after 1920 were mainly given to writings on politics, education, and social ethics.

One of the books Russell wrote in this period was *Marriage and Morals* (1929), in which he had some good words to say for sex (he was only the third philosopher to do so, after La Mettrie and Nietzsche). He also stated the opinion that episodes of infidelity should not necessarily be regarded as incompatible with satisfactory marriages, and recommended that young people might find it advantageous to contract informal trial marriages, which would be especially desirable among college students, who would thereby be relieved of obsession with sex and (so Russell thought) be able to study more efficiently.

In 1938 Russell came to the United States to teach at the University of Chicago and then at the University of California at Los Angeles, where he declined a permanent appointment in favor of an offer from the College of the City of New York. There was an outcry at this appointment from the local Bishop of the Episcopalian Church, the Catholic hierarchy and lay groups, and the Hearst newspapers. A housewife of the Bronx brought suit to have the appointment revoked on the ground that if her daughter attended classes conducted by Professor Russell her morals might be corrupted. A judge upheld the complaint in a vituperative decision stating that the Board of Higher Education in appointing Russell was "in effect establishing a chair of indecency." Mayor LaGuardia and other officials prevented the Board from appealing the decision.

The title page of the British edition of Russell's fiftieth book, published the following year, reads as follows.

AN INQUIRY

INTO

MEANING AND

TRUTH

BY

BERTRAND RUSSELL

M.A., F.R.S.

Holder of the Nicholas Murray Butler Medal of Columbia University (1915), the Sylvester Medal of the Royal Society (1932) and the de Morgan Medal of the London Mathematical Society (1933). Honorary Member of the Reale Accademia dei Lincei. Fellow (1895–1901) and Lecturer (1910–1916) of Trinity College, Cambridge. Herbert Spencer Lecturer at Oxford (1914). Visiting Professor of Philosophy at Harvard University (1914) and at The Chinese Government University of Peking (1920–1921). Tarner Lecturer at Cambridge (1926). Special Lecturer at the London School of Economics and Political Science (1937) and at The University of Oxford (1938). Visiting Professor of Philosophy at the University of Chicago (1938–1939). Professor of Philosophy at the University of California at Los Angeles (1939–1940). Occasional Lecturer at the Universities of Uppsala, Copenhagen, Barcelona, the Sorbonne, etc., etc.

Judicially pronounced unworthy to be Professor of Philosophy at the College of the City of New York (1940)

Subsequently Russell was awarded the Order of Merit, one of the highest British honors—bestowed on the personal initiative of the King—and the Nobel

Prize for literature, 1950, with the citation "One of our time's most brilliant spokesmen of rationality, and a fearless champion of free speech and free thought in the West."

Russell wrote that "The secret of happiness is to face the fact that the world is horrible." He tried to make it less horrible. His last quarter century was occupied with movements attempting to limit the production and proliferation of nuclear weapons. Earlier, during the time when the United States had exclusive possession of the bomb, Russell took the position that we would have been justified in using the threat of nuclear war to obtain from other countries, notably the Soviet Union, enforceable agreements to outlaw nuclear war.

In 1961, for having taken part in a nuclear disarmament sit-in demonstration in Trafalgar Square, Russell served his second jail sentence, this one of six days. The next year he received a unique if backhanded honor: the committee arranging to celebrate his ninetieth birthday was refused use of the Royal Albert Hall on the ground that his Lordship's presence might provoke a riot, with damage to the furnishings. The festivities took place instead in the Royal Festival Hall without incident.

Logical Atomism

In the latter part of the nineteenth century, followers of Hegel dominated philosophy in Great Britain. Russell was brought up in this tradition and taught to regard the British "empiricists" as shallow. While still an undergraduate, however, he began to have doubts about Hegel when he discovered (so he tells us) that what Hegel had to say about mathematics was nonsense. G.E. Moore, a year younger than Russell and his closest philosophical companion, encouraged him in revolt. Russell was ever afterwards an analytic philosopher, the direct heir of Locke, Hume, and Mill.

Yet he was also a member of the class of philosophers who were mathematicians: Pythagoras, Plato, Descartes, and Leibniz—men impressed with the rigor and clarity of mathematical method and the certainty of its results, who strove to generalize its procedures and with them attain comparable benefits in other departments of knowledge. Russell, coming after Hume, became convinced reluctantly that mathematical statements are exempt from uncertainty only at the cost of inability to describe any matters of fact. But if he recognized a great gulf fixed between mathematics and natural science, he believed nevertheless—at least in his earlier period—that philosophy itself not only might benefit from mathematics but could even be absorbed into it. For, he maintained, philosophy is at bottom logic, and logic is indistinguishable from mathematics.

He argued that mathematics is a branch of logic since arithmetic, and therefore all the rest of mathematics, can be developed as a system of deductions from axioms which are purely logical, such as (letting p and q stand for any two propositions) "If p is true then p-or-q is true." The traditional logic of Aristotle can be considered as the doctrine of the relations of class membership and class inclusion. The syllogism

> All men are mortal;
> Socrates is a man;
> Therefore, Socrates is mortal.

can be rewritten as

> The class of men is included in the class of mortals;
> Socrates is a member of the class of men;
> Therefore, Socrates is a member of the class of mortals.

Russell held that numbers can be defined as classes of classes: 2 is the class of all couples, 12 the class of all dozens, and so on. Arithmetic is, then, a part of the calculus of classes, which is a branch of logic. The establishment of the definition of number and the working out of simple arithmetical propositions from a set of axioms for logic were arduous enterprises, carried out in outline in *The Principles of Mathematics* and in detail (not to everyone's complete satisfaction) in *Principia Mathematica*.

Russell held that "every philosophical problem, when it is subjected to the necessary analysis and purification, is found either to be not really philosophical at all, or else to be . . . logical."[2] It may be not philosophical because it belongs to a natural science, for instance the problem (which exercised Berkeley) whether we perceive depth directly or by inference. But if it is a philosophical problem, it turns out to be a question of logic. This is so because "every metaphysical theory has a technical counterpart."[3] To use a favorite example of Russell's—the Hegelian contention that to know anything is to know everything—this belief is a consequence, so Russell tells us, of the assumption that every proposition is of the subject-predicate form; that is, every proposition asserts that some subject has some attribute. If that were so there could not be more than one substance, for the proposition "There are two substances" does not ascribe a predicate to anything, hence asserts nothing. Otherwise put, belief in the Hegelian Absolute, or in integrative philosophies generally, results from the doctrine of *internal relations*, which is the contention that a proposition asserting a relation, such as "The cat is on the mat," is really an ascription of properties of spatial location to the cat and to the mat. Now since everything is related to everything else, it follows that if relations are really properties and if knowing a thing is the same as knowing all its properties, nothing can be known completely until its relations to everything else are known—in short, until everything is known. But the doctrine of internal relations is simply a logical mistake. The relation in the example is signified by the preposition 'on', which cannot be eliminated by rewording; even to specify exact latitudes, longitudes, and altitudes of cat and mat would presuppose a coordinate system in which places are located only in relation to a center. (As we have seen, Peirce had earlier reached the same conclusion about relations.)

In the Hegelian view the cat enters into the nature of the mat and vice versa, so that remarks about the cat that do not mention the mat cannot be entirely true. Moreover, the cat's being on the mat is a fact only in relation to the consciousness of the knower, and depends essentially on that relation. To deny the doctrine of internal relations is therefore not only to make analytic philosophy possible, but also to restore philosophical acceptability to such beliefs of common sense as that things do not necessarily depend on consciousness, and that particular propositions can be true—completely true—on their own and apart from what else may be the case.

> With a sense of escaping from prison, we allowed ourselves to think that grass is green, that the sun and stars would exist if no one was aware of them. . . . The world, which had been thin and logical, suddenly became rich and varied and solid.[4]

Alas, this revel on the green grass was not to last, and the Russellian world was to become even thinner and more logical.

One purpose of philosophy, Russell said, is to "give an account of science and daily life." Philosophers are expected to tell us what, ultimately, there is in the world. But instead of attempting to enumerate the kinds of things there are, Russell, taking the world to be whatever makes our true statements true, and noting that truth pertains to propositions not names, concluded that it is more profitable to consider facts as the ultimate constituents. Since every true proposition states a fact, and conversely every fact can (presumably) be stated by a true proposition, the question of what there is in the world reduces to the question of what kinds of propositions there are. This is another example of the principle that every metaphysical theory has a technical logical counterpart.

Logic tells us what kinds of propositions there are. The simplest kind, which Russell calls "atomic," ascribes a simple property to an individual, or asserts a relation to hold between two or more individuals: This is red; This is longer than that. Complex or "molecular" propositions are built up of atomic propositions by conjunction ("This is red and this is longer than that"), disjunction ("Either this is red or this is longer than that"), and implication ("If this is red then this is longer than that"). A molecular proposition is said to be a *truth function* of its atomic constituents; this means that the truth value (*i.e.* the truth or falsity) of the molecule can be derived, according to rules, from the truth values of the atoms. A conjunction is true if and only if both conjuncts are true, an alternation if and only if at least one alternate is true, and an implication is true in every case except that in which the antecedent (the atomic proposition following the 'if') is true and the consequent false. The import of this, and the reason for calling the theory "logical atomism," is that each atomic proposition is true (or false) strictly on its own: truth of molecular propositions depends on truth of atomic propositions, but never vice versa.

Unfortunately for neatness and simplicity, Russell found himself obliged to admit that there are other irreducible propositions besides the simple kind just described. There must be negative propositions, such as "There are no lions in this room," "Unicorns do not exist;" and there must be general propositions, "All crows are black." One might suppose that the last would be equivalent to "This crow is black and that crow is black and the other crow is black and . . . ," that is, the conjunction of propositions ascribing blackness to each and every crow. But the equivalence would not hold unless to the complete enumeration were added the proviso ". . . and these are all the crows there are," which is a general proposition. Even more troublesome are propositions such as "Democritus believed that the earth is flat," "Socrates hoped that the souls of the just would go to heaven," which seem to be complex but cannot be truth functions of their apparent components—they are both true, although it is false that the earth is flat and it is (perhaps) unknown where the souls of the just go.

If this logical doctrine is to serve as a metaphysics or theory of knowledge, one must specify what can qualify as the *this*es and *that*s of the atomic propositions, and what kinds of properties and relations can be predicated of them. Russell showed himself to be in the Cartesian-Lockean inside-out tradition. Our knowledge of the world, he held, must be built up from our experience of the world—and experience is to be construed as immediate awareness, which Russell calls "acquaintance." "Every proposition which we can understand must be composed wholly of constituents with which we are acquainted." The 'acquaintance' intended is not the relation between a person and his or her neighbors and colleagues but between a mind and a "hard datum"—by which is meant something known without inference. One kind of hard datum is the *sense-datum*; following G.E. Moore, Russell used this expression to designate what Berkeley spoke of as 'idea', Hume as 'impression', Mill and Mach as 'sensation'. Hard data include also recent memories, principles of logic, and some universals. Russell did not deny that our neighbors have lives of their own out of our attention, but what we know of them consists of awareness of the colored patches that make up their appearances in our visual fields, the sounds that seem to issue from their vicinity, and so on, together with inferences we base on these sense-data, such as that they have not gone to bed yet. Our neighbors considered as physical objects are "what cause the sense-data." We know them only by this *description*—that is, we know one or more truths about them.

Locke and others in the British tradition had supposed that our knowledge of physical objects, such as it is, is inferential. It sounds odd to speak of the tree at which I am gazing or the neighbor with whom I am quarreling as an inferred entity. Russell, a dexterous man with Ockham's Razor, wished to reduce inferred entities to a minimum. To this end he enunciated the Principle of Abstraction, or as he preferred to call it the "principle by which we dispense with abstractions": "Wherever possible, substitute logical constructions for inferred entities." The notion of the logical construction is not an easy one. In the case of the tree it comes to this: we can consider the tree not as inferred cause of certain sense-data but simply as the class of all the sense-data, both actual and possible, that we ordinarily consider to be associated with the tree. In earlier writings Russell distinguished between the sense-datum and the awareness of it by some conscious subject, but later he gave this up. If we are to speak philosophically we will not say "I saw a flash of lightning" but "A flash of lightning occurred." Thus the notion of event becomes fundamental.

It is possible in this way to dissolve the distinction between mind and body, Russell believed. The flash, in a certain context, is an event in (as we would say) the physical world; in another context, it is a mental event—but it is the same flash in both cases. The world need not be conceived as containing physical events and mental events, but as made of a "neutral stuff" prior to each, which can enter into either the one or the other depending on its relations to other events—whether they are thunderstorms or memories, for example. This doctrine Russell called *neutral monism*. It is essentially the same as Mach's view that "sensations" constitute the world.

In the version of this theory that Russell developed in the 1940s, even expressions such as "This is red" are under suspicion, because the word "this" suggests substance, a forbidden category. When observing a tomato we should not say "This is red" but rather "Red is compresent with round, juicy, . . ." The minimum vocabulary in which we could state all facts would contain words for qualities, compresence, succession, and observed spatial relations. Proper names—a class of words in which, according to Russell, 'this' and 'that' are comprised—could be dispensed with.

Ethics

Young Russell's announcement to his family that he was a Utilitarian was greeted with such derision that afterwards he kept his serious opinions to himself. Nevertheless he remained a Utilitarian all his life, though with a strong admixture of Spinozism with regard to ultimate values. During his lifetime he was best known to the public as a moralist, a shocker of right-thinking citizens, and a frequent spokesman for intellectual groups in desperate attempts to persuade men of power to follow policies less likely to lead to destruction.

A stock objection to anyone who like Russell rejects religion and thereby the will of God as the basis of morality is that his own pronouncements then can be no more than personal opinions. Russell replied that "it is heretical, and very properly so, to hold that right and wrong are *constituted* by God's decrees, since in that case they might just as well have been the opposite of what they are."[5] God's decrees are, in fact, reported variously in different cultures, or in the same culture at different times or by different reporters. The Utilitarian, then, is at no disadvantage with regard to fixity and coherence of standards.

Nevertheless, Russell's principal concern in philosophical ethics was with the avoidance of subjectivism. Accepting Hume's arguments for the thesis that moral judgments are founded on emotions and cannot be true in the ordinary sense of correspondence to fact, he was driven to conclude that moral judgments are not assertions at all—not even of the speaker's attitudes, but are expressions of those attitudes. "Cruelty is bad" is not so much the assertion "I dislike cruelty" (though perhaps that can be inferred from it) as the interjection "Would that no one were cruel!" or "Cruelty—alas!" However, Russell found it intolerable that the analysis of moral judgments should result in something so subjective. In his last work on ethics, *Human Society in Ethics and Politics* (1955), he argued that an objective ethical theory could be built on an emotive basis after all, because as a matter of fact there is general agreement about ultimate values. Nobody (he held) really denies that pleasure is the good that right conduct ought to aim at maximizing; apparent disagreement is due to confusion of pleasure with the means of producing it, which in the case of the sadist may be bad; or with concern for painful consequences, as of hangovers after imbibing or of pleasant diversions which are thought to lead to hellfire. There may be disagreement too between those who hold that the happiness of all mankind is the good and those who recognize only the pleasure of their nation or in-group or simply of themselves. About this, however, rational argument is possible. Russell sought to show that policies aimed at restricting enjoyment to selected parties are likely, on account of resentments generated in those left out, to result in diminished happiness even for the favored group. If all disagreements about end values are of these two types—confusions that can be cleared up and misapprehensions of the factual consequences of actions—then ethics can be objective in the sense that questions about what ought to be done become questions of means, which are in principle capable of being resolved by essentially scientific methods.

Yet, Russell characteristically conceded, it does look as if there can be genuine differences about end values. He cited disagreement as to whether punishment ought always to be awarded only with a view to reform and deterrence, or whether the infliction of pain on evildoers—retribution—is an intrinsic good. In *A History of Western Philosophy* (1945), he imagined a dialogue between Nietzsche and the Buddha, and commented

> For my part, I agree with Buddha as I have imagined him. But I do not know how to prove that he is right by any argument such as can be used in a mathematical or scientific question. . . . I think the ultimate argument against [Nietzsche's] philosophy, as against any unpleasant but internally self-consistent ethic, lies not in an appeal to facts, but in an appeal to the emotions.[6]

49

Existentialism

THE THREE PRINCIPAL TWENTIETH-CENTURY existentialist philosophers are Karl Jaspers (1883–1969), Martin Heidegger (1889–1976), and Jean-Paul Sartre (1905–1980). The two Germans are said to have disagreed on every point save disapproval of the Frenchman, the only one of the three who was willing to be called an existentialist.

Existentialists are supposed to be foes on principle of systematic philosophy, yet each of the three wrote at least one bulky and systematic treatise—they are in fact the longest winded of recent philosophers; one book by Jaspers runs to 1,100 pages. Jaspers was a Protestant, a believer in the existence of God; Heidegger was agnostic; Sartre characterized existentialism as "nothing else but an attempt to draw the full conclusions from a consistently atheistic position."[1]

For all that, existentialists form a more tightly knit family than any other ists except Thomists and Marxists. They share a common descent from Kierkegaard; an emphasis on the problems of man and human relations, to the exclusion of philosophy of science and most of what has traditionally been thought of as theory of knowledge; a common insistence that the world is irrational, "absurd"; that man in this world is not only free to choose but must choose what he is to become, with responsibility never to be evaded by blaming heredity, upbringing, other people, God, or even rational standards; and a common jargon, largely inherited from Hegel.

In centering their philosophy on man—man not as an object of study but as an actor in the world—with implied and sometimes explicit criticism of other philosophies as irrelevant to the main concerns of living, existentialists remind us of the Stoics. They too offer a worldview that many feel to be more appropriate than supernaturalist religion to our times.

Kierkegaard

Søren Aabye Kierkegaard (1813–1855) was the youngest son of well-to-do and pious parents. He was small and his body was misshapen. Intending to become a pastor, he studied philosophy and theology at the University of Copenhagen. Philosophy at that time and place meant Hegel. Kierkegaard found that Hegel did not speak to him; he conceived a violent antipathy to the system wherein one concept engenders another, everything particular and individual having importance only as illustration of the general. In disgust at this dominant rationalism the young man left the University and the church, and for a time led an extravagant life as a playboy. This period did not last long. Kierkegaard returned to the University, wrote his dissertation, preached sermons, and got engaged to a beautiful young woman. Again this did not last. Again he left the church; broke his engagement; thereafter led a solitary and withdrawn life as a writer—though with characteristic paradox he made a point of appearing in public as often as possible. He wrote voluminously: essays, criticism, satires, fiction, homilies, under numerous pseudonyms, sometimes under one name attacking his own work under another.

Systems and Individuals

Hegel said that the real is the rational. But only systems of general truths can intelligibly be said to be rational. Hence what is real is conceptual structure. The business of the philosopher, in Plato's phrase "the spectator of all time and existence," is to perceive and categorize this structure. No doubt the structure has a content of particular individuals, but they derive their whole reality just from their place in it. The philosopher can be interested in world-historical individuals such as Napoleon—not because they are individuals, however, but because they happen to embody the world spirit. The individual as such has no more significance for the philosopher than some particular stone in an avalanche has for the geologist.

The Hegelian viewpoint implies furthermore that choice is illusory, for all human activity is determined beforehand by the march of the dialectic. At any rate the rationality, therefore rightness, of a choice depends upon its being made in accordance with objective norms derived from the Absolute. The State reflects the Absolute. To find out what I should do, then, I must ask what the State requires of me.

All this was anathema to Kierkegaard. Individuals are the fundamental reality, from them all concepts take their significance. Concepts express only possibilities; actuality, existence, is always of individuals. And in man, what is actual depends on the will, not on the intellect. Nor can man be understood when viewed as an object. The human reality can be seen adequately only from the inside. The actor, not the spectator, must be the philosopher.

What the actor-philosopher sees with unmistakable clarity is the reality of choice. Any system, therefore, that questions choice must give a false picture of man. Nor is it just one fact among others about a man that he chooses; choice makes the man, a man chooses what he is to be. In a rationalist philosophy such as Plato's there is a concept, Man, that individual men participate in more or less adequately. Correspondingly the individual has a character, an essence, that determines his particular actions. This is the view that essence precedes (or determines or guides or is more real than) existence—the teaching of Plato and Hegel among others. We have seen how Aristotle protested that substance, basic reality, is the individual; however, he was constrained by Platonic scruples to qualify his individualism practically to the point of abandoning it. Kierkegaard did not vacillate: *Existence precedes essence* is the foundation of existential philosophy.

At any point in his life a man has a character, which is the summation of the choices he has made so far. That is his essence, and it is what it is. However, it is constantly being added to, and the past does not determine the future of a being who chooses. Nothing does. Not even rational or ethical criteria do. For if I make my choice in accordance with a certain rule for choosing, I thereby choose that rule of choice rather than some other. A man is entirely on his own resources, whether he wants to be or not. To have to choose without any external guidance is *anguish*.

But was Kierkegaard not a Christian? And is not Christianity a way of life, a framework of prescriptions for choices? Yes, but first it is necessary to choose to be a Christian. How that is to be done, and what it involves, was the problem that obsessed Kierkegaard throughout his life. Moreover, as we have seen, to live is to choose. To choose even to become a Christian cannot be to make one big choice that relieves one from the burden of having ever to choose again. On the contrary, the first choice must be renewed at every moment, for the past does not determine the future. Time is real.

Notoriously, most people think otherwise. They do not resolve every problem in inner agony, but choose according to their habits, or do what is customary, or excuse themselves on the ground that history or environment or society or human nature forces them in one direction. All this is evasion, Kierkegaard insisted. There is no sloughing off responsibility. If you conform it is because you have chosen to conform; all that has happened is that you have made matters worse, for you have decided that your existence is to be *unauthentic*. The truth to live authentically by must be yours—not supplied by society or a philosopher or even God and passively accepted. "Truth is subjectivity"; "The crowd is untrue."

Stages on Life's Way

Following his own experiences, Kierkegaard discerned three stages in life, which he labeled the aesthetic, the ethical, and the religious. Man in the aesthetic stage assumes the pose of the spectator, lives for enjoyment, and refuses to commit himself to anyone or anything beyond himself. In the ethical stage a system of moral values is regarded as imposed from without, of paramount importance, and the guide to all decisions. But morality, in the end, is not enough. Beyond morality lies religion, complete commitment to God. Sometimes Kierkegaard represented these stages as constituting a natural progression, one developing into the next from inner necessity in Hegelian fashion. On the whole, however, Kierkegaard seems to have thought of the transition from one stage to another as a conversion, dramatic or even catastrophic. The difference between the ethical and the religious he illustrated with the story of Abraham's obeying the Lord and preparing to sacrifice his only son in contravention of the moral law. In contending that God—without ceasing to be the Perfect Being—could demand such a "teleological suspension of the ethical" and that Abraham was right to obey, Kierkegaard reminds us of the medieval voluntarists, as does indeed his philosophy in general.

Religion to Kierkegaard did not mean the church. The professed Christianity of the middle-class churchgoer was to him the low point of the unauthentic life. On his deathbed he refused ministerial solace, remarking of the Lutheran pastors—who in Denmark were paid by the State—that "Government officials have nothing to do with Christianity." He proposed for his tombstone the simple inscription, "That Individual."

Heidegger and Sartre

Kierkegaard was not an academic or technical philosopher, and certainly had no wish to be one. He was afraid that one day he would fall into the hands of the professors. He seldom argued, and when he did he disdained mere logic; "The conclusions of passion," he said, "are the only reliable ones." He did not concern himself with metaphysics.

Professor Martin Heidegger, wrestling with the Aristotelian problem of Being, arrived by a metaphysical route at a worldview coinciding markedly with Kierkegaard's, as well as with that of Nietzsche, who in ignorance of the Dane's existence had likewise come to similar conclusions. Nietzsche, it will be recalled, proclaimed the death of God and the necessity of finding a new basis for values— though it does not appear that he proposed to leave so important a matter up to every individual.

Heidegger reiterated the question Leibniz had asked: Why is there any Being at all? Why is there not, instead, simply nothing? He did not, however, give the Leibniz answer, that contingent being exists because there is Necessary Being Who creates it. Heidegger explicitly denied the principle of sufficient reason. Being exists for no reason, it is brute fact, "absurd." Man likewise exists without any reason. He finds himself "thrown" into the world, a finite being, temporal, destined for death—a return to nothingness. Consciousness of this fact—fear not of anything definite, but of death, annihilation, "Nothing"—is *dread*. Existentialist man is doomed to freedom.

In-Itself and For-Itself

Heidegger was an inside-out philosopher. Investigation of the problem of being, he held, cannot begin otherwise than with the being of the questioner. Sartre concurred: the starting point must be the conscious subject, which (following Hegel) he called being-for-itself, or simply the for-itself. He explicitly acknowledged the inevitability of the Cartesian *Cogito* as the base on which all knowledge must be constructed, from the resources of the single isolated subject. But Sartre parted company with Descartes immediately after this. There is no need to prove the existence of something other than the subject's consciousness, for this other—being-in-itself—is already implied in the concept of consciousness, which must have an object. The in-itself, that which is a thing, includes the past of the for-itself; that is to say, my past history, my character as so far formed, is an object of study like any other. The in-itself limits the freedom of the for-itself but does not determine it.

The duality of consciousness and its object implies separation. But what separates them? Nothingness. This is not to be taken as meaning that there is no separation; rather that nothingness, nonbeing, which consciousness "secretes," comes between the for-itself and the in-itself. Sartre argued moreover that since the in-itself is being and the for-itself is separated from and contrasted with it, the for-itself must be nothingness, "a hole in being."[2] (This is, apparently, another sense of nothingness. One scholar[3] claimed to discern more than twenty distinct meanings for that word in Sartre's book *Being and Nothingness*.) Sartre meant that the for-itself is continually being transformed into the in-itself; that is to say, the present, in which alone there is consciousness, continually becomes the past, which is purely in-itself. This transition is in fact the generation of time. But the for-itself, as long as it is the for-itself, is nothing; it is mere potentiality, freedom. Yet it is my very existence—it precedes my past, my essence, my historical self. The for-itself is "that which is not what it is and is what it is not." This fact is, not unnaturally, the source of the feeling of *dread*. In yet another sense, nothingness is the instant between past and present; inasmuch as this moment is the separation between the for-itself and the in-itself, Sartre could write that "consciousness is being present to oneself as distant from oneself; and this distance is Nothingness." When I try to think of myself as for-myself, I succeed only in thinking of my past self, my in-myself. The free self is, as for Kant, not a possible object of experience—still another sense in which it is Nothing.

In other words, there can be no such thing as conscious self-identity. This follows of necessity, we are told, from the distinction between the for-itself and the in-itself. But God, by definition, is such a conscious self-identity: that which is in itself and conscious of itself as it is in itself—that is to say, the in-itself-for-itself. Therefore the notion of God is self-contradictory; God necessarily does not exist.

Dreadful Freedom

Sartre argued that from the nonexistence of God it follows that man's existence precedes his essence. For it is the other way around only where a product is in question: the essence of the house exists (in the architect's consciousness) before the house exists. But God does not make man as a craftsman makes a paper knife; there is no God. Sartre pointed out that the contrary view of man persisted in the men of the French Enlightenment who rejected God but still supposed there is such a thing as a common human nature. But "man first of all exists, encounters himself, surges up in the world—and defines himself afterwards. . . . There is no human nature, because there is no God to have a conception of it. Man simply is."[4]

Thus man is condemned to be free. Everything depends upon choice, in particular upon choice of an ideal. If you try to excuse yourself—to blame the in-itself—this is self-deception, "bad faith." Bad faith can, to be sure, be chosen; Sartre maintains that the man who chooses it is really aware of what he is doing.

In one respect Sartre's doctrine of choice goes beyond Kierkegaard's and joins hands with Kant. To choose, according to Sartre, is to legislate for everyone. If I decide upon a course of action as the right one for me, I have by that very fact proclaimed that it is right for every other for-itself in similar circumstances. Thus Sartre attempted to parry the charge of relativism and the objection that to an existentialist one choice must be as good as another: "your values are not serious, since you make them up." Sartre replied in Nietzschean fashion that since we have rejected God, someone has to do the job. This does not mean that the philosopher can or ought to prescribe what others should do. Rather, the task of philosophy is to show people the possibilities of authentic choice. One person cannot judge the absolute worth of another's values, but can say of the other, perhaps, that she deceives herself.

Dreadful freedom and like concepts are employed liberally and rather theatrically in existentialist writings, which tend moreover to dwell on gloomy themes. The impression is almost inevitably created that existentialism is a philosophy of despair. Sartre insisted passionately that on the contrary existentialism is an optimistic form of humanism, since "the destiny of man is placed within himself."[5]

50

Wittgenstein and the Linguistic Turn

WITH NEGLIGIBLE EXCEPTIONS, PHILOSOPHY in the twentieth century has been the exclusive province of academics—'professionals' teaching the subject in universities. This is a feature shared with the scholastic philosophy of the middle ages. Some peculiarities of this professionalism are also shared: technical jargon, minute argumentation, subtle distinctions, striving for exactitude of expression, and preoccupation with the relation of words to things.

The last is a legitimate philosophical concern for, since philosophy is an inquiry not into matters of fact but into concepts, philosophical errors are bound to be logical or linguistic in a broad sense. If a philosophical theory seriously put forward fails to make sense, the trouble must arise in one or the other or both of two ways: either the source of error lies in the ordinary language itself—Greek or German or English—that the philosopher uses, or the philosopher has misunderstood certain features of the language and has inadvertently misused it in such a way that nonsense has resulted. There has been a broad division of philosophers, especially in the present century, between those sometimes called Analysts, who believe that ordinary language should be reformed for philosophic and scientific purposes, and Ordinary Language philosophers, who hold that the cure for philosophical perplexity is understanding how natural languages work.

The central contention of Analysis is that some linguistic forms are more right than others: they are inherently better pictures of facts and are free from the misleading features of ordinary expressions. It is the work of philosophy to discover these correct forms. As an example, let us take the Theory of Descriptions of the leading twentieth-century practitioner of Analysis, Bertrand Russell.

Consider the sentence "The golden mountain does not exist." It is meaningful and true, and purports to assert nonexistence of the golden mountain. But true sentences must be *about* something. What is this one about? "The golden mountain"—what else? So we are led to conclude that in some sense there must *be* a golden mountain because at least one thing can be truly said about it, namely that it does not exist. Reflections of this sort led the Austrian philosopher Alexius von Meinong (1853–1920) to hold that besides the realm of existing things there must also *subsist* all the nonexistent things that can be referred to—even the round square. Russell, appalled at this extravagant multiplication of entities, proceeded to scrutinize sentences asserting (or denying) existence of unique objects.

First he developed the notion of the *propositional function*. This is a form of symbols, such as "*x* is golden," that is not a proposition but becomes one when a word is substituted for *x*. In this example if for the 'variable' *x* we substitute the 'value' "the British Crown," the resulting proposition "The British Crown is golden," is true; when *x* stands for "the (notoriously iron) Lombard Crown," the proposition is false.

Russell asserted that phrases of the form "the so-and-so," which he called *definite descriptions*, are incomplete symbols: their real form is "the one and only value of *x* that satisfies [*i.e.* makes a true proposition of] the propositional function '*x* is so-and-so'", and they have no reference in isolation. Then the real form of "The golden mountain does not exist" is "There is no value of *x* such that the propositional function '*x* is golden and *x* is mountainous' is true when *x* has that value and false otherwise." This sentence has the same meaning as "The golden mountain does not exist," but it does not even purport to mention a golden mountain. Therefore there is no need to provide a metaphysical landscape for such an entity to subsist in.

This is an example of how, according to Russell, an ordinary sentence can be rephrased to reveal its true form. He held further that some ordinary modes of speech are not merely misleading but downright wrong, embodying "the metaphysics of the stone age." The subject-predicate form of sentence entails that reality consists of substances having attributes. Since this is wrong—for reality (according to his lordship) consists of bundles of actual and possible sense-data—a philosophical language should eschew sentences such as "This tomato is red" and "I am thinking" in favor of "Red is compresent with round, juicy, subacid, . . ." and "A thought is occurring." Ordinary language is even logically inconsistent, Russell claimed, in that it allows logical paradoxes to be stated, such as:

The sentence below the line is true.

_____

The sentence above the line is false.

If the sentence above the line is true, it is false; and if it is false, it is true. Russell maintained that ordinary language must be replaced for philosophical purposes by an artificially constructed symbolism with rules forbidding the generation of such monstrosities. (This idea goes back at least to Leibniz, of whose philosophy Russell was a leading scholar.)

Working out the principles of an ideal language for science and philosophy has been a major part of the program of the philosophical movement somewhat loosely referred to as Logical Positivism. But an opposite moral can also be drawn from the tale of the golden mountain. Ordinary speakers of ordinary language find nothing troubling in a remark designed merely to put a curb on the excesses of imagination. "The golden mountain does not exist" is not 'about' anything—that is its point! (Which after all is the same conclusion that Russell reached by his elaborate analysis.) Only philosophers are troubled by it, and only because they try to force this form of expression into a simple all-purpose mold—in other words, because *they have an oversimplified model of how ordinary language works*. (Recall the origin of Platonic Ideas in the notion that words can mean only by being names of real things.) This line of thought eventuated in the Ordinary Language or Oxford philosophy, mostly after World War II.

Wittgenstein's *Tractatus*

The man regarded by many as (so far) the most important philosopher of the twentieth century wrote two major works, the first of which is *almost* a piece of Logical Positivism; the second takes *almost* the Ordinary Language viewpoint and repudiates most of the first.

Ludwig Wittgenstein (1889–1951), of a wealthy and cultured Viennese family, was educated at home until fourteen and then attended technical schools. In 1908–1911 he went to England to do aeronautical engineering research at Manchester, where he designed a propeller and a jet engine. His interests, however, turned toward pure mathematics. In 1912 he gave up engineering to enter Cambridge University and study under Russell, whose *Principles of Mathematics* he had read with consuming interest.

Russell recognized his extraordinary ability. Wittgenstein remained in Cambridge as a student for less than two years at this time, however. Always finding personal relationships difficult, he retired to seclusion in the Norwegian countryside to work on logic. At the outbreak of the war in 1914 he returned to Austria at once and joined the army. He continued work on his book during military service, completing it in August 1918. He sent the manuscript to Russell from the Italian prison camp in which he was interned at war's end. It was not published until 1921, in a learned journal that ceased publication with that issue.

The *Tractatus Logico-Philosophicus* (*Logisch-Philosophische Abhandlung*), though only 80 pages long, is a survey of all reality, a metaphysics in the grand style. Its brevity is due to its containing few arguments. The author asserts his philosophy dogmatically, contenting himself with the hope that a few spirits who have gone through the same process of thinking will one day be enjoyably surprised to find their thoughts set out in it.

The book begins with the assertion that "The world is everything that is the case"; that it consists of "facts, not things." Soon, however, the discussion turns to the "pictures we make for ourselves of the facts": propositions or sentences. The question that generated Wittgenstein's meditations was: How is it possible to *mean*? How can one fact—the sentence—be a symbol for another?

This was a novel way of putting the ancient question. Previous philosophers of language had asked how *words* mean. The usual reply was that they are labels, imposed arbitrarily on things—bodies or universals or classes or ideas. The meaning of a sentence was thought to be derivative from the meanings of its constituent words: Hobbes, for instance, held that a sentence was true if the predicate was a name of the same thing that the subject named. This theory and others of the sort taking the word as the unit of meaning seemed unsatisfactory for several reasons: they could not plausibly be applied to relational (as opposed to subject-predicate) propositions, and they failed to explain why, in verifying propositions, we have to look at the world—why not simply look in the dictionary? Why should we have to look beyond words to find out whether they have the same meanings?

Gottlob Frege (1848–1925), the German mathematical logician who anticipated much of Russell's work and next to Russell was the greatest influence on Wittgenstein, improved this kind of theory by turning it around: "Only in the context of a sentence," he declared, "does a word have a reference." 'Cat' has no reference in isolation, but it refers to a definite animal in "The cat is on the mat." Still, in Frege's view meaning was naming—the sentence as a whole named one of two objects, the True or the False.

Ludwig Wittgenstein, *1930.*

However, Wittgenstein objected, I cannot know what a name such as 'cat' means unless it has been explained to me. Hence if a sentence is a name, how could I know what some particular sentence means without explanation? Yet I do—I can perfectly well understand sentences I have never heard before, if I am familiar with the words in them.

Wittgenstein held that this understanding is possible only if the proposition is a *picture* of the fact: in his words, they share the logical form, the form of representation. The theory was suggested to him by the use of dolls and toy cars in a court of law to reconstruct an accident that was the basis of a suit for damages.

To see a pattern of colors *as* a picture is to understand what certain things must be like if this pattern is a picture of them. In the same way, to hear sounds or see marks as a sentence is to understand what things must be like if the sentence is true. That is why we can understand a sentence we have not previously heard: we understand that the words and their arrangement show the sense of the sentence as the toy cars show the situation in the accident. Now there can be a picture of anything, with one important exception: a picture cannot depict its own relation to what it pictures. The picture *shows* the form of representation, but it does not picture it. Likewise the sentence shows its sense, its relation to the fact, but it does not and cannot *say* what that relation is. The relation of language to the world cannot be put into words.

As in Russell's philosophy, propositions are either complex or elementary. An elementary proposition is one that cannot be analyzed into constituent propositions. It consists of names, each of which names an object; its structure shows the structure of the atomic fact—that is, it states the fact. Wittgenstein concluded, *a priori*, that atomic facts must exist, and that elementary propositions must state them, because the complex presupposes the simple. He gave no example in the *Tractatus* either of atomic facts or of objects, though from his notebooks it seems that he considered whether points in the visual field, or perhaps even watches, might not be objects in his sense. Objects are whatever there are, or can be, names of. Since the possibility of being named is a logical possibility, the same for every possible world, the objects are said to "exist necessarily" and to be the "substance" of the world. Propositions, which are contingent, state the connections that obtain between the objects. The world, it must be remembered, consists of facts not of objects. If we suppose that "The cat is on the mat" is an atomic proposition, and if the cat really is on the mat, then the cat's being on the mat is an atomic fact, one of the constituents of the world. There are other atomic facts into which the cat and the mat enter. But it is impossible to identify an object, except in a fact, by a name that refers to the object in the context.

All propositions that are not elementary are truth functions of elementary propositions—as in Russell's philosophy, but without Russell's restrictions and qualifications. There are some complex propositions that are true whatever the truth of their constituents: for example "It is raining or it is not raining." These Wittgenstein called *tautologies*: degenerate cases of propositions as it were, for they do not tell us how the world is. Logical identities and mathematical equations are tautologies. Although they are helpful to us in elucidating structure, in the description of the world they can be dispensed with.

All atomic facts are independent of one another. Hence, as for Hume, there can be no necessary connection between facts: "Outside of logic everything is accidental." Nor can there be value in the world: values are not facts. "In the world everything is as it is and happens as it does happen. *In* it there is no value—and if there were, it would be of no value."[1] Ethics cannot be expressed, values are "transcendental." Wittgenstein appears to have meant that to make a judgment of value is to take an attitude toward the world, toward "what is the case," from outside. If I say that eating people is wrong, what I express is not a fact, although it is a fact that I uttered the expression.

Philosophical writings, since they consist neither of tautologies nor of statements of fact, are without sense. There are no philosophical propositions. Wittgenstein explicitly applied this conclusion to his own book.

> He who understands me finally recognizes [my propositions] as senseless, when he has climbed out through them, on them, over them. (He must so to speak throw away the ladder, after he has climbed up on it.)[2]

He concludes

> Whereof one cannot speak, thereof one must be silent.[3]

Wittgenstein has been accused of self-contradiction—after all, his book was hardly a case of being silent—or at least of having purported to have invented a special brand of deeply significant nonsense. He has been defended as having been too hard on himself; why did he not note that after all it *is* possible to make significant linguistic remarks? Although the *Nude Maya* does not and cannot depict its relation to the Duchess of Alba, there is no reason why there could not be a painting of Goya painting the *Nude Maya*. Why then can there not just as well be meaningful sentences describing the relation of other sentences to the nonlinguistic facts? The *Tractatus*, despite its author's disparagement, seems to consist largely though not wholly of such unexceptionable statements.

Logical Positivism

Ernst Mach's positivist view of science, in particular his rejection of atoms, was so influential as to amount to orthodoxy in later nineteenth-century physics—Ludwig Boltzmann (1844–1906), the founder of statistical mechanics, almost alone upholding the reality of the atom and in consequence suffering a virtual ostracism that drove him to suicide. Mach was, furthermore, a man of eminence in the affairs of the Austro-Hungarian empire: a member of the upper house of parliament, and after 1896 holder of a professorship of philosophy of science created especially for him in the University of Vienna.

The second holder of the chair, appointed in 1922, was Moritz Schlick (1882–1936), principal organizer of the Ernst Mach Society, after 1929 known as the Vienna Circle. This group of philosophical scientists and philosophers of science held regular meetings and published the journal *Erkenntnis* (*Knowledge*), in which they developed and propagated the philosophy generally known as Logical Positivism. The Circle included among others Rudolf Carnap (1891–1970), Otto Neurath (1882–1945), Herbert Feigl (1902–1973), Friedrich Waismann (1896–1960), and Kurt Goedel (1906–1978). A.J. Ayer (born 1910) attended many sessions in the 1930s, and introduced Logical Positivism to England in his sensational book *Language, Truth and Logic* (1936). Hans Reichenbach (1891–1953) led an affiliated group in Berlin.

The aim of the logical positivists, as of Hume, Comte, and Mach, was to show that all genuine knowledge is comprised in logic, mathematics, and the natural sciences. There is not and cannot be any metaphysical knowledge of a reality above or behind or otherwise transcending what is given in experience. The novelty of *logical* positivism was its rejection of metaphysical statements as not merely unwarranted or false but as literally nonsensical—they do not really mean anything though they may seem to.

The weapon by which the logical positivists hoped to eliminate metaphysics was adapted from Peirce, the Verifiability Principle: the meaning of a proposition is the method of its verification. The method of verifying "The cat is on the mat" consists in looking at the mat and seeing the cat thereupon. If you know that this is how to verify the proposition, you know its meaning, and if you know its meaning, you know how to verify it. "How" must be interpreted leniently. If you are in prison, you may not know how to get out and examine the hearthside. You know, however, what kind of procedure would count as "verifying 'the cat is on the mat'", and that is enough.

The positivists denied the possibility of specifying conditions that would verify pronouncements of metaphysicians, such as "The Absolute is perfect," "An unperceivable substance underlies the qualities given in sense experience," "Causes are not merely conjoined with their effects but produce them." Sentences such as these look like assertions of fact, but by the criterion of meaning are seen to have no empirical content. They are, therefore, only *pseudo-propositions*. It is not true that the Absolute is perfect, but it is not false either; no assertion has been made with those words.

The positivists recognized the necessity for explaining and qualifying their principle. First, the propositions of mathematics, though without empirical content, are nevertheless meaningful. They accounted for this *à la* Hume: mathematical statements are analytic, asserting nothing beyond the consequences of the conventions we have adopted governing the use of mathematical symbols. Second, unless general statements—of which science consists—were to be condemned as meaningless, "verification" could not be taken as meaning "conclusive establishment of truth"; for no matter how many black crows are observed, with never a white one, the next may still surprise us. The Logical Positivists consequently concluded that general statements of matter of fact are at best only highly probable hypotheses. But observation of just one black crow *confirms* the generalization; that is, it increases the probability that all crows are black. Possibility of confirmation in this sense was taken as sufficient for satisfying the verifiability criterion.

The principle, if accepted, has the desired effect of eliminating metaphysics—including religion, for "A transcendent God exists"; "I have an immortal soul"; "In the most holy sacrament of the Eucharist, there takes place a wonderful and singular conversion of the whole substance of the bread into the Body, and of the whole substance of the wine into the Blood, of our Lord Jesus Christ, the species of bread and wine alone remaining"; and the like crucial dogmas, are unverifiable. The positivists allowed that such utterances typically have powerful emotional effects—"emotive meaning," some called it—but they denied their possession of cognitive meaning, any feature whereby they could be properly considered to be either true or false.

The fate of ethics aroused controversy within the movement. Schlick held it to be a fact about human beings that they desire, in the end, only pleasure; so that utterances containing the words 'good', 'right', and the like, refer to the presence or production of pleasure and are verifiable. Ayer on the other hand regarded ethical (and aesthetic) utterances as nothing but expressions of the speakers' emotions. There could be no question, then, of their verification, nor indeed could there even be such a thing as ethical disagreement, for emotions and their expressions do not stand in logical relations to one another. My liking for rice pudding and euthanasia cannot *contradict* your horror of them.

But what verifies a proposition? Experience. The positivists, who claimed to be more rigorous than other philosophers, were bound to give a precise and detailed account of what was to count as experience. Here another controversy arose. Schlick held that if a statement is meaningful to *me*, it must be verifiable by *me* in *my* experience. What verifies (or confirms) "All crows are black" for me is the existence of a certain black patch in my visual field. But if the statement in question is to be a probable empirical hypothesis, scientific and public, other members of the public must have like experiences in the presence of crows. How can I tell whether they do? How can I know that your experience, when looking at crows and coal, is not qualitatively like what I undergo when I look at tomatoes and blood—and vice versa? If it were, you and I would nevertheless use the same color *words* and apply them to the same objects. We would never be able to find out that our color experiences were reversed in this way. Indeed it seems that by the verifiability principle, the statement "Our color experiences are reversed" is meaningless. Therefore, so is its contradictory opposite, "Our color experiences are the same"!

Schlick accepted this paradoxical consequence and tried to establish a distinction between form and content of experience, according to which the structural elements of experience—"this is above that," "this noise is louder and later than that"—are communicable, even though the actual sense content—color, timbre, taste—is not. Otto Neurath on the other hand, followed by Carnap, declared that propositions can be compared only to other propositions. What verifies the crow generalization is a "protocol sentence," a singular statement reporting an individual observation: "Otto's protocol at 9.47 / Otto's speech-thought at 9.46 was / In the tree at 9.45 a black crow was perceived by Otto."

Neurath thus sought to avoid the subjectivism, indeed solipsism, implied by Schlick's restriction of verification to the experience of the verifier. "A black crow was perceived by Otto" is supposed to be an objective scientific statement; its truth does not have to be established by having Otto's experience. It is enough to observe Otto, the body, and his, its, behavior—for example, its uttering the words "I see a black crow." If this kind of observation is deemed insufficient, one could in principle observe Otto's physiological characteristics, including his brain states, while he was pointed in the direction of the crow. Even so, someone might object, it could not be considered certain that Otto was observing a black crow. Neurath admitted the point but denied its force as an objection: no scientific statement is incorrigible, not even the protocol sentence. Its probability is to be judged in relation to the accepted statements of science. To demand absolutely certain foundations—basic sentences not liable to be corrected—is to be a metaphysician, Neurath claimed. In giving up the requirement of firm foundations, Neurath rejected the whole traditional quest for certainty stemming from Descartes' *Cogito*. The break with Cartesianism was completed in Neurath's demand that protocol sentences be expressed in "physicalist" terms, that is, in such a way as to make no reference to a mind distinct from body. Neurath was an outside-in philosopher, really a materialist.

Most positivists, however, were less radical in this direction, where they feared metaphysics still lurked. Carnap, for example, who at one time wanted to get rid even of the name philosophy, substituting 'Logic of Science', accepted physicalism but only in the sense that the progress of science would be furthered if scientists adopted a standard terminology. The task of "logic of science," as he saw it, was to construct an artificial language in which every symbol referred unambiguously to one concept and whose syntactical rules did not permit the formation of unverifiable sentences. But also, he suggested, metaphysicians would do well to construct a similarly precise vehicle for the expression of whatever they might want to say!

In 1936 Schlick was murdered in the University of Vienna by a mentally deranged student whose dissertation Schlick had refused to approve. The Catholic government of Austria publicly expressed satisfaction at this event. When in 1938 Nazi Germany annexed Austria, the Vienna Circle was broken up. Feigl had emigrated to America in 1930; he was followed by Carnap, Goedel, and Reichenbach. Waismann and Neurath went to England. The general outlook of the movement was congenial to the dominantly Russellian "analytic" philosophy practiced in England and the United States, and in time the sharper edges wore off.

Ryle and Ordinary Language Philosophy

The analytic approach was dominant in Anglo-American philosophy before World War II, Ordinary Language in the generation afterward. The transition can be observed in the work of Gilbert Ryle (1900–1976), who was oarsman, rowing coach, and finally Waynflete Professor of Metaphysical Philosophy in Oxford University. In an early article "Systematically Misleading Expressions" (1932), he held like Russell that "Unpunctuality is reprehensible" is philosophically defective and should be replaced by "Whoever is unpunctual deserves reproof." But his book *The Concept of Mind* (1949) is concerned to "rectify the logical geography" of the concepts we use in talking about minds; the general conclusion is that when we have done this, our ordinary ways of speaking will be seen as quite correct. If philosophers have been misled by ordinary language, it is their fault for not having paid attention to the way it operates.

Mind and Body

The "official theory" of mind and body, according to Ryle, stems from Descartes. It holds that a person is a body and a mind. Mind and body are distinct and separable. Bodies are in space and subject to mechanical laws; minds are not in space and not subject to mechanical laws. Bodies are publicly inspectable; minds are inspectable only by their owners. This theory Ryle stigmatized "with deliberate abusiveness" as "the Dogma of the Ghost in the Machine." According to Descartes, human bodies are complicated assemblages of material substance, subject to the laws of physics: "machines." But unlike clocks, they are haunted by immaterial entities called "souls" or "minds" that somehow direct the clockwork. Ryle also called this the "double-life theory" and, because the ghosts themselves are supposed to be causal agents and subject to laws (though not the laws of mechanics), the "para-mechanical hypothesis."

Ryle contended that the official theory resulted from a "category mistake." This kind of error consists in representing the facts as belonging to one "logical type or category . . . when they actually belong to another." A category mistake would be made by a visitor to a university who, after seeing the classrooms, laboratories, dormitories, and administrative offices, inquired "But where is the University?"— as if the University were another building, not the organization of the building (and so on) already inspected. Or a philosophically confused spectator of a ball game might ask which player did the pitching, which the catching, and which the exercising of the team spirit. To suppose that the mind is an invisible member of, or ghostly counterpart to, the body is to be confused in a similar way. Ryle did not deny that minds exist and bodies exist, but these assertions ought to be made, he cautioned, in "different logical tones of voice."

Ryle discussed one after another and in detail some ways in which the terms we actually use in describing mind behave, his object being to show that in no case does the usage presuppose the official theory. Intelligence, for example, is a property of minds. The official theory of intelligence is that while it can only be detected and evaluated by performances, its real nature is different: it is the mind's apprehension of rules and criteria. But, Ryle pointed out, rules and criteria can themselves be applied intelligently or stupidly; so that if my intelligence consisted in selecting the right rule and applying it, I must already have considered a rule of rule-selection, which itself was intelligently selected and applied in the light of a still previous rule of selection of selection rules—and so on endlessly. Intelligent behavior is not an external symptom of an interior and unwitnessable activity of theorizing; it is acting according to a certain disposition, an intelligent capacity. "Overt intelligent performances are not clues to the workings of minds; they are those workings. Boswell described Johnson's mind when he described how he wrote, talked, ate, fidgeted and fumed."[4] That intelligence cannot be a property of a mind, witnessable only by the mind's owner, is shown also by the undoubted fact that other people can know how intelligent you are as well as you can, perhaps even better, and that you can find out how intelligent you are only in the same way the others evaluate you: by observing your performances.

The so-called problem of other minds—how do I know that other people have minds as I have, when all I can observe is their behavior?—is solved, so Ryle claimed, by the simple observation that

> in making sense of what you say, in appreciating your jokes, in unmasking your chess-stratagems, in following your arguments and in hearing you pick holes in my arguments, I am not inferring to the workings of your mind, I am following them.[5]

Volitions

In attacking the problem of the will and its supposed freedom or lack of it, Ryle made the claim that those mental acts called volitions are mythical—a submyth in fact of the Ghost in the Machine myth.

> Volitions have been postulated as special acts, or operations, "in the mind," by means of which a mind gets its ideas translated into facts. I think of some state of affairs which I wish to come into existence in the physical world, but, as my thinking and wishing are unexecutive, they require the mediation of a further executive mental process. So I perform a volition which somehow puts my muscles into action. Only when a bodily movement has issued from such a volition can I merit praise or blame for what my hand or tongue has done.[6]

Against this theory Ryle marshaled several objections. No one talks this way, he claimed, except philosophers talking about the theory; yet we manage to decide what was voluntary and what was not, even in difficult cases. If we did talk about our acts of volition we would not know what to say about them, because none of the adjectives and adverbs—such as sudden, weak, fatiguing, inefficient, and habitual—that describe ordinary activities apply to volitions. If there were such acts, there would be no way for anyone other than the agent to find out whether they occurred or not; even a confession would not help, because we would have to know whether the confession was voluntary, that is, preceded by a volition to confess; and so *ad infinitum*. It would be impossible to conceive how the volition could cause a bodily action: the "interaction problem" that beset Descartes, to which no plausible solution has ever been proposed. Finally, if volitions are actions, it must make sense to ask whether *they* are voluntary or involuntary.

> In short, then, the doctrine of volition is a causal hypothesis, adopted because it was wrongly supposed that the question, "What makes a bodily movement voluntary?" was a causal question.[7]

Then what kind of question *is* "Was it voluntary?" It is, said Ryle, the same kind as "Could he have helped it?" It arises in two kinds of circumstances: when we want to know whether he did it (as opposed to its being something done to him, something he was compelled to do) or when we want to know whether the blame-worthy thing he did was something he was competent to avoid. Both these questions can be settled without reference to introspection of mental acts, and in fact they are settled in that way not only by judges and juries but by the agents themselves.

Like Hume and others, Ryle considered the problem of the freedom of the will to be a "tangle of largely spurious problems."[8] Because Descartes and his successors were alarmed by "the bogy of Mechanism," they postulated nonphysical causes of overt actions. But since the question remained whether these nonphysical causes were not nevertheless themselves effects of physical happenings, the problem persisted.

Ryle sought to get rid of this bogy by pointing out that even if every happening can be explained in terms of the laws of physics, it does not follow that some may not also be explained in terms of "life, sentience, purpose or intelligence . . . Men are not machines, not even ghost-ridden machines. They are men."[9] We say, rightly, of the marksman who pulled the trigger, "'He did it' and not 'He did or underwent something else which caused it'."[10]

This reassurance, Ryle believed, ought to allay the qualms of those who fear that science has somehow ruled out life, sentience, purpose, intelligence, and responsibility from the world, and left people to be mere automata.

Knowledge

As there is no act of volition, neither are there acts of knowing and believing, Ryle argued. To know is not to perform any act but to be in a position (or have a capacity) to get things right. Knowing is to learning as winning is to running: 'know' is a success word. Nor is knowing the superlative degree of believing. To believe is to have a tendency to behave in certain ways; we ask *how* you know but *why* you believe.

Ryle did not deny that there are mental acts. He rejected only the "Privileged Access Theory," the contention that there are *private* mental acts, occurrences "in the mind," witnessable by the mind's owner but by no one else. Some mental acts such as learning and problem solving are witnessable, but by outsiders as well as by the performers, and in the same way. Others such as feeling or perceiving are not witnessable by outsiders; but, Ryle contended, neither are they witnessable by the agents. It is indubitably a fact that you and I feel itches, hunger, anger, and grief; likewise it is a fact that I cannot feel your itches. It is not a fact, however, but a theory that feeling an itch is an occurrence in which one entity, the mind, is related as spectator to another entity, the itch.

Philosophers from Descartes to Russell have built their philosophies on the supposition that we are directly aware of our own sensations because we observe them without any intermediaries. Some indeed have held that we are not, strictly speaking, ever aware of anything else. Ryle to the contrary argued that sensations are precisely things that are not and never could be observed. Sensations are *had*, sometimes *noticed*, but never *witnessed*. This is not a merely verbal point, for the notion of observation presupposes two things: something observed and an observer. If the sensation is the thing observed, then some entity entitled "the mind" must be cast in the role of observer. The philosopher is trying to explain our awareness of our sensation by duplicating the familiar facts of awareness of the external object. This will not do. Admittedly, if I am to observe a tomato, I must have a sensation (of red, say). If, then, having a sensation is also a case of observing, I must have another sensation of the sensation under observation. But then I must have still a third sensation of the sensation of the sensation . . .

In this manner Ryle dissolved the "beloved but spurious question, 'How can a person get beyond his sensations to apprehension of external realities?'"[11] For if we do not observe sensations, there can be no problem of how to justify inferences from those observations. The external realities are there, and we see them, hear and smell them, not at one or more removes but "immediately"—if we must use this inappropriate word at all. Hume, as we noted, put mankind back into the cave of appearances from which Plato had tried to rescue them and conduct them to a realm of higher reality. Ryle attempted a second rescue. If the world into which he allowed us to escape is merely the everyday world, we should be none the less grateful—if this time we can stay in it.

Imagination

Perhaps most people will be easily convinced that when they are in the situation ordinarily described as looking at a tomato, what they really see is a tomato, not some internal copy or effect of a tomato, nor some nonphysical entity intermediate between the tomato and the mind. The situation is rather different with sensuous imagery, hallucinations, and dreams; for it is common enough to talk about seeing elephants in a dream, seeing pink rats in delirium, and seeing the old homestead in the eye of memory. Ryle held that the verb *see* in such locutions is understood to have quotation marks around it, signaling metaphorical use; and perhaps in speech we give the word some faintly off-color inflection or are otherwise aware that we are not using it in its normal sense. But again, maybe we do not. It seems easy for philosophers to convince ordinary folk that there are two species of seeing (and hearing, and so forth), and that since one of these—the seeing of mental images—is admittedly seeing something "in the mind," therefore so is the other kind. If seeing imaginary or hallucinatory or dream tomatoes is seeing, in the same sense as seeing grocery-store tomatoes, then we might as well embrace skepticism without further ado.

Ryle sought to show that one does not see imaginary objects *at all*. "Imaging occurs, but images are not seen. . . . There are no such objects as mental pictures."[12] Imagining is not having sensations, not even faint ones. When we close our eyes and imagine Mount Shasta, the experience is not at all like being in a dark movie theater when the screen suddenly lights up—brightly or dimly.

But if imagining Mount Shasta is not seeing an internal picture, what then is it? Ryle begins his answer by pointing out the hosts of widely divergent sorts of behavior that can be described as imaginative. Some involve sensuous imagery, but some, such as pretending, do not. If I am to pretend to do A, I must know how A is actually done by someone not pretending. Pretending to do A is a higher order act that involves the thought of the lower act. Yet while I am pretending to do A, I am not necessarily theorizing or describing to myself how A is done. Pretending to do A is one kind of exercise of the knowledge how to do A.

Remembering how a tune goes, "having the tune running through your head," is a similar exercise of knowledge. To know a tune when it is heard is to listen to it in a certain frame of mind—to listen with the right expectations as to what is coming next. Remembering how the tune goes is being in this frame of mind, having these right expectations successively, though without the external stimulus of the music. It is realizing how the tune *would* sound if played. Similarly, remembering or imagining the appearance of Mount Shasta is realizing how it would look if you were looking at it. "So far from picturing involving the having of faint sensations, of wraiths of sensations, it involves missing just what one would be due to get, if one were seeing the mountain."[13]

The Later Wittgenstein

In the Preface to the *Tractatus*, Wittgenstein declared that "the *truth* of the thoughts communicated here seems to me unassailable and definitive. I am, therefore, of the opinion that the problems have in essentials been finally solved." With disturbing consistency he thereupon abandoned philosophy, gave his large personal fortune to his sisters, and for six years taught the equivalent of fourth grade in an Austrian country school. However, the English philosopher Frank Ramsey (1903–1930) sought him out and discussed philosophy with him for several days. Wittgenstein's interest was rearoused. In 1929 he returned to Cambridge, acquired the degree Doctor of Philosophy by submitting the *Tractatus* as his dissertation, and joined the faculty, becoming Professor of Philosophy in 1939. Except for one year spent in Norway and three years during World War II during which he served as hospital orderly and laboratory assistant, he lectured until his resignation on account of ill health in 1947. After that he lived for a while in Ireland but returned to Cambridge when it became clear that he was suffering from cancer. When he expressed a fear of dying alone in a hospital, his physician, Dr. Ernest Bevan, and Mrs. Bevan took him into their home, where he lived for some months until April 29, 1951. His last words, to Mrs. Bevan, were "Tell them I've had a wonderful life!"

The *Philosophical Investigations*

Shortly after his return to Cambridge and philosophy, Wittgenstein published a paper "On Logical Form" which is in keeping with the *Tractatus* conception of language. Nothing else by him was printed during his lifetime, although he wrote an enormous amount, much still unpublished today. However, in the academic year 1933–1934, he dictated a set of notes to his class which students duplicated and distributed without authorization. These soon were well known in the philosophical world as "The Blue Book." Another set, dictated the following year, became "The Brown Book." After their author's death these works were given official publication. Their importance at the time was their showing how Wittgenstein was in process of subjecting the ideas of the *Tractatus* to fundamental criticism and rejection in favor of a radically different theory of language and of philosophy.

Wittgenstein expounded his new conception in paragraphs that he was not able to join together in a way satisfactory to himself. Nevertheless, he authorized their postmortem publication under the title *Philosophical Investigations* (1953).

It is roughly true to say that the movement from the *Tractatus* to the *Investigations* is from philosophical analysis to ordinary language philosophy. The *Tractatus* has much in common with Russell's logical atomism and the antimetaphysical doctrines of the Vienna Circle. On two crucial points, however, they differ. First,

Wittgenstein held that the relation of language to the world could be shown but not said; while Russell and the positivists believed, in Ramsey's words, that "what can't be said can't be said, and can't be whistled either." Second, Russell and Carnap looked toward the ideal of an artificial and precise language for science, free of the ambiguities, vaguenesses, and irrational quirks of ordinary English or German. The *Tractatus*, on the other hand, declared that "All propositions of our colloquial language are actually, just as they are, logically completely in order."[14] Wittgenstein never dreamed of replacing ordinary expressions by elementary propositions. These, and the simple objects that they pictured, were postulated to explain why the language of daily life and of science works.

At the other end, to classify the *Investigations* as a work of ordinary language philosophy can be misleading if taken as implying that the author found some Rousseauian virtue in the talk of ordinary folk, by reference to which philosophical perplexities could be dissolved at once. He did not. (But, then, neither did Ryle nor others associated with the "Ordinary Language School"—a bad label, retained only because the alternatives "Oxford Philosophy" and "Linguistic Analysis" are worse.)

The young Wittgenstein had supposed that analysis clarifies, that it consists in dividing down to absolute simples, and that these simples are reached in one way only. Wittgenstein in middle age pointed out that "Bring me the broomstick and the brush which is fitted on to it" is not clearer than "Bring me the broom"—that simplicity is always relative to context (is white simple, or a mixture of pigments, or a summation of the spectral colors?), and that whether we are to divide up the world into facts, or objects, or events, or in some other way, is a decision we must make, one not dictated by the world out there. Young Wittgenstein reasoned that since there is no indefiniteness in facts, the propositions that picture them must likewise have perfectly definite senses that can be revealed by complete analysis. Wittgenstein of the thirties perceived the futility, even absurdity, of the demand for exactitude.

> Am I inexact when I do not give our distance from the sun to the nearest foot, or tell a joiner the width of a table to the nearest thousandth of an inch?
> No *single* ideal of exactness has been laid down; we do not know what we should be supposed to imagine under this head.[15]

Wittgenstein rejected the picture theory of meaning as an error and a source of error.

> (*Tractatus Logico-Philosophicus*, 4.5): "The general form of propositions is: This is how things are."—That is the kind of proposition that one repeats to oneself countless times. One thinks that one is tracing the outline of the thing's nature over and over again, and one is merely tracing round the frame through which we look at it.
> A *picture* held us captive. And we could not get outside it, for it lay in our language and language seemed to repeat it to us inexorably.
> When the philosophers use a word—"knowledge," "being," "object," "I," "proposition," "name"—and try to grasp the *essence* of the thing, one must always ask oneself: is the word ever actually used in this way in the language-game which is its original home?—
> What *we* do is to bring words back from their metaphysical to their everyday use.[16]

Language sometimes may be *used* to picture the world, but that is only one of its manifold uses. Words may name, but the surgeon's "Forceps!" is an order, and not an abbreviation for one. Meaning is use. Wittgenstein turns us from the contemplation of linguistic pictures to the bewilderingly varied manifold of activities in which we use words: "language-games," the "forms of life" that confer meaning on sounds and marks. The analogy to games was carefully chosen, for there is no common element in all games by virtue of which they are called games.

> Consider for example the proceedings that we call "games." I mean board-games, card-games, ball-games, Olympic games, and so on. What is common to them all?—Don't say: "There *must* be something common, or they would not be called 'games'"—but *look and see* whether there is anything common to all.—For if you look at them you will not see something that is common to *all*, but similarities, relationships, and a whole series of them at that. To repeat: don't think, but look!—Look for example at board-games, with their multifarious relationships. Now pass to card-games; here you find many correspondences with the first group, but many common features drop out, and others appear. When we pass next to ball-games, much that is common is retained, but much is lost.—Are they all 'amusing'? Compare chess with tic-tac-toe. Or is there always winning and losing, or competition between players? Think of solitaire. In ball games there is winning and losing; but when a child throws his ball at the wall and catches it again, this feature has disappeared. Look at the parts played by skill and luck; and at the difference between skill in chess and skill in tennis. Think now of games like ring-around-the rosey; here is the element of amusement, but how many other characteristic features have disappeared! . . .
> And the result of this examination is: we see a complicated network of similarities overlapping and criss-crossing: sometimes overall similarities, sometimes similarities of detail.
> I can think of no better expression to characterize these similarities than "family resemblances"; for the various resemblances between members of a family: build, features, color of eyes, gait, temperament, etc. etc. overlap and criss-cross in the same way.—And I shall say: 'games' form a family.[17]

Traditional philosophy, however, has not been a language-game in its own right; philosophical puzzles have resulted from failure to comprehend and observe the rules of various language-games. Perplexity, "mental cramp," comes from trying to treat words in isolation from their contexts of use. Suppose someone, who knows how to find out what time it is in London when it is five o'clock in San Francisco, asks "But is it five o'clock on the sun?" The question is senseless because the word 'time', which had work to do in the former situation, is now "on holiday." It literally has no meaning in this situation (although we could devise a language-game in which the expression "five o'clock on the sun" would play a role). The example (Wittgenstein's) is artificial and simpleminded; yet it is relevant to the puzzlement of St. Augustine, who confessed: "What is time? If no one asks me, I know; but if I would explain it to someone who asks, I know not." What Augustine needed, according to Wittgenstein, was a reminder of something he knew quite well: the grammar of the word 'time'.

> What is your aim in philosophy?—To show the fly the way out of the fly-bottle.[18]

For example, in a long series of meditations, imaginary dialogues, thought-experiments, and rhetorical questions, Wittgenstein tries, like Ryle, to cure us of the conception we seem inevitably to succumb to, that thinking is a process—like digestion only not a corporeal process. This, he says, is to make the difference "look *too slight*." What happens when you are trying (as you say) to find the right expression for your thought? If you say what you think, must you first have thought out what you wished to say—are you reciting a previously composed sentence? Must Germans, who put all the verbs at the end of the sentence, have really thought out the sentence in a more natural order, which they then revised to conform to their eccentric linguistic custom?

Wittgenstein struggled against the conception of sensations as private occurrences witnessable only by the conscious subject and known about or conjectured by others only by inference—the "Privileged Access Theory" that Ryle also battled. Wittgenstein's main line of argument was based on the impossibility (so he claimed) of a "private language"—a language that I can understand, but that it would be logically impossible for anyone else to understand. We are asked to suppose that everyone has a box; what is in a person's box we call a "beetle." No one can look into anyone else's box, and nothing like the things in the boxes exist outside them. Then each person may be said to know what a beetle is only by looking into his box. In these conditions, if people talk to one another about beetles, the word "beetle" could not be for them the name of a *thing*—it could mean, at most, "whatever is in my box"; what was, in fact, in the box would be irrelevant to this meaning. The content of a box might keep changing, or the box might even be empty; it would make no difference.

The same would have to be the case if "pain," say, were the name of a private sensation, which I can observe but you cannot. But, then, there could be no need for rules or criteria of correct linguistic usage according to which my use of the word could be judged as right or wrong; for whenever it seemed to me that I was using the word rightly, I *would* be using it rightly. Since, however, it is essential to the conception of a language that there are criteria of correct usage, talking of sensations in this way would be private; it would be talk that no one else could understand, but it would not be a *language*.

How are we to understand an expression such as "I am in pain"? Wittgenstein conceived of such talk as something we learn as a replacement for writhings and groans. Pain talk is substitute pain behavior. We learn the word 'pain' by being told that it is the appropriate word for what we feel when we are writhing and groaning. If we felt pains but never overtly behaved differently when we did, we could not be taught the word. Pain behavior, then, is essentially involved in the concept of pain. Whether anything else is involved, and if so what, no one has yet been able to say.

> I can be as *certain* of someone else's sensations as of any fact. . . . "But, if you are *certain*, isn't it that you are shutting your eyes in face of doubt?"—They are shut.[19]

Notes

Chapter 32   *The Renaissance*

[1]*Pensée* 91.

[2]Munro translation.

[3]*New Organon*, Book I, Aphorism 42.

[4]Same, 54.

[5]Same, 43.

[6]Same, 61.

[7]Same, 44.

[8]Same, Book II, Aphorism 13.

[9]Same, 17.

[10]Same, 15.

[11]Same, 20.

[12]Same, Book I, Aphorism 61.

[13]*Encyclopaedia Britannica,* 11th ed.

Chapter 33   *Descartes*

[1]From the *Discourse on Method*. Other quotations in this chapter, unless otherwise noted, are from the *Meditations*, by permission of the Open Court Publishing Company, La Salle, Illinois.

[2]By Richard Popkin in his *History of Scepticism from Erasmus to Descartes*.

[3]*Principles of Philosophy*, Sec. 45.

[4]*Man on His Nature* (Cambridge University Press, 1963), p. 248.

Chapter 34   *Hobbes*

[1]Aubrey, *Brief Lives*, ed. Oliver Lawson Dick (London: Secker & Warburg; Ann Arbor: University of Michigan Press), p. 150 of London edition.

[2]Same, p. 156.

[3]Hobbes, verse autobiography.

[4]Hobbes, *Leviathan*, Chapter 5.

[5]Aubrey, p. 156.

[6]Same, pp. 156 and 159.

[7]*Concerning Body*, Chapter 1, Section 2.

[8]Same, Chapter 5, Section 10.

[9]Same, Chapter 8, Section 1.

[10]Same, Chapter 8, Section 2.

[11]Same, Chapter 25.

[12]*Human Nature*, Chapter 2.

[13]*Leviathan*, Chapter 1.

[14]Same, Introduction.

[15]*Human Nature*, Chapter 12, Section 5.

[16]*Leviathan*, Introduction.

[17]*Concerning Body*, Chapter 15, Section 2.

[18]*Leviathan*, Chapter 11.

[19]Same, Chapter 6.

[20]Aubrey, p. 157.

[21]*Human Nature*, Chapter 9, Section 21.

[22]*Leviathan*, Chapter 13.

[23]Same.

[24]Same.

[25]Same, Chapter 17.

[26]Same, Chapter 19.

[27]Same, Chapter 9.

[28]Same.

[29]W. G. Pogson Smith, in the essay prefixed to the Oxford University Press edition of *Leviathan*, p. xxix.

[30]Chapter 12.

[31]*Leviathan*, Chapter 6.

[32]Same, Chapter 32.

Chapter 35 *Spinoza*

[1]Willis, *Benedict de Spinoza* (London 1870), pp. 35–36.

[2]Letters 53 and 54, Elwes translation.

[3]Letter 19. Elwes translation.

[4]*Theologico-Political Treatise*, Chapter 20.

[5]*On the Improvement of the Understanding*, beginning. Elwes translation.

[6]Same, near end.

[7]Letter 35. Wolf translation.

[8]*Ethics*, Part I, Proposition 17. White-Stirling translation.

[9]Same, Scholium.

[10]Same, Proposition 29, Scholium.

[11]Same, Proposition 16.

[12]Same, Proposition 33.

[13]Same, Proposition 29.

[14]Same, Part 2, Proposition 7, Scholium.

[15]Same, Part 3, Proposition 9, Scholium.

[16]Same, Proposition 59, Scholium.

[17]Same, Part 4, Proposition 4.

[18]Same, Appendix 4.

[19]Same, Part 5, Proposition 3.

[20]Same, Proposition 20, Scholium.

[21]Same, Proposition 5.

[22]See 5.

Chapter 36 *Locke*

[1]*Essay*, Book 2, Chapter 1, Section 2.

[2]Same, 2-1-3.

[3]Same.

[4]Same.

[5]Same, 2-1-1.

[6]Same, 2-4-6.

[7]Same, 2-8-13.

[8]Same, 2-8-10.

[9]Same, 2-8-13.

[10]Same, 2-8-17.

[11]Same, 2-12-1.

[12]Same, 2-11-9.

[13]Same, 2-23-1.

[14]Same, 3-6-2.

[15]Same, 4-3-13.

[16]Same, 4-1-2.

[17]Same, 4-2-14.

[18]Same, 4-4-18.

[19]*Second Treatise*, Section 93.

[20]Same, 19.

[21]Same, 202.

[22]Same, 225.

Chapter 37   *Leibniz*

[1]*The Principles of Nature and of Grace*, 7. In Duncan, *Philosophical Works of Leibniz* (New Haven, 1890).

[2]Fifth Letter to Clarke, Paragraph 9. In Duncan, p. 256.

[3]*The Principles of Nature and of Grace*, 10.

[4]Same, 2.

[5]"First Truths," quoted in Smith and Grene, *From Descartes to Locke*, p. 302.

[6]Same, p. 306.

[7]Same, p. 303.

Chapter 38   *Berkeley*

[1]James Boswell, *Life of Samuel Johnson, LL.D.*, 1763.

[2]C. M. Turbayne, *Berkeley's Principles, Dialogues, and Correspondence* (Bobbs-Merrill, 1965), page xxxiii.

Chapter 39   *Hume*

[1]Quoted in E. C. Mossner, "Philosophy and Biography: The Case of David Hume," in V. C. Chappell, ed., *Hume* (Doubleday, 1966), p. 7.

[2]*Treatise of Human Nature*, Book I, Part 4, Section 7.

[3]*Enquiry Concerning Human Understanding*, Section 1.

[4]*Treatise*, 1-1-1.

[5]*Enquiry*, Section 2.

[6]*Treatise*, 1-1-1.

[7]*Enquiry*, Section 2.

[8]*Treatise*, 1-1-4.

[9]Same, 1-2-6.

[10]*Concerning Body*, Chapter 9, Section 3.

[11]*Treatise*, 1-3-3.

[12]Same, 1-3-6.

[13]Same, 1-3-14.

[14]Same.

[15]Same.

[16]Same, 1-3-6.

[17]Same.

[18]Same, 1-3-8.

[19]Same, 1-4-7.

[20]Same, 1-3-11.

[21]Same, 1-3-15.

[22]*Enquiry*, Section 7, Part 1.

[23]Same, Section 4, Part 2.

[24]*The Natural History of Religion*, Section 3.

[25]*Treatise*, 1-4-2.

[26]Same.

[27]Same.

[28]Same.

[29]Same.

[30]Same, 1-4-6.

[31]Same, 1-4-2.

[32]Same, 1-4-7.

[33]*Natural History of Religion*, "General Corollary."

[34]*Enquiry*, Section 10, Part 1.

[35]Same, Part 2.

[36]*Dialogues*, Part 9.

[37]Same.

[38]Same, Part 2.

[39]Same.

[40]Same, Part 5.

[41]Same, Part 10.

[42]Same, Part 11.

[43]Same, Part 12.

[44]*Treatise*, 3-1-1.

[45]Same, 2-3-3.

[46]Same.

[47]Same, 3-1-1.

[48]Same, 3-1-2.

[49]*Enquiry Concerning the Principles of Morals*, Section 9, Part 1.

[50]Same, Part 2.

[51]Same.

[52]*Intellectual Powers*, Essay 2, Chapter 12.

[53]Same, Essay 1, Chapter 1, Section 6.

[54]Hume, *Enquiry Concerning Human Understanding*, Section 1, Part 1.

[55]*Intellectual Powers*, Essay 2, Chapter 14.

Chapter 40 *The Enlightenment in France*

[1]*A History of Philosophy*, 6, Part 1, Chapter 1 (New York: Image Books, 1960).

[2]Quotations in this section are from La Mettrie's *Man a Machine* (La Salle, Illinois: Open Court Publishing Co., 1912).

[3]*Discourse on the Arts and Sciences*, Part 2.
[4]Same.
[5]*The Social Contract*, Book 1, Chapter 6.
[6]Same.
[7]Same, Chapter 7.
[8]Same.

Chapter 41 *Kant*

[1]*Prolegomena to Any Future Metaphysics that may Come Forth as a Science*, Section 5.
[2]Same, Section 22.
[3]*Critique of Pure Reason*, B165, trans. Kemp Smith (New York: St. Martin's Press) p. 173 *f.*
[4]*Prolegomena*, Section 36.
[5]*Critique of Pure Reason*, A426/B454.
[6]Same, A427/B455.
[7]*Foundations of the Metaphysics of Morals*, trans. Lewis White Beck (Liberal Arts Press, 1959), p. 14.
[8]Same, p. 16.
[9]Same.
[10]Same.
[11]Same, p. 17.
[12]Same, p. 20.
[13]Same, p. 22.
[14]*Principles of Morals and Legislation*, Chapter 1.
[15]*Foundations*, p. 28.
[16]Same, p. 29.
[17]Same, p. 33.
[18]Same, p. 39.
[19]Same, p. 46.
[20]Same, p. 47.
[21]*Critique of Pure Reason*, A599/B627.
[22]*Treatise*, 1-2-6.
[23]*Critique of Pure Reason*, A600/B628.
[24]Same, A602/B630.

Chapter 44 *Marx and Engels*

[1]Karl Marx, "Theses on Feuerbach," XI.
[2]Quoted in Robert Payne, *Marx* (Simon & Schuster, 1968), pp. 155 *f.*
[3]*The German Ideology*, I. In Eugene Kamenka, ed., *The Portable Karl Marx* (Viking Penguin, 1983), p. 177.
[4]"Contribution to the Critique of Hegel's Philosophy of Right," Introduction, Kamenka, p. 119.
[5]*Communist Manifesto*, I.
[6]"On the Jewish Question," Kamenka, p. 110.
[7]See 4, p. 121.
[8]See 5.
[9]*Critique of Political Economy*.
[10]"Address of the Central Committee to the Communist League" (1880), Kamenka, pp. 251 *f.*
[11]See 5.

[12]See 10, p. 250.

[13]*The German Ideology*, Kamenka, pp. 192 *f.*

[14]Continuation of passage cited in 3.

[15]"Theses on Feuerbach," II.

[16]*Physics and Reality.*

[17]Hebrews 11:1.

[18]See 4, p. 115.

[19]"On the History of Early Christianity." In Lewis S. Feuer, ed., *Marx & Engels: Basic Writings on Politics & Philosophy* (Anchor Books, 1959), pp. 168 *f.*

Chapter 45   *The Utilitarians*

[1]Bentham, *Principles*, Chapter 4. In *Works*, 1, p. 16.

[2]Bentham, *Deontology*, 1, p. 12.

[3]Bentham, *Principles of Penal Law*. In *Works*, 1, p. 415.

[4]See *Works*, Introduction, pp. 18–19.

[5]*Autobiography.*

[6]Same.

[7]*Utilitarianism*, Chapter 2.

[8]*On Liberty*, Chapter 1.

[9]Same.

[10]Same, Chapter 3.

[11]*Autobiography*, Chapter 7.

[12]*A System of Logic*, Book 3, Chapter 21.

[13]Same, Chapter 8.

[14]*Examination of Sir William Hamilton's Philosophy*, 1, Chapter 11.

Chapter 46   *The Will in Germany*

[1]*The World as Will and Idea*, Book 1, Section 1.

[2]Same, Section 2.

[3]Same, Book 2, Section 18.

[4]Same, Book 3, Section 38.

[5]Same, Book, 4, Section 57.

[6]"The Problem of Socrates," Section 5. In *Twilight of the Idols*, trans. W. Kaufmann, in *The Portable Nietzsche* (New York: Viking Press, 1954), p. 476.

[7]*The Will to Power*, Section 493, trans. A. M. Ludovici. In O. Levy, ed., *The Complete Works of Friedrich Nietzsche*, 15 (New York: Russell & Russell, 1964).

[8]*The Gay Science*, Book 5, Section 344. In Kaufmann; see 6, p. 449.

[9]Same, p. 450.

[10]*Thus Spoke Zarathustra*, First Part, Prologue; *The Gay Science*, Book 5, Section 343; and elsewhere.

[11]*Thus Spoke Zarathustra*, First Part. In Kaufmann, p. 159.

[12]Same, p. 160.

[13]Same, pp. 211. *ff.*

[14]*The Birth of Tragedy*, 18, trans. Francis Golffing (New York: Doubleday Anchor Books, 1956), p. 110.

Chapter 47   *Pragmatism*

[1]"Percept and Concept—The Import of Concepts," in *Some Problems of Philosophy.*
[2]"The Fixation of Belief."
[3]*The Meaning of Truth*, Preface.
[4]"Experience, Knowledge and Value: A Rejoinder." In P. A. Schilpp, ed., *The Philosophy of John Dewey* (Northwestern University, 1939), p. 597.
[5]Same, p. 544.
[6]Same, p. 524.
[7]Same, p. 542.
[8]*The Quest for Certainty*, p. 255.

Chapter 48   *Russell*

[1]Russell, "My Mental Development." In Schilpp, ed., *The Philosophy of Bertrand Russell* (La Salle, Illinois: Open Court), p. 9.
[2]*Our Knowledge of the External World*, Lecture II (George Allen and Unwin, 1926), p. 42.
[3]"My Mental Development," p. 13.
[4]Same, p. 12.
[5]*Human Society in Ethics and Politics*, Chapter 6 (New York: Simon and Schuster, 1955), p. 54.
[6]*A History of Western Philosophy* (New York: Simon and Schuster, 1945), pp. 772–3.

Chapter 49   *Existentialism*

[1]Jean-Paul Sartre, *Existentialism and Humanism*, trans. Philip Mairet (London: Methuen, 1948), p. 56.
[2]*Being and Nothingness*, trans. Hazel Barnes, p. 78.
[3]Stephen Pepper.
[4]*Existentialism and Humanism*, p. 28.
[5]Same, p. 44.

Chapter 50   *Wittgenstein and the Linguistic Turn*

[1]*Tractatus*, 6.41.
[2]Same, 6.54.
[3]Same, 7.
[4]*The Concept of Mind* (London: Hutchinson; New York: Barnes & Noble, 1949), p. 58.
[5]Same, p. 61.
[6]Same, p. 63.
[7]Same, p. 67.
[8]Same, p. 71.
[9]Same, p. 81.
[10]Same, p. 82.
[11]Same, p. 223.
[12]Same, pp. 247 and 254.
[13]Same, p. 270.
[14]*Tractatus*, 5.5563.
[15]*Philosophical Investigations* (New York and London: Macmillan, 1953), #88.
[16]Same, #114–116.
[17]Same, #66–67.
[18]Same, #339.
[19]Same, #224.

Index

This index covers both volumes of *A New History of Philosophy*. Pages 1–249 are in Volume I; pages 250–485 are in Volume II. Page numbers in **boldface** refer to the more central discussions.

A 6
B 7
C 8
D 9
E 0
F 1
G 2
H 3
I 4
J 5